Early Reading Development and Dyslexia

Dedication

This book is dedicated to my mother
Mary Muter

Early Reading Development and Dyslexia

VALERIE MUTER M.Phil PhD

Consultant Clinical Psychologist,
Great Ormond Street Hospital for Children
Research Fellow, University of York

Consultant in Dyslexia
PROFESSOR MARGARET SNOWLING
University of York

W
WHURR PUBLISHERS
LONDON AND PHILADELPHIA

© 2003 Whurr Publishers

First published 2003 by
Whurr Publishers Ltd
19b Compton Terrace, London N1 2UN, England and
325 Chestnut Street, Philadelphia PA 19106, USA

Reprinted 2003 and 2005

British Library Cataloguing in Publication Data

A catalogue record for this book is available from the
British Library.

ISBN 1 86156 327 2

Printed and bound by CPI Antony Rowe, Eastbourne
Transferred to digital print on demand, 2007

Contents

Preface

The past 20 years have seen an enormous amount of research into reading development that has greatly advanced our knowledge of the processes involved. Great strides have also taken place in terms of our understanding of reading difficulties and disorders. Not surprisingly, books about reading and reading disorders (in particular, dyslexia) proliferate.

Two years ago, my close colleague, Professor Margaret Snowling, suggested that I write a book that addressed reading development in the age range in which I have an especial interest, that is, children aged 4 to 7 years. The research work that I have conducted over the past 10–15 years has concentrated on the processes involved in the earliest stages of learning to read. Similarly, my work as a clinical psychologist, which has been conducted over a much longer period of 25 years, has become increasingly focused on assessing the needs of the younger child with reading difficulties.

From the beginning, I wanted this book to reflect my dual interest in the academic and practitioner aspects of reading development and disorders. I also wanted to write a book that I hoped would meet the needs of a broad readership, that is, psychologists, speech and language therapists, teachers and parents. In trying to achieve these two aims, I have come to recognize how intimately connected are the academic and practitioner strands of the field of reading, and how they can, and should, inform each other's development.

I would like to acknowledge my academic colleagues, who have taught me a great deal over the past decade or so about research methodology, and who have introduced me to the vast research literature in the field of reading and its associated disorders. In particular, I would like to thank Margaret Snowling, Charles Hulme, Jim Stevenson and Faraneh Vargha-Khadem.

My journey as a practitioner psychologist has been a much longer one, beginning with my introduction to the field of reading difficulties at the Institute of Psychiatry, continuing through my work at the Nuffield Hearing and Speech Centre, then the Dyslexia Institute and, most recently, Great

Ormond Street Children's Hospital. I would like to acknowledge the contributions to my clinical practices made by the staff of these institutions.

My warmest thanks of all goes to Margaret Snowling, who read the first full draft of the book, and who made many helpful comments and recommendations that greatly assisted me in the final stages of its preparation.

A final thanks must go to the hundreds of dyslexic children and their parents with whom I have worked and who have given me many insights into reading and the difficulties that so concern them.

Valerie Muter
London
September 2002

CHAPTER 1

Introduction

Why learning to read is so important

Most modern societies recognize that reading is the key route through to learning and knowledge. It follows that successful reading acquisition is a fundamental goal for all children entering education. However, reading is a skill that in evolutionary terms has appeared relatively recently in human development, far later than has spoken language communication.

Indeed, learning to read is not the same as learning to talk. The majority of pre-school children acquire spoken language simply by being exposed to speech at home. They do not need to be taught explicitly how to speak. They rapidly acquire the structure and rules of spoken language without apparent conscious effort and with no teaching as long as they are raised in an environment where speech is used in a meaningful and appropriate way. In a sense, the learning of spoken language in man can be regarded as 'instinctual' (Pinker, 1994). This is not the case for written language, which for humankind is a far more recently acquired skill; children need to be taught explicitly how to read.

Systematic writing forms have existed since approximately 3500 BC, with books (in the sense of paper-like materials bound between boards) being in evidence since approximately 200 BC. In the fascinating and very readable book on psycholinguistics, *The Ascent of Babel*, (Altman, 1997), the development of the written word is rated as one of mankind's greatest achievements, along with the discovery of uses for fire and the invention of the wheel. As Altman (1997, p. 160) points out, 'science and technology would hardly have progressed beyond the dark ages were it not for the written word — science simply relies on too much information for it to be passed down through the generations by word of mouth alone'. Not all knowledge and learning can be committed to memory; we need a permanent record to refer back to and to pass on to others. To borrow again from the book, 'it is only through writing that almost all that is known today is known at all' (Altman, 1997, p.179).

1

Learning to read is perhaps the single most important educational challenge children face during their first two to three years of formal schooling. Although learning to read presents few difficulties for the majority of youngsters, who by the age of 7 will be able to access a remarkable range of reading materials, there are substantial numbers of children who have enormous problems acquiring this fundamental skill.

Epidemiological or large-scale population studies have shown that as many as one in six young children are at risk of failing to read at a level that enables them to access their school curriculum meaningfully. Such failure has serious implications for educational development, and emotional and behavioural adjustment. Conversely, children who experience early success in learning to read appear to have positive attitudes to reading experiences that can stretch well into early adulthood. Indeed, Cunningham and Stanovich (1997, p. 934) claim that 'rapid acquisition of reading abilities might well help the development of the lifetime habit of reading'. In support of their argument, these authors report the findings of a study that looked at children's first-grade reading skills, when they were approximately 6 years of age. They then followed this same group of children over a 10-year period to see how much reading for pleasure they did and how well they understood and recalled what they had read. The children who had made a good start in reading in grade 1 read more and understood what they were reading far better in grade 11 than those who were slow to start. Making a successful early start in reading clearly has a long-term sustaining effect, an observation that carries huge implications for the cultural, economic and educational future of any society.

All children need to learn to read. It is an ability that is highly valued in our society, yet substantial numbers of children find this a difficult skill to acquire. Having considered the importance of reading and the prevalence of reading failure (albeit briefly), let us address the aims of this book, which are threefold. First, the process of learning to read is examined during the first two to three years of formal schooling, that is, between the ages of 4 and 7 years. The second aim of the book is to relate what we know about normal reading development to patterns of learning in children whose reading is delayed or deviant, in particular dyslexic children. Finally, what we know about normal and deviant reading development will be related to practitioner issues of screening for reading failure, early identification of reading problems, assessment and intervention.

How common are reading problems?

Not surprisingly, the importance of recognizing reading failure at the earliest stages of schooling has become a serious focus of researchers, educators and even politicians during the course of the past 10 years. Substantial numbers of children have serious problems learning to read, the incidence of which has been determined through epidemiological research. Epidemiology refers to the study of large representative samples of children. For instance, in the well-known Isle of Wight epidemiological study (Rutter, Tizard and Whitmore, 1970), the entire 9- to 10-year-old population of the Isle of Wight was screened for reading underachievement. Prevalence rates do vary from one epidemiological study to another, although generally speaking, somewhere between three and 10 per cent of the child population has reading difficulties, depending on how the reading problem is defined.

Most studies distinguish between children who are backward readers and those who have a specific reading difficulty. Because it is accepted that there is a relationship between intelligence and ease of learning to read, we need to take this into account when defining types of reading problems. In general, brighter children learn to read earlier and with greater ease than less able children, though this is true for any newly learnt task. Children who are backward in reading may be achieving some way below their chronological age requirement, but nonetheless their reading skills match their developmental level as indicated by, say, an IQ test. In other words, their reading attainments, though poor, are in line with those to be expected given their age and ability level. Children who have specific reading difficulties are those whose attainments are well below the level to be expected given their ability; so, these are the children who are often of good general ability but whose reading is weak. Dyslexic children fall into this specific reading-retarded category, and it is this particular group of poor readers with whom the second half of this book is concerned.

In epidemiological research, the placement of the cut-off point for the difference between a child's actual and expected levels of reading achievement is to some degree arbitrary — and this in itself may account for some of the variation in prevalence rates in different studies. In the Isle of Wight study (Rutter and Yule, 1975), the authors used a fairly stringent cut-off point. They used a statistic that reflects dispersion around the mean or average — the standard error of measurement which represents the average amount of deviation from the mean for a given individual. The use of a cut-off whereby children's actual reading scores were at least two standard errors of measurement below their expected attainment scores resulted in a prevalence rate for specific reading retardation of 3.1 per cent for 10-year-olds. This figure was doubled when the same methodology and cut-off point was used for children living in an inner-city part of London. This latter finding suggests that prevalence rates can be affected by geographical, social and presumably other environmental factors. A more recent study of 414 children in the USA (Shaywitz et al., 1992a) used a less stringent cut-off of 1.5 standard errors of

measurement below expectation, which yielded a higher incidence rate of
5.4 per cent for their 10-year-olds. These authors also point out that prevalence is not a stable entity, but can vary from year to year; the prevalence rate
for the 8-year-olds in this study was rather higher at 7 per cent. It may
depend, for instance, on the specific and, indeed, changing demands of the
literacy process as children proceed through the schooling system. In the
early years of learning to read, the critical components of learning to read
include learning about letters and building up a sight vocabulary. In the later
years, reading speed and fluency as well as reading for understanding
become more important features of the reading process. So the nature of the
child's reading difficulty and the impact this has on his or her performance
and progress may vary according to the age or stage at which the reading
skills are being measured. It is also possible that, for any given population of
children, the level and quality of teaching input and the extent to which the
children are themselves able to compensate might affect prevalence rates
during the school years in which children are learning to read.

Advantages of early identification of reading failure

It is not difficult to enumerate the advantages to be gained when children
who are at risk of reading failure have their difficulties identified at a very
early age. Children whose 'at-risk' status has been recognized at ages 5 or 6
will have far less educational ground to make up than those children identified later in their schooling. Reversing one year's underachievement in
reading in a 7-year-old will be faster and easier than remedying three years'
underachievement in a late-diagnosed 10-year-old. Furthermore, from the
perspective of the evaluating teacher or psychologist, assessing a child of 5, 6
or 7 may yield a 'purer' and, therefore, easier to interpret learning profile. In
contrast, the profile obtained from an older child may reveal a learning
pattern that has become distorted through experiential factors, for example
different teaching methods or compensatory strategies the child has developed. Most teachers acknowledge the greater ease of working with younger
children who have not yet experienced excessive frustration and feelings of
failure that can adversely affect their motivation and responsivity to instruction. Also, teachers often find it easier to work with youngsters who have not
had the opportunity to establish too many 'bad habits' that have to be
unlearnt before they can be replaced by new and more effective strategies.
Additionally, there may be negative behavioural consequences of untreated
persisting reading problems. Many failed readers who have effectively 'given
up' are significantly at risk of emotional and behavioural problems. Indeed,
recent research has demonstrated a substantial link between early reading
failure and later social adjustment problems and even delinquent behaviour

(see Maughan, 1994, 1995). When reading difficulties occur alongside a behavioural disorder, the effect on psychological functioning and employment prospects is far greater than when a behavioural disorder occurs in the absence of reading problems (Maughan, 2000). Finally, there is the economic advantage of early identification. Implementing a twice- or thrice-weekly teaching programme over a one-year period for a 6-year-old is clearly far cheaper than having to provide long-term daily help (or even specialist schooling) to a late-diagnosed 10-year-old whose behaviour is becoming increasingly antisocial.

Some terminology

Approaches to reading research

There has been an enormous amount of research over the past 20 years looking at how young normally developing children acquire reading skills. What is understood about early reading processes and how they can go wrong stems largely from research that takes what might be termed a 'predictor approach', both in normal and high-risk populations. 'Predictors' are skills or abilities that have been demonstrated to contribute to reading development, and which are definable, measurable and potentially modifiable through teaching. For very young children, the predictors indicate what underlying cognitive skills or abilities children need to have in place to enable them to begin to learn to read. These predictor measures are also helpful because they are tools that enable us to predict (albeit with some degree of error) which children will find reading easy and which children may find it difficult. The predictor skill or ability is then related to later reading (the 'outcome measure'). The most-studied of the predictors of early reading skill is that which is usually termed 'phonological awareness': children's sensitivity to the speech sound structure of words. The nature of the connection between phonological awareness and reading will be the primary focus of the next chapter.

Most predictor research takes the form of correlational studies which examine the relationship between predictor abilities and reading (outcome) skills. A correlation provides a measure of the strength of the relationship between two variables. It is possible to distinguish between two types of correlational research studies. The first, concurrent correlational research, looks at the relationship between predictor and reading skills at the same timepoint. However, this type of correlational research does have its limitations. A significant correlation between measures assessed at the same timepoint merely means that they are occurring simultaneously and that they have some consistent relationship with one another. However, it cannot tell us about the direction of the relationship. Nor can claims be made about prediction over time. Because of these disadvantages, most predictor research is conducted longitudinally. In longitudinal correlational research, children are seen and assessed at a given point in time, very often as pre-schoolers, at which time they are given tasks to do that are thought to measure the predictor skills. Their reading skills are then assessed some time later to see if how they performed on the predictor measures affects, or contributes to, their subsequent progress in learning to read. Longitudinal studies establish not only the presence of a relationship between the two measures but, even more importantly, the direction of that relationship.

It is tempting to conclude that longitudinal research allows us to establish a causal relationship between a predictor skill and an outcome measure. However, this is not the case. Both types of correlational research are susceptible to the problem of the unknown third factor. There is the danger that both the predictor and outcome measure might be affected by some unknown, and therefore unmeasured, third factor. Thus, despite an apparent positive correlation between the two measures, there may be no real connection between them. For instance, it might be possible to find a positive correlation between children's phonological awareness and their reading ability even if there were no connection between these skills. This is because bright children would do better on both the phonological and reading tests, whereas less able children would do badly on both. In this case, the correlation between phonological and reading skills would be quite spurious; they would be related only because both are determined by the same third factor, the children's intelligence level.

Bradley and Bryant (1983) suggested that a way round the third factor problem is to combine two types of research that essentially complement each other and cancel out each other's disadvantages. Longitudinal research establishes the presence and direction of a relationship in the real world, but cannot equivocally confirm causation because of the third factor problem. Bradley and Bryant (1983) proposed that longitudinal studies should be carried out in conjunction with experimental training studies. Experimental studies manipulate events in a highly controlled way, with the result that third-factor problems are minimized. However, experimental studies may be criticized on the grounds of artificiality. They do not necessarily mirror what would happen in real life. Since the strengths and weaknesses of longitudinal and experimental studies are complementary, they can, in combination, provide strong evidence for the existence, direction and strength of specific cognitive influences in beginning reading. Throughout this book both longitudinal and experimental training studies are drawn upon to demonstrate the relationship between reading and its related skills and abilities.

If predictors of early reading skills are established to be valid, they may form the basis for screening of pre-school or grade 1 populations. Alternatively, the predictors might be used for initial diagnostic assessments of young children whose histories suggest they are 'at risk' (for example, where there are other family members with literacy problems). If a child shows a significant difficulty in a predictor skill that is known to be closely related to reading progress, this provides important clues about how to remediate the reading problem.

Before embarking on a discussion of reading and related language skills, it is important to introduce some terms relating to spoken and written language that will be used throughout this book.

Some spoken language terminology

Words may first of all be composed of 'morphemes' which are units of meaning. A single word may have one morpheme, as in *dog*, or two or more morphemes; *dogs* has two morphemes, *dog* to indicate the animal in question and *s* to indicate that there are more than one, that is, to indicate pluralization.

At the level of the sound system, words may be composed of 'syllables', 'onset' and 'rimes' or 'phonemes'. A syllable is a vowel flanked by one or more consonants — *dog* has one syllable (*dog*), *carpet* has two (*car* and *pet*) and *unhappy* has three (*un*, *happ* and *y*). Syllables can be further subdivided into onsets and rimes. The onset is the initial consonant or consonant cluster and the rime is the following vowel and any succeeding consonants. So, in the word *dog* the onset is *d* and the rime is *og*. The rime can be further subdivided into the 'peak', which is usually the vowel, and the 'coda' which comprises any following consonants. In the rime *og* from our example word *dog*, the *o* is the peak and the *g* is the coda. The smallest unit of speech sound to which we shall refer is the 'phoneme'; so in the word *dog* there are three phonemes /d/, /o/ and /g/. The hierarchical structure of a two-syllable word is presented diagrammatically in Figure 1.1.

The writing systems of the world are known as 'orthographies'. In alphabetic languages, 'graphemes' record phonemes in written form. In English, there are 26 letters but 44 phonemes; combinations of letters are used to represent some of the phonemes, for example **chimpanzee**, **hush**, **bring** and so on. The phonemes of a language are usually written using an internationally agreed set of symbols, known as the International Phonetic Alphabet (see Table 1.1).

Some orthographies, such as Spanish and Italian, are referred to as 'phonologically transparent'. Phonemes within these language are represented consistently by graphemes. So, when a certain sound in Spanish is heard it is almost always represented by the same configuration of letters. This is not the case for

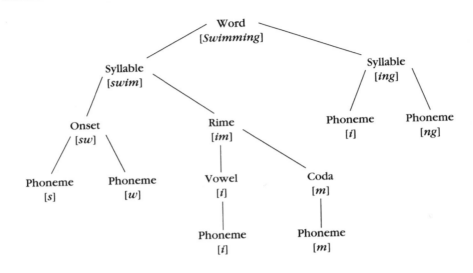

Figure 1.1 Hierarchical structure of a two-syllable word *swimming*.

English, which has a 'morpho-phonological' orthography in that its spelling is based partly on phoneme–grapheme relations and partly on morphological consistencies within the language. So, for instance, the word *health* contains certain predictable phoneme–grapheme relations, that is [h], [l], [th], but the vowel combination appears to be 'irregular' and is certainly not consistent with how [ea] is used in words such as *meat, feat, beat* and so on. However, what we need to appreciate is that *health* is written with [ea] and not [e] because it is preserving its morphological unit of origin — *health* is morphologically related to its base unit word *heal* which has the vowel combination [ea].

Some reading terminology

The outcome measure to be considered throughout this book is that of reading level or competence. There are a number of components of reading skill which may be assessed and quantified. Some of these may be measured by standardized tests for which normative data have been obtained on large numbers of children; several of these will be discussed in a later chapter. Others take the form of experimental measures that have been developed by researchers in order to test a specific hypothesis related to reading. The outcome measures that will be discussed in the context of early reading are single word recognition skills, prose reading ability, reading comprehension, reading speed and non-word reading.

'Single word reading' measures require the child to read words in isolation and out of context. These tests aim to assess the breadth of the child's

Table 1.1 The phonemes of the English Language*			
Vowels (20)		*Consonants (24)*	
Symbol	*Sound (or value)*	*Symbol*	*Sound (or value)*
aɪ	try - write	b	back - rubber
aʊ	noun - now	d	day - rudder
ɑ	father	dʒ	judge - George - raj
ɒ	wash - odd	ð	this - other
æ	cat - trap	f	few - puff
eɪ	day - steak - face	g	got - bigger
əʊ	go - goat	h	hot
ɛ	get	j	yet
ɛə	fair - square	k	car - key - clock - trekked - quay
ɜ	her - stir - word - nurse	l	lip
i	he - see	m	much - hammer
ɪ	ship	n	now - runner
ɪə	hear - here	ŋ	sing
o	force	p	pen - pepper
ɔ	north - war	r	round - sorry
ɔɪ	noise - toy	s	see - missed
u	lunar - pool	ʃ	ship - mission
ʊ	foot - put	t	ten
ʊə	pure	tʃ	church - latch
ʊ	bud - blood - love	θ	three - heath
		v	very
		w	will
		z	zeal
		ʒ	decision - treasure
(Total = 44)			

*From Doyle (1996).

word recognition knowledge; the words may be read either as whole word units (sight word reading), through decoding or 'sounding out' strategies, or through 'analogizing' to similarly constructed words already known by sight. 'Prose reading' tasks require the child to read whole sentences or passages, usually within a story context. This is obviously a much more naturalistic reading task that assesses the skills children bring to bear on their everyday reading experiences. Individual words within a sentence or story may be read by whole word recognition, decoding or analogizing strategies or even with the help of the context cues that are readily available in prose reading material. 'Reading comprehension' refers to children's understanding, retention and recall of what they have read. Arguably, a child's ability to read for meaning is the most important reading skill of all. Children's reading comprehension skills can be measured by asking children to, for instance, retell a story they have read or to answer specific questions that assess their understanding and recall of the content of the reading material.

Hoover and Gough (1990) proposed 'The Simple Model' that views reading comprehension as a product of reading accuracy skill and listening comprehension. Reading accuracy refers to children's ability to recognize words in printed form accurately. Listening comprehension is a term used to denote children's ability to understand language in spoken form; naturally, this is dependent on the child's development of oral language skills.

'Reading speed' is not an aspect of reading that will be considered in much depth here, bearing in mind the very young age of the children under scrutiny in this book. However, the ability to read fluently and quickly becomes an increasingly important skill as children get older, when they often have to read under time-constrained conditions, such as written examin-ations. Finally, psychologists are very fond of asking children to attempt to read nonsense words or 'non-words', literally made-up words that do not actually exist. The aim of this seemingly pointless exercise is to assess directly and in a 'pure' form a child's ability to decode or 'sound out' words that are new or unfamiliar. Examples of non-words are: puk, lisk, swesp, tispet and cratfert. Clearly, children cannot recognize these non-words visually, having never seen them before; nor can they make use of context-based information to help them to read them as the non-words have no meaning. Non-words were first used in experimental studies to look at reading processes in children and adults. They are now used routinely in standardized test formats to assess a given child's use of decoding strategies in reading. It will be seen later that non-word reading is an important diagnostic tool when assessing the difficulties of the dyslexic child.

A child's performance on a given test of reading may be described in a number of ways. Most simply, one can add up the total number of words read correctly to yield a raw score. However, this is of little clinical or educational value since the number of words read correctly will be influenced by the length of the word list or text and by the level of difficulty of the material. The value of raw scores is generally limited to research purposes.

Alternatively, a child's performance on a reading test may be described in terms of a reading age equivalent. A reading age equivalent is computed by finding the average reading level for a group of children of a given age. Thus, an eight-year-old poor reader who obtained the same reading score as a group of six and a half-year-olds would be described as having a reading age of 6½ years. In general, the use of age-equivalent scores is discouraged by experts because they can be very difficult to interpret and even be positively misleading. An age equivalent tends to convey the impression that any child who scores below age level has a problem when, in fact, a large proportion of children must score below average by definition. To illustrate, after excluding those children whose reading age is precisely at age level, 50 per cent of the remainder will read below age level and 50 per cent above. Also, reading ages may be difficult to interpret because the clinical significance of a discrepancy between chronological age and reading age depends on the variation in scores for a given test at a given age. This variation or spread of scores around the mean (which can be expressed as a standard deviation) may vary according to age and also the particular test being used. This makes it very hard to compare children's reading performance at different ages and across different measures. While acknowledging the difficulties with reading age scores, they may be "clinically" useful because they are readily understood by parents and teachers.

Because of the problems inherent in the use of age equivalents, most professionals prefer to report results of tests by use of either percentiles (sometimes called 'centiles') or scaled and standard scores. A percentile indicates the percentage of the distribution that is equal to or below that particular score. For example, if a child obtains a percentile of 60, this means that 60 per cent of children in the same age range of the normative (or standardization) sample scored at or below that child's score. Scaled or standard scores give the clearest indication of a child's reading level because they are based on a distribution that has a prescribed mean and standard deviation. In effect, the standard deviation becomes the unit of measurement. It is, therefore, possible to make comparisons across different tests and at different ages. Scaled scores usually have a mean of 10 and a standard deviation of three, whereas standard scores have a mean of 100 and a standard deviation of 15.

Summary

- Although the majority of young children acquire reading skills without difficulty, as many as one in six children will be 'at risk' of failing to read at a level that enables them to access their school curriculum.
- Identifying reading failure in young children may help to prevent not only later educational underachievement but also the development of behavioural and emotional problems.
- Longitudinal correlational research and experimental training studies have allowed us to develop valid predictor measures that can be used to screen for, and assess the presence of, early reading problems.
- In English orthography, 26 letters record the 44 phonemes that are the smallest units of speech sounds in our language; children's awareness of the phonemic structure of words is critical to their success in learning to read.
- Reading is a multi-component skill that includes single word recognition, prose reading ability, reading comprehension and decoding ability.

CHAPTER 2

Phonology, reading and the alphabetic principle

What is phonological awareness and how do we measure it?

The previous chapter discussed how a predictor approach to reading might help in the eventual development of screening and assessment instruments as well as teaching methods for children whom we suspect will find reading difficult. But what might be good candidates for predictor variables, and how would they be measured in young children? This and the next chapter describe how a set of measures that tap phonological processing skill are important to understanding early reading development. This chapter will concentrate on phonological awareness and its interaction with letter knowledge acquisition, whereas the following one looks at related skills, such as phonological processing speed and short-term verbal memory.

Within the population of young normal readers, the most extensively studied of the predictors of early reading skill over the past 20 years has been that of phonological awareness. Research into individual differences in children's sensitivity to speech sounds within words has led us to the conclusion that these are causally related to the normal acquisition of beginning reading skill.

Phonological awareness refers to children's appreciation of, and ability to process and manipulate, the speech sound segments of words. In her seminal book on beginning reading, Adams (1990) divided phonological tasks that successfully predict reading skill into four main types. This categorization still holds good more than 10 years later.

First, there are rhyming tasks that at the most rudimentary level might include even knowledge of common nursery rhymes, such as 'Jack and Jill' and 'Humpty Dumpty' (MacLean, Bryant and Bradley, 1987). In research conducted with Margaret Snowling and Charles Hulme, children's rhyming ability has been assessed by asking them to produce as many rhyming words as they can for a presented word. So, for instance, 'What words do you know that rhyme with *day*?' to which the child might respond '*may, say, lay*' and so on. Another task involves asking young children to select from a choice of three words (for example *cow, tree, door*) the one that rhymes with *key*, the correct response being *tree*. This task appears in picture format in the Phonological Abilities Test (PAT) (Muter, Hulme and Snowling, 1997) (Figure 2.1).

Figure 2.1 A picture item from the Phonological Abilities Test (PAT) Rhyme Detection subtest. (Source: Phonological Abilities Test; Muter, Hulme and Snowling, 1997.)

However, most of the research into rhyming and its role in early reading development has been conducted by Bryant and colleagues, using an 'odd word out' or sound categorization task. Children are asked to select from an array of three or four words the one that is the 'odd one out' or non-rhyming word (Bradley and Bryant, 1983), for example the odd word out in the series *cat, pat, fan* is *fan*. Bryant and colleagues found that this test given to 4- and 5-year-old children proved a powerful predictor of reading at ages 6 and 7 years.

Second are syllable and phoneme segmentation tasks, in which the child taps, counts out or identifies the constituent syllables and/or phonemes within words. Liberman et al. (1974) asked young children to tap out with a dowell the number of syllables in multisyllabic words or the number of phonemes in single syllable words. In the word, *sandwich*, the children tapped twice to indicate the syllables *san* and *wich*. In the word *cat*, the children tapped three times to indicate the three constituent phonemes /c/, /a/, /t/ within the word. Other segmentation tasks might require the child to say the initial syllable or phoneme in a word, for example *pen* in *pencil* and /p/ in *pen*, respectively (Fox and Routh, 1975). For the PAT, a syllable and phoneme segmentation task was developed using pictures (Muter, Hulme and Snowling, 1997); the procedure was originally suggested in a study by Stuart (Stuart and Coltheart, 1988) using concrete objects. In the PAT task children were shown a picture of a two-syllable word, such as *sandwich*; the examiner said the first syllable *san* and the child was asked to 'finish off' the word by supplying the second syllable *wich*. In the phoneme segmentation part of the task, children were required to supply the final phoneme of a single-syllable word; so, for instance, the examiner showed the child a picture of a cat, said the initial two phonemes /ca/ and then asked the child to supply the final phoneme /t/. It has been found consistently that tasks such as this are strongly related to how easily children learn to read. So children who are good at syllable, and in particular, phoneme segmentation tasks learn to read more rapidly than children who find these segmentation tasks difficult.

Third are phoneme manipulation tasks that require the child to delete, add, substitute or transpose phonemes within words. For instance, in a consonant deletion task, the word *cat* without the /c/ says *at* (Bruce, 1964). In a more difficult version of this task the child might be asked to delete a medial (embedded) sound from a word, for example *winter* without the /t/ says *winner* (item taken from the Elision subtest of the Comprehensive Test of Phonological Processing (CTOPP); Wagner, Torgesen and Rashotte, 1999). Phoneme deletion tasks have been shown to be very powerful predictors of early reading development (between the ages of 5 and 7 years). In a study conducted by Share and colleagues (Share et al., 1984), kindergarten children's phoneme deletion ability was the best of a number of predictors of reading measured one year later.

Sometimes phoneme manipulation tasks ask the child to 'add' a phoneme to a word rather than delete it, for example /b/ added to the beginning of the word *in* becomes *bin*. A subtest from the Phonological Assessment Battery (PhAB) (Frederickson, Frith and Reason, 1997) assesses phoneme substitution ability; here, the child is required to replace the first phoneme of a presented word with another specified phoneme, for example *make* with /t/ gives *take*. The authors of this test refer to it as a 'semi-spoonerism task'. A more advanced version for older children who have more developed reading skills is a 'full spoonerism task' in which the child is required to 'swap over' the initial phoneme of two words. For instance, *fed man* becomes *med fan* (item also taken from the PhAB).

Finally, there are sound blending tasks in which the examiner provides the syllables or phonemes of a word and the child is asked to put them together, for example *san-wich* blends to give *sandwich*; /c/-/a/-/t/ blends to yield *cat*. Sound blending tasks such as these have been found to predict beginning reading skills in studies conducted by Perfetti et al. (1987), Lundberg, Olofsson and Wall (1980), and more recently by Wagner, Torgesen and Rashotte (1994).

What must be apparent from the description of the above tasks is that some phonological awareness tasks are easier than others. Some children aged as young as 2 and 3 years are able to demonstrate skills of syllable blending, syllable segmentation and some aspects of rhyming skill (at least knowledge of nursery rhymes). Other skills that are very much more advanced do not emerge until later in development, and may depend on children being exposed to printed material (initially alphabet letters and then reading books) and even upon explicit reading instruction. Phoneme segmentation and, in particular, phoneme manipulation tasks are the most challenging of these and are unlikely to be carried out successfully by pre-school children. There may be an intermediate stage between the ability to segment syllables and phonemes in which children demonstrate an ability to blend and segment onsets and rimes (Treiman, 1985). Table 2.1 depicts the developmental progression of phonological awareness skills and relates it to both chronological age and experience of printed form.

Table 2.1 Developmental progression of phonological awareness skills

Age (years)	Developmental progression of phonological skill	Print experience		
4	Nursery rhymes	Learning letters		
	Rhyme recognition			
	Syllable blending			
	Syllable segmentation			
5	Alliteration			
	Beginning sound matching			
	Onset-rime segmentation			
	Rhyme production			
5½	Syllable manipulation		Building sight vocabulary	
	Identification of beginning and end phonemes			
	Phoneme blending			Developing decoding skills
	Phoneme segmentation			
6	Phoneme addition			
	Phoneme deletion			
	Phoneme substitution			

The above discussion, with Table 2.1 depicting the continuum of phono-logical development, points to there being a two-way interactive process between phonological skills and learning to read. So, phonological awareness promotes reading development, but reading also helps develop phonological skills. One of the earliest studies that pointed to this reciprocal relationship between reading and phonology was that carried out by Morais et al. (1979). These workers found that illiterate Portuguese adults had much more diffi-culty in deleting or adding phonemes within words than did those who had already benefited from an adult literacy programme. They concluded that the ability to analyse sounds in words depends to a significant extent on the experience of learning to read.

Of perhaps more obvious relevance to children's development is a study by Mann (1986) in which the performance of 6-year-old Japanese and American children was compared on a phoneme awareness task. The Japanese-speaking children, who were being taught a syllable-based written language, encountered much greater difficulty on the phoneme awareness task than the American children, whose reading experience was based much more on alphabetic sounds. Goswami and Bryant (1990) suggested that some forms of phonological awareness pre-date and, in fact, facilitate reading development, whereas other (more advanced) forms of phonological skill are caused, or at any rate influenced, by exposure to print. It seems reasonable to propose that learning to read draws children's attention to the sound struc-ture of words, which then in turn improves their phonological awareness (Perfetti et al., 1987; Cataldo and Ellis, 1988).

How stable and robust are phonological skills?

Although some phonological skills are available at a rudimentary level to children as young as 2 and 3 years of age, they are not necessarily stable abili-ties at that age. Lonigan et al. (1998) studied the phonological awareness skills of over 300 children aged from 2 to 5 years. The measures used included rime oddity, syllable and phoneme blending, and syllable and phoneme deletion. While there were enormous individual differences within this large group of children, in general significant numbers of 2- and 3-year-olds were able to demonstrate syllable sensitivity and many 4- and 5-year-olds were able to analyse words at the level of the phoneme. Lonigan and colleagues (1998) were able to demonstrate that phonological sensitivity becomes increasingly stable during the pre-school years. Certainly, the 2- and 3-year-olds varied quite a lot in their performance within and across the different phonological tasks. However, by the time the children were 4 years of age they were beginning to show stability in their phonological sensitivity across the different tasks and across time, with their responding becoming increasingly consistent and reliable. Lonigan et al. (1998) also showed that lower levels of sound sensitivity (at the level of the syllable) are developmental precursors of phonological sensitivity (that is, of phonemes). The children's ability to perform blending or deletion operations at the level of the syllable was correlated with their later ability to blend and delete at the level of the phoneme. This is consistent with the developmental model of the progression of phonological awareness skills shown earlier in Table 2.1.

Once children reach the elementary school years, their phonological skills become, and indeed remain, very stable indeed (Stuart, 1990; Stuart and Masterson, 1992; Wagner, Torgesen and Rashotte, 1994; Wagner et al., 1997; Muter and Snowling, 1998). Thus, children who are weak in phonological skills at the beginning of school will continue to be relatively weak in these abilities in the fourth or fifth grades. In a longitudinal study (Muter and Snowling, 1998), an initial phoneme deletion task was given to 38 children when they were 4, 5 and 6 years old; examples of items included: *cat* without the /c/ says *at*; *bus* without the /b/ says *us*. We had the opportunity to follow up 34 of these children nearly three years later when they were aged 9. At follow-up they were given a similar, though admittedly much more difficult, phoneme deletion task which involved deleting a specified sound from a nonsense word in order to produce a real word (after McDougall et al., 1994). Some of the items were relatively easy, necessitating only the omission of the initial or final phoneme, 'bice' without the /b/ says *ice*, 'bloot' without the /t/ says *blue*. Other items were much more difficult and required the child to take away a phoneme from the middle of the nonsense word, for example 'clart' without the /l/ says *cart*; 'hift' without the /f/ says *hit*. The children's performance on the phoneme deletion task given at ages 5 and 6 (but not at age 4) correlated significantly with their performance on the more complex deletion task at age 9.

Similarly, large-scale cross-sectional and longitudinal studies carried out by Wagner and colleagues demonstrate very convincingly that measures of phonological awareness are good concurrent and longitudinal predictors of reading ability throughout the elementary school years (Wagner, Torgesen and Rashotte, 1994; Wagner et al., 1997). This is not necessarily the case for other predictors of reading skill which we will come to later. Short-term memory, naming speed tasks and letter identification tend to exert only a transitory influence over reading skill, predicting reading ability at particular stages in literacy development. As Wagner and associates conclude, the ability to segment and analyse sounds within words should be viewed as a stable and coherent individual difference variable. They suggest that phonological skill may be as stable an entity as IQ, which has been shown to be highly consistent in children and adults in both the short and the long term. Bearing in mind the observed stability and the established long-term predictive power of phonological skills, it may be argued that tasks that tap these abilities are prime candidates for inclusion in any early screening or assessment battery of reading achievement and in teaching programmes designed to remediate reading problems. On a cautionary note, Muter and Snowling (1998) found that phonological measures taken at age 4 years did not predict reading skill at age 9. Arguably, therefore, it may be appropriate to delay screening for children at risk for reading failure until the end of the pre-school period.

We have seen that phonological awareness measures are both powerful and stable long-term predictors of reading achievement. Another way to look at the robustness of phonological awareness is to demonstrate that its influence over reading is the same even in very varied and disparate groups of children. This can be achieved through replication of the phonology-reading association with different samples of children, and with those from multilingual backgrounds. In a study of 55 5- to 6-year-old children who were attending an international school in Switzerland (Muter and Diethelm, 2001) half the sample had English as their mother tongue, but came from a number of English-speaking countries, including the UK, the USA, South Africa and Australia. The majority of the non-English mother tongue group was French-speaking, though there were also children who were native speakers of Italian, Spanish, Japanese, Arabic and Scandinavian languages. All the children were being educated in the school's English language programme. The children were given a range of phonological awareness tasks at ages 5 and 6, and their reading skill at age 6 was also examined.

The tests of phonological awareness required the children to supply the final phoneme of single-syllable words and to delete beginning and end phonemes from words (taken from the PAT). The children's scores on these tests at ages 5 and 6 were significantly predictive of their reading skills at age 6. This was true not only irrespective of the language background of the children but also irrespective of their oral proficiency in English. Their vocabulary levels at both ages 5 and 6 were assessed by giving them a well-known picture vocabulary test (British Picture Vocabulary Scale (BPVS); Dunn, Dunn and Whetton, 1982); this proved a relatively weak (and non-significant) predictor of early reading skill. Thus there was good evidence for the phonology-reading association being a powerful and robust one that can transcend even language differences and social backgrounds. It is also important to realize that children's proficiency in spoken language is not, on its own, a reliable indicator as to how easily they will learn to read.

Which phonological skills most influence early reading development?

This chapter has presented strong arguments for phonological skills being causally related to the development of beginning reading skills. Indeed, few psychologists would disagree with this statement. However, the nature of phonological skills and their precise bearing on reading is not as yet clear; it is, in fact, an area of some controversy and at times heated debate. How many sorts of phonological skill are there? If there are different sorts, which play the most important role in the beginning stages of learning to read? Do different phonological skills influence reading at different stages of development? It is possible to carry out a statistical procedure called 'factor analysis' (sometimes referred to as 'principal components analysis') to determine whether different tasks essentially measure a single skill or underlying ability, or alternatively whether certain tasks measure different components of phonological skill. If phonological awareness tasks are all tapping into the same underlying global ability then presumably it does not matter which particular task a child is given in order to measure his or her level of sensitivity to speech sounds. However, if there are different subskills within the phonological domain, it is important to know what these are because they might affect reading development in different ways.

In general, early correlational studies of phonological awareness tasks suggested that a single factor accounted for variance in phonological ability (Stanovich, Cunningham and Cramer, 1984; Wagner and Torgesen, 1987). More recent studies have indicated that it may be possible to derive multiple factors within the phonological domain. Yopp (1988) uncovered two factors from a principal components analysis of 10 phonological awareness tests given to 96 kindergarten children. The factors were highly correlated, that is they were related, not independent, factors and they appeared to reflect two levels of difficulty rather than two qualitatively different kinds of skill. Yopp (1988) termed the first factor 'simple or implicit phonemic awareness'. The tasks that loaded on this factor required only one cognitive operation, such as blending sounds together to form a word. The second factor, 'complex or explicit phonemic awareness', was derived from tasks that involved more than one cognitive operation and placed a heavier burden on memory. For instance, a phoneme deletion task requires the child to isolate a given sound, and then to hold the resultant sound in memory while performing the deletion operation. Yopp (1988) found that measures of both of these kinds of ability accounted for variations in the children's ability to read nonsense words.

Other studies have claimed to identify differing types of phonological ability. For instance, the longitudinal study by Wagner, Torgesen and Rashotte

(1994) uncovered two factors in first and second grade readers, namely phonological 'analysis' (breaking words down into sounds) and phonological 'synthesis' (blending sounds). These factors were described by the authors as 'non-redundant' in that they were independent of one another, and they separately made a contribution to reading skill development during the first two years at school.

Clearly, how useful it is to make distinctions between highly correlated phonological ability factors really depends on the nature of their predictive relationships with reading. If different factors differ in their predictive power then it may be important to distinguish between them. If they do not, it is simpler merely to consider differences in phonological skill as a unitary or global construct. Also, it is important to emphasize that although different phonological skills may be highly interrelated, this is not incompatible with a developmental model in which these skills develop at different times. We have already seen that blending and rhyming skills develop at an earlier age than phoneme manipulation skills. Finally, different phonological skills could have quite different causal relationships with reading ability that are dependent on the age of the child and the stage he or she has reached in the reading process. We shall come back to this point later when we look at the evidence that tasks that measure phoneme awareness have a considerable bearing on reading during the first year at school. In contrast, rhyming tasks seem to predict reading skill later on when children are learning about word families, what we now usually refer to as 'analogies' (for example *fight, sight, might*).

Relevant to my own research is the influential theoretical position held by Goswami and Bryant (1990) who proposed that awareness of different phonological units of spoken words develops at different rates. Specifically, Goswami and Bryant (1990) proposed that tasks of rhyming skill tap the child's understanding of onset and rime units within words; as seen earlier, the onset refers to the consonant or consonant cluster that precedes the vowel, whereas the rime consists of the vowel and succeeding consonants. Rhyming tasks may be performed by children as young as 4 and 5 years old, and are considered highly predictive of later success in reading. One of the most important and oft-reported studies that demonstrated a link between early phonological (including rhyming) skill and later reading development was that conducted by Bradley and Bryant (1983, 1985). These authors studied approximately 400 children who were either 4 or 5 years old when the study began and either 8 or 9 years old when they were seen for the last time three to four years later. When the children were aged 4 or 5 years they were given the rime oddity task described earlier, with tests of vocabulary and memory. Three years later they were given tests of reading and arithmetic together with an IQ test. Bradley and Bryant (1985) uncovered a very strong and specific relationship between the children's rhyme oddity scores at ages 4 and 5 years, and their reading (but not arithmetic) scores at ages 8 or 9. In Goswami and Bryant's (1990) model, the ability to segment phonemes within words is a very different skill that develops later, partly as a consequence of learning to read, and is thought to be particularly closely related to learning to spell.

In a study of 38 normal children during their first two years of learning to read, Muter et al. (1998) carried out a principal components analysis of scores from a battery of phonological measures initially administered when the children were pre-readers. The researchers wanted to cover the full four categories of phonological awareness tasks described by Adams (1990), as discussed in the earlier part of this chapter. Two measures of rhyming skill were included in the study. First, the children were asked to select from three choices the word which rhymed with a given presented word (rhyme detection). Second, the children were asked to produce as many rhyming words as they could for a given presented word (rhyme production). The children were also asked to blend phonemes to form words, to supply the final sound of a presented incomplete single syllable word, and to delete the initial sound of a word.

In this study Muter et al. (1998) identified two distinct and relatively independent factors: rhyming (defined by the measures of rhyme detection and rhyme production) and segmentation (defined by the measures of phoneme completion, phoneme blending and phoneme deletion). Segmentation was strongly correlated with attainment in both reading and spelling at the end of the first year of learning to read, whereas rhyming was not.

It is sometimes helpful to depict the predictive relationships between the phonological and reading measures through the use of a path diagram, as shown in Figure 2.2.

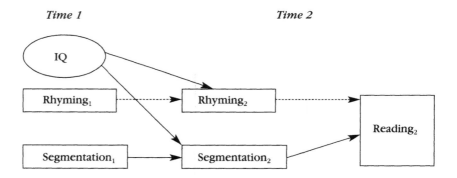

Figure 2.2 Path diagram depicting the relationships between phonological segmentation, rhyming, IQ and reading during the first year at school.

Figure 2.2 charts the relationships between IQ measured at Time 1 when the children were aged 4 years, rhyming and segmentation skill assessed at both Times 1 and 2 (ages 4 and 5) and reading measured at Time 2 (5 years). The arrows in a path diagram indicate putative causal connections between variables. The model moves from left to right, with the left-sided measures being causally related via arrows to those on the right. The solid black lines indicate significant predictive relationships, whereas the broken lines indicate non-significant relationships. We can see from the path diagram that rhyming has no impact on the first year of learning to read, whereas segmentation at age 4 is predictive of segmentation ability a year later which, in turn, then influences reading after a year at school. Note that the effect of IQ on reading is indirect. It appears that its impact is mediated by segmentation ability. In other words, brighter children find segmenting words into sounds easier than less able children, and it is this skill in segmentation that promotes reading development.

The relative contribution of rhyming and segmentation to reading was evident even in the long term with this same sample of children. Recall that 34 of the original sample of 38 children were followed up until they were 9 years of age (Muter and Snowling, 1998). Consistent with the results of the earlier phases of the study, it was the segmentation measure (in this case beginning phoneme deletion) administered at ages 5 and 6 years that was predictive of reading skill in the later elementary school years. The rhyming scores obtained at ages 5 and 6 did not predict reading skill at 9 years old.

The relative salience of rhyming and segmentation skill to beginning literacy development has generated heated debate in the scientific literature (see Bryant, 1998; Hulme, Muter and Snowling, 1998). A number of other recent studies also suggest that segmentation may be a more influential phonological skill in the beginning stages of learning to read than rhyming (Wimmer, Landerl and Schneider, 1994; Duncan, Seymour and Hill, 1997; Seymour and Duncan, 1997). The longitudinal studies by Seymour and colleagues followed a group of children who had well-established rhyming skills at nursery school through their first two years of learning to read. These workers conducted a series of experiments that showed that the introduction of letters and the alphabetic principle (learning to connect letters with their sounds) resulted in the children becoming more proficient in identifying smaller phonemic, rather than larger rime, units within words. So, even when children start school with established rhyming skills, they are not necessarily disposed to use this knowledge in their initial attempts at reading. Indeed, it was only during the children's second year at school that they began to take advantage of rime units in their reading attempts. Wimmer, Landerl and Schneider (1994) found that rime awareness was only minimally predictive of reading and spelling achievement at the end of grade 1 in German-speaking children, but that it gained substantially in predictive importance for reading and spelling achievement in grades 3 and 4. Although these findings should be treated with some caution, bearing in mind that German has a more phonologically transparent orthography than English, nonetheless they add weight to the view that rhyming skills may have relevance at a later rather than an early stage in reading development.

Clearly, the resolution of this controversy is crucial not only from a theoretical standpoint but also in respect of knowing which phonological skills to prioritize, both for the development of early screening instruments and in the teaching of reading to children in their early years at school. Recently, an attempt has been made to resolve this controversy in two subsequent studies. The first of these involved a larger scale replication of an earlier study (Muter et al., submitted). A range of phoneme and onset-rime awareness measures was given to 90 children, initially on entering primary school; the average age of the children at the outset of the study was 4 years 9 months. These tasks were similar to those used in the original study (Muter et al., 1998) in that an initial phoneme deletion task was used, with measures of rhyme detection and rhyme production. However, two new tasks were added — a test of final phoneme deletion and a rime oddity task similar to that used in the study by Bradley and Bryant (1985). The data were analysed by use of a complex statistical procedure called 'Structural Equation Modelling' (SEM). In essence, SEM is a combination of factor analysis and the statistical procedure used in prediction research, that of multiple regression. It permits the creation of theoretical models of learning against which the 'goodness of fit' of the actual data to the model may be determined. In keeping with the results of the earlier study, two independent (that is, uncorrelated) phonological factors were derived from the Time 1 (4-year-old) data: a rhyme factor on which the rhyme detection, rhyme production and rhyme oddity tests loaded highly, and a segmentation factor on which the beginning and end phoneme deletion tests loaded highly. When the predictive relations between the phonological factors at age 4 and the children's reading one year later were examined, it was again found that it was the children's earlier segmentation scores that predicted their later reading, not their rhyming scores.

The second study that has attempted to resolve this controversy was conducted by Hulme et al. (2002), in response to a suggestion made by Bryant (1998) in a critique he made of the earlier longitudinal study by Muter et al., (1998). Bryant (1998, p. 37) proposed that 'if one wants to compare the predictive powers of onset-rime and phoneme tasks, one should ensure that both sets of tasks involve exactly the same procedure apart from the difference in the phonological unit which children have to detect'. In the study by Hulme et al. (2002) 5- to 6-year-old children were given three tasks which employed the same set of nonsense words — one task required deleting a sound unit from the non-word; one required the selection of a non-word that sounded like the stimulus non-word; and the third required the child to select the 'odd word out' from a list of three non-words. Each task tapped awareness of four phonological units — initial phoneme, final phoneme, onset and rime. The children were followed up about seven months later in order to determine which phonological unit best predicted progress in learning to read. In keeping with the findings of earlier studies, it was the measures of phoneme awareness that proved to be the best predictors of later reading, with the onset and rime measures proving far weaker predictors.

But where does rhyming come in?

The evidence presented so far presents a compelling case for phonological segmentation skills being far stronger predictors of beginning reading than rhyming abilities. That is not to say that rhyming does not play a role in later reading processes. As seen earlier, Wimmer, Landerl and Schneider (1994) found that rhyming did not predict reading in German speaking children in grade 1 but it did predict both reading and spelling in grades 3 and 4. Similarly, Seymour and colleagues found that children pay attention to, and use, smaller phonemic units during the first year at school, but that they begin to take note of larger rime units within words in their second year. It is also possible that different phonological skills influence different components of the reading process.

Goswami (1990) proposed that rhyming tasks measure children's awareness of the onset-rime boundaries of words and this level of awareness is critical to their use of analogical strategies in reading. When reading by analogy, readers generate the pronunciations of new words based on their knowledge of known words with similar letter patterns (Glushko, 1979). Thus, a child who knows how to read the word *beat* can, through the process of analogy, infer the pronunciation of similarly spelled words, such as *meat* and *heat*. Goswami (1986) devised an elegant experimental paradigm for demonstrating young children's ability to analogize. She presented 5- and 6-year-old children with a clue word, for example *beak*, and then asked them to read other words, some of which were analogous to the clue word, for example *peak, weak*, whilst others were control words that could not be read by analogy but were equally visually similar in that they shared three letters, for example *lake, pake*. Goswami (1990) found that beginner readers read correctly more analogy than control words. In fact she went so far as to say that children as young as 5 could make use of analogy in the absence of existing reading skill. She hypothesized that there is a causal link between early rhyming ability and children's subsequent use of analogy in reading; she found that children's rhyme awareness, as measured by the rhyme oddity task, was more closely related to their success in making analogies than was their performance on a phoneme deletion task. Goswami then went on to design teaching materials (published through Oxford Learning Tree) which promote children's development of rhyming, onset-rime awareness and analogical skill, and which could form the core of an elementary school reading programme.

The teaching of rhyming and analogical skills has had a not inconsiderable impact on teaching methods adopted in British schools over the past five years. However, a number of other authors have questioned the significance of early reading by analogy. First, Ehri and Robbins (1992) suggested that children need some decoding skill, that is, knowledge of sound-to-letter correspondence before they can read words by analogy. These authors found that, although 6-year-old children who had well-established decoding skills were able to read analogy words after training on 'clue' words, other children who had limited decoding skills were no better at reading the analogy than the control words.

In virtually all of Goswami's analogy studies, the clue word has been exposed to the child throughout the experiment so that he or she can refer to it when later shown the test analogy and control words. Snowling and I queried whether young children would be quite so adept at analogizing if they did not have this prompt in front of them. After all, in a naturalistic reading setting children attempting to use analogies would not be carrying prompt clue word cards around with them! We began by training 36 6-year-old children to read a series of clue words (Muter, Snowling and Taylor, 1994). The children were then asked to read a series of analogy and control words based on the trained clue words (post-test). So, for instance, for the clue word *land*, the analogy words were *sand, grand, hand, band*, whereas the control words were *lean, nail, lend, bald*. Half the children had the clue word in view during the post-test session while the other half did not.

It was found that the analogy effect was much reduced when the clue word was not placed in front of the children post-test. This finding led us to doubt that young children spontaneously use analogies with any degree of frequency. Indeed, the extent to which they do depends critically on their reading level. Ten of the children in our study failed to demonstrate any analogy skills at all; these children were the poorest readers in the sample. We would thus agree with Ehri and Robbins (1992) that children need some decoding skill to enable them to use analogical processes in reading. We also had some doubts about the connection between rhyming ability and use of analogy. We looked at the association between the children's rhyme detection and production skills at ages 4, 5 and 6, and their ability to use analogies at age 6. There was a significant concurrent relationship between rhyming ability and analogizing at age 6, but we could not uncover a predictive relationship between the children's rhyming scores at ages 4 and 5, and their ability to use analogies at age 6. Without this important longitudinal connection, we cannot be truly confident that there is a causal relationship between early rhyming skill and the later ability to use analogical strategies in reading.

In Goswami's model, children make analogies based on the shared spelling patterns of the clue and target words. An alternative explanation is one in terms of what is referred to as 'phonological priming'. In this view, the sound of the clue word acts to 'ready' or prime the pronunciation of the target, regardless of the shared letter sequences between the clue and the target. So, hearing the word *beak* before attempting to read the word *peak* may help a child to decode *peak*, without their having any knowledge that these two words share a common spelling pattern.

In order to test which of these explanations account for analogy effects, Nation, Allen and Hulme (2001) carried out an analogy experiment with 5- and 6-year-old children in which there were three different presentations of the prompt word. In the combined prompt condition, the clue word was exposed in the training phase and was also in view and spoken by the examiner in the test phase. In the phonological prompt condition, the clue word was exposed in the training phase but was hidden from view and simply spoken aloud by the examiner in the test phase. In the pure phonology condition, the clue word was never exposed at either the training or the test phase, but instead was spoken aloud by the examiner in both phases. In this experiment, the same number of 'analogy' responses were made by the children regardless of whether the clue word was seen or just heard. The authors concluded that there is no evidence that children in the beginning stages of learning to read genuinely make orthographic analogies based on shared spelling patterns. Rather, it is the simpler mechanism of phonological priming that explains the findings of this study.

Nation, Allen and Hulme (2001) do, however, concede that children are making some use of orthographic information in an analogy experiment such as this. The children in their study had developed the rudiments of letter-to-sound knowledge and used this to attempt to decode mostly the initial or final consonants of the word. They could not, however, decode the vowels, which in this instance were rather difficult vowel digraphs, such as 'ea' and 'oa'. Nation, Allen and Hulme (2001) suggest that what the children were doing was to attempt a partial decoding of the word which, when combined with the phonological prime, was enough to elicit the correct pronunciation. They conclude by suggesting that analogy experiments of the type developed by Goswami probably overestimate the extent to which beginning readers make true orthographic analogies. That is not to say of course that the spontaneous use of analogies does not play an important role in later reading and spelling when it becomes a relatively sophisticated strategy for children who already have a sizeable reading vocabulary.

It is tempting to conclude that there is little point in bothering with the measurement and training of children's rhyming skills, and that instead we should concentrate only on training phoneme-level skills to beginning readers. However, Hulme et al. (2002) caution against taking this stance. They have pointed out that there is good evidence that the development of phonological skills in young children proceeds from early awareness of large units (like rimes and syllables) to later awareness of small units (phonemes). Thus, 'interventions to improve children's phonological skills need to respect this developmental sequence and begin by training children to appreciate larger units before moving on to smaller units' (Hulme et al., 2002, p. 20). In other words, it may be important to train rhyming skills in children with limited phonological awareness before moving on to more developmentally advanced phonological skills such as segmenting or manipulating phonemes. Relevant to this view is the finding of the longitudinal study conducted by Bryant and colleagues (1990), namely that children's early rhyming ability was predictive of their later phoneme detection skill. Bryant (2002), in his recent response to the paper by Hulme et al. (2002), continued to argue a case for rhyme awareness having an indirect impact on reading via its effect on phoneme awareness. It is suggested that rhyming might be construed as a developmental precursor of more advanced phoneme awareness ability; it would, therefore, be entirely appropriate to train up rhyming ability as an early step towards the eventual development of the child's awareness of phonemes.

Where does phonological awareness come from?

In achieving a better understanding of how phonological abilities influence reading skill, and in particular how phonological deficits might be avoided through intervention, we need to know more about the precursors of phonological awareness. There is good evidence that the development of phonological skills proceeds from early awareness of large units, such as syllables, to later awareness of small units, such as phonemes (Liberman et al., 1974; Treiman, 1985; Goswami and Bryant, 1990). Studies such as these have shown that children are aware of the syllabic structure of words by the age of 4, they can split words at the level of onset and rime by age 5, and they are beginning to segment words at the level of the phoneme by age 6.

Fowler (1991) maintains that the internal representation or coding of speech sounds by the brain is initially global or holistic (essentially whole words). During the pre-school years, these representations are gradually reorganized into increasingly smaller segments — syllables, then onsets and rimes, and eventually, phonemes. So, in essence, phonological representations become increasingly fine-grained. This awareness of segmental size is assumed to be driven by earlier vocabulary growth, specifically a growth spurt that takes place between 18 months and 3 years of age (Walley, 1993). The child's first 50 words or so are acquired slowly, and one at a time, but from about 18 months of age there is a large and sudden increase in the number of words they can produce and comprehend (Reznick and Goldfield, 1992). As a growing number of words overlap in their sound-based properties, there should be considerable pressure to implement fine-grained or segmental representations of these.

Evidence for the relationship between vocabulary growth and phonological development comes from a correlational study by Metsala (1999) that showed that performance on phonological awareness tasks was related to vocabulary size. So, in effect, growth in vocabulary drives both segmental restructuring (from large to small units) and the subsequent development of phonological skills. Byrne (1998) suggested that vocabulary growth contributes to the early stages of phonological awareness development but that it does not play a continuing role. It could be that in the early stages, children develop rudimentary phonological skills (for instance, awareness of syllables and onsets and rimes) that are themselves driven by vocabulary. However, the further growth of refined phonemic awareness may simply depend on those earlier established phonological skills. It may be that early phonological skills somehow pave the way for children becoming aware of smaller phonemic units, and also for drawing their attention to the sound structure of words in a very general way

Letter knowledge and learning to read

A further predictor candidate that relates strongly to reading skill, and which may be an even more powerful determiner of beginning progress in learning to read than phonological segmentation ability, is letter knowledge acquisition. Early large-scale studies found pre-readers' letter knowledge to be a very good predictor of first-grade reading skills (Bond and Dykstra, 1967; Chall, 1967). More recently, Byrne et al. (1997) found that letter knowledge contributed far more to children's performance on a reading decoding task in a teaching experiment with pre-school and kindergarten children than did a measure of phonemic awareness. Analyses from our recent longitudinal study of nearly 100 normal children have highlighted letter knowledge skill on entry to school as the best single predictor of word recognition one year later (Muter et al., submitted).

It is clear that knowledge of letter names or sounds is an important prerequisite for children learning to read and spell in an alphabetic orthography
such as English. Knowledge of letter sounds is necessary for children to
understand that there is a systematic relationship between the spelling
patterns of words and their pronunciations. In our study (Muter et al., 1998)
not only did segmentation and letter knowledge make separate and specific
contributions to the first year of learning to read, but there was also an
additional significant contribution from the product term 'Letter knowledge
× Phonological segmentation', reflecting the interaction of these two component skills. The product term exerted a small, but significant, additional influence on reading (with an even bigger effect on spelling). It seems, therefore,
that in order to progress in reading, children need to forge meaningful
connections between their developing phonological skills and their appreciation of print — what Hatcher, Hulme and Ellis (1994) refer to as 'phonological linkage'. It is not simply having adequate phonological awareness and
letter knowledge that permits good progress in learning to read. Rather, both
of these factors are important and they act in an interactive fashion. Figure
2.3 depicts the relationship between phonological segmentation skill and
letter knowledge and their joint impact on beginning reading and spelling.

It may be seen from this path diagram that both letter knowledge and
phonological segmentation skills exert separate and significant influences on
reading during the first year of learning to read. There is an additional, and

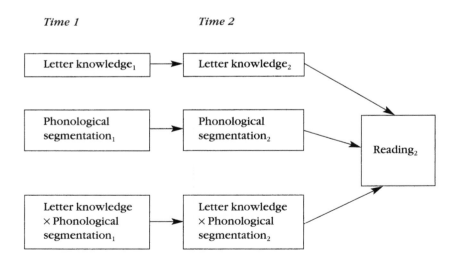

Figure 2.3 Path diagram depicting the relationships between phonological segmentation,
letter knowledge and reading during the first year at school.

indeed quite separate, significant path to reading that is explained by the interactive term, 'Letter knowledge × Phonological segmentation'. This latter path embodies children's ability to form explicit connections between their emerging segmentation skills and their experience of print.

Although letter knowledge is a far more powerful predictor of reading success in the first year or so at school than is phonological awareness, it drops out of the picture as children reach a full knowledge of their letters and head towards becoming more fluent readers. In our most recent longitudinal study (Muter et al., submitted), it was found that letter knowledge contributed greatly to children's progress in learning to read during their first year at school, but played a diminishing role by the time they had reached the end of their second year. These findings are in keeping with those of Wagner et al. (1997) who also found that letter knowledge had only a temporary, albeit powerful, effect on young readers' progress in reading. This is unlike phonological awareness, which appears to contribute to, and predict, reading ability throughout the elementary school years.

Given the evidence that letter knowledge is a critical predictor of beginning reading success, an important question we need to ask is what are the determinants of the ease with which letter–sound connections are acquired? It is tempting to think that the relationships between phonemes and graphemes are learned purely in a rote fashion, a kind of 'paired-associate' learning. So, in effect, being repeatedly told that the phoneme /s/ is represented in print by the letter *s* should eventually enable a child to forge a connection between the sound /s/ and the letter *s*. This being the case, it might be assumed that given equal exposure, /w/-*w* and /t/-*t* are learned equally quickly. However, as Treiman, Weatherston and Berch (1994) point out, it is easier for kindergarten children to learn letter–sound correspondences when the sound of the letter is contained in its name (for example *p, b, k*) than when the letter name does not help to specify the sound (for example *h, w*). These authors go on to suggest that more extensive teaching is needed for some phoneme-grapheme correspondences than for others. Consequently, teachers may need to spend more time on the sounds of letters such as *y* and *w* than on the sounds of letters such as *b* and *v*.

Treiman, Weatherson and Berch (1994) also suggested that children's phonological awareness skills are intimately involved in their learning of phoneme-grapheme correspondences. However, the direction of influence between phonological awareness and letter knowledge acquisition remains an area of dispute. Treiman, Weatherson and Berch (1994) and indeed others (Rack et al., 1994), have suggested that phonological awareness skills help to promote letter–sound knowledge acquisition. However, Barron (1991) and Johnston, Anderson and Holligan (1996) have proposed that learning the alphabet may cause children to become explicitly aware of the phonological structure of words. Johnston, Anderson and Holligan (1996) found that letter knowledge contributed to phoneme awareness in 4-year-old non-readers. Clearly, there is an interactive relationship between children's emerging letter–sound knowledge and their phonological awareness. The bi-directional nature of this relationship has been explored by Burgess and Lonigan (1998) in a one-year longitudinal study of children aged 4 and 5 years. Their analyses revealed that phonological sensitivity predicted growth in letter knowledge, and that letter knowledge predicted growth in phonological sensitivity when controlling for children's age and oral language skills. However, the effect of letter knowledge on phonological sensitivity was less than the effect of phonological sensitivity on growth in letter knowledge.

There has been an enormous amount of research into the role of phonological awareness in influencing literacy development. Far less attention has been given to the process of letter knowledge acquisition and specifically how it affects beginning reading. Given the status of letter knowledge as the most powerful predictor of beginning reading, it is critical to direct greater research effort towards a better understanding of how children acquire letter knowledge and which early factors affect its growth. One way of doing this would be to conduct a fine-grained longitudinal study in which children are assessed at four- to six-monthly intervals during their acquisition of letter knowledge from age $3^{1}/_{2}$ to approximately 5 years. This would allow for the study of the interactive influences of measures, such as paired associate learning skills, vocabulary growth, phonological awareness and perhaps even environmental factors (such as exposure to alphabet picture books at home or nursery school), on letter knowledge growth.

Putting phonological awareness and letter knowledge together — acquiring the alphabetic principle

The forging of connections between phonological skills and letter knowledge is captured in an important concept that has been studied in depth by Byrne and colleagues – this is the notion of the 'alphabetic principle' (Byrne, 1998). This notion refers to the idea that 'the letters that comprise our printed language stand for the individual sounds that comprise our spoken language' (Byrne, 1998, p. 1). This seems both obvious and simple. However, the acquisition of the alphabetic principle is no mean feat for young children encountering print for the first time. It is thought that the acquisition of the alphabetic principle forms the foundation upon which all subsequent literacy skill development is built. Before embarking on a more comprehensive discussion of this concept, it may be helpful to briefly digress to discuss stage models of reading. Familiarity with these can help to put the acquisition of the alphabetic principle into a broader developmental perspective.

One particular model is of especial relevance to the study of early reading development and dyslexia. This is the model proposed by Frith in 1985. In Frith's (1985) model, children learn to read logographically at first. They pay attention to salient visual cues within words, such as word shape and length, initial and final letters, and in this way build up a sight vocabulary. So, a child in the logographic stage of learning to read who has learned to recognize the words *fruit* and *photograph* might read the newly presented words *fast* and *policeman* also as *fruit* and *photograph* because of their visual similarities to known words. When children learn the alphabet, and assuming they have sufficient phonological skills to enable them to split words into sounds, they proceed to the alphabetic stage. With an improved appreciation of sound-to-letter relationships, they begin to phonically decode or 'sound out' unfamiliar words they encounter. It is the acquisition of the alphabetic principle that enables children to proceed from the limited logographic stage into the alphabetic stage. This latter stage affords them an independent strategy for tackling new words and in so doing enables them to build up what will eventually become a massive reading vocabulary.

Dyslexic children are conceptualized within Frith's (1985) model as failing to make an easy transition from the logographic to the alphabetic stage of reading. In essence, they remain 'arrested' in the logographic stage for far longer than they should (most children proceed to alphabetic reading by the time they are 6 years old) and so fall further and further behind their contemporaries. The final stage of Frith's (1985) model, the orthographic stage is not reached until children are well into the later primary school years, and is, therefore, beyond the age range covered by this book. This latter stage is characterized by a child becoming aware of more complex graphemic clusters, for example 'tion', 'ove', and morphemic and analogical units within words, such as 'ight'.

Given the importance of the alphabetic principle in determining the ease with which children begin to broaden their reading vocabulary, we need to consider the conditions necessary for its acquisition. Our writing system represents spoken language at the level of the phoneme but also at the level of onset-rime, syllable, morpheme and words. It is not obvious to children when they first encounter words that they need to focus on the alphabetic nature of their written language and not, for instance, on its morphological structure. In other words, they need to concentrate on the sounds of the letters they see, not what they might represent in terms of meaning.

Byrne (1996) has shown that in their first attempts at learning to read, children are far more likely to focus on the morphemic representations of letters than on their phonological representations. In this study, pre-reading children were required to learn to read a pair of words distinguished by the letter *s* that in English represents both the phoneme /s/ and also the morpheme for regularized pluralization, for example *hat–hats* and *book–books*. Children were then shown the pair of words *cup–cups* and asked which said *cup* and which *cups*. Children could be successful on this 'transfer task', irrespective of whether they were basing their response on a morphological or a phonological representation, because there was a one-to-one mapping or correspondence between the morphemes and the phonemes. In fact, the children were able to perform this transfer task without any difficulty. However, they were then given a second transfer task in which they were required to distinguish two words in which the final *s* played only a distinguishing phonological, not morphemic, role, for example *pur–purs*. Most of the children failed the task. They did not notice the phonological role of the letter *s*. Instead, the children focused on its morphological function, that is, its role in indicating pluralization. Byrne (1996) went on to argue that children do not induce the alphabetic principle for themselves simply through exposure to reading materials or through the acquisition of a sight vocabulary. Rather, they need to have their attention directed towards the phonological role of letters by being taught alphabetic sound-to-letter relations.

Byrne and colleagues went on to use the above type of experimental transfer task to determine exactly what skills and knowledge children need to have in place in order to acquire the alphabetic principle. In a classic study, Byrne and Fielding-Barnsley (1989) first taught children how to read the words *mat* and *sat*. They were then asked to decide whether the printed word *mow* should be pronounced as *mow* or *sow*. Success on the transfer task was achieved only by those children who could phonemically segment the speech items, who identified the initial sound segments, and who had learned the graphic symbols for the sounds 'm' and 's'. Thus, phoneme awareness and grapheme–phoneme knowledge are needed in combination for successful acquisition of the alphabetic principle. This is very similar to the concept of 'phonological linkage' raised earlier; that is, the notion that children need to forge meaningful connections between their developing phonological skills and their appreciation of print. Indeed, it is this combination of phoneme awareness and phoneme–grapheme knowledge that enables the child to proceed from the logographic to the alphabetic stage in reading acquisition.

One of the limitations of most stage models of cognitive development is that they rarely make explicit how a child moves from one stage to the next. In other words, stage models are rarely able to specify the conditions for stage transition or the processes involved. However, Byrne has been able to achieve this in respect of understanding how children move from logographic to alphabetic reading. We shall see later how we can use this knowledge to devise teaching programmes to help children for whom this transition is difficult to achieve. One point worth noting before leaving our discussion of stage models and the alphabetic principle is that some children appear to bypass the logographic stage and go straight from pre-reading into the alphabetic stage (Stuart and Coltheart, 1988). Byrne explains this by suggesting that if children do not have a usable knowledge of the sound structure of words they will read logographically at first — in a sense, the 'default option'. However, this stage can be circumvented if the child has an understanding of the sound representation of letters and has begun to appreciate how letters symbolize sounds; the child is then able to proceed straight to alphabetic reading. Byrne would argue that dyslexic children fail to acquire the alphabetic principle and so stay 'stuck' in the logographic stage.

Connectionist models of reading development

We have looked at a stage model that attempts to explain how acquisition of the alphabetic principle enables children to move from crude notions about word identification to a more sophisticated concept of complete phoneme–grapheme relations which then forms the foundation for the subsequent expansion of their reading vocabulary. Another way of conceptualizing reading acquisition is embodied in connectionist or parallel distributed processing models. These models are derived from the idea that the brain is a large neural network whose function can be simulated by computers. These computer simulations are carried out on the premise that if we can replicate the way humans read by studying how a computer functioning as a neural network might acquire a reading vocabulary, we might come to know more about the complexities of human reading. The computer simulated models very much reflect our current way of thinking about skilled reading and more recently about how children learn to read. The ideas represented in these models are quite complex to convey and not all that easy to understand, and some readers may after a cursory glance feel more comfortable moving on to the next chapter of the book. However, to exclude altogether a consideration of connectionist models would fail to recognize what is currently an important way of attempting to understand reading and its underlying processes.

Connectionist models postulate that the learning of new words takes place within a neural network that permits associations or connections between three sets of units – graphemes or letter strings, phonemes or sound strings, and intermediate units (sometimes called 'hidden units') which connect between the graphemic and the phonemic units (Figure 2.4).

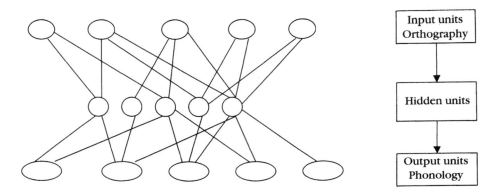

Figure 2.4 Connections within the reading neural network.

Computer simulations usually begin by assuming that as yet the network has learned nothing. When the network 'sees' a word, it activates the graphemic units, giving each unit a particular amount of activation. Each letter of the alphabet (or in some models, triples of letters) has its unique pattern of activation. There is then a spread of activation from the graphemic units, via the intermediary or hidden units, to the phoneme units. To begin with, this pattern of excitation is random. As the network learns, the strength of the associations is encapsulated as a weight on the phoneme–grapheme connections. It is these weights that govern the spread of activation across the units. Through the connection weights, those words containing the grapheme will be activated. Because the pattern of activation is unique for each word in the network's lexicon or 'dictionary', after training, the system will eventually settle on the correct printed word for the given spoken word. The training procedure is through a learning algorithm (a kind of mathematical formula) which works by altering the weights on the connections in such a direction as to reduce error. Eventually, the error is reduced to zero so that a perfect match appears between the spoken word and its printed representation. This forms a knowledge base which can be drawn upon when the network is presented with a new word to read; in so doing, this model of reading seems to exhibit rule-like behaviour which we see in humans. However, it is important to realize that learning does not take place in a conscious way.

One model of this type was developed by Seidenberg and McClelland in 1989. Their phonemic units are represented as sets of triples, with each triple specifying a phoneme and its flanking phonemes; for example, the word *make* consists of the phoneme triple /mAk/ and is coded as _mA, mAk and

Ak_. Graphemic representation is also in the form of triples, this time of letters, with each unit consisting of 10 possible first letters, 10 possible second letters and 10 possible third letters. The Seidenberg and McClelland (1989) model was demonstrated to learn 97% of the words from the training set by the end of the learning process, though it did seem to have rather more difficulty in reading phonemically regular non-words than would a normal human reader. A further concern is that this model assumes that at the start of learning the phonological representations are completely unstructured. This is not the case for humans; we have seen that even very young children come to the reading task with some degree of segmental organization of their phonemic representations. Consequently, as Hulme, Snowling and Quinlan (1991) point out, early connectionist models had not taken on board the vast body of evidence on early phonological awareness and its powerful predictive effect on subsequent reading development. These authors suggested that a way to resolve this problem would be to incorporate a pre-structured phonological store that would facilitate the learning of mappings between the phonological and graphemic units. In fact, Harm and Seidenberg (1999) did just that; their phonological network was pre-trained before learning trials began, thus simulating the child's phonological development prior to beginning to learn to read.

Although the connectionist models emphasize incremental learning, it is worth noting that they do not preclude describing the development of reading in terms of a series of stages. Indeed, Ehri's (1992) stage model of reading makes references to 'connections' that could be seen to be compatible with those described in the above connectionist models. Her first stage is the visual cue phase which, like the logographic stage of Frith (1985), involves children taking note of salient visual cues in and around the word and connecting these by rote memory to its meaning and pronunciation. In the second phase, phonetic cue learning, children learn about letter names or sounds and use these to form systematic visual–phonological connections between letters and sounds. To begin with, these connections are incomplete as only some letters (usually initial and/or final ones) are linked to sounds. Consequently, certain letters and consonant clusters are frequently omitted. When readers' phonemic segmentation and decoding skills improve, they are in a position to form complete visual–phonological connections in learning to read sight words, and so enter the cipher sight word reading phase. In the early part of this stage, the children apply grapheme-to-phoneme correspondence rules when encountering new words. Later on, after they have recoded the word several times, they will retain an awareness of the letter–sound relations within the word so that these links can participate in a more rapid reading by memory operation.

Specific connections between visual cues within words (sequences of letters, essentially) and their pronunciation in memory are set up. The connections are formed out of the reader's knowledge of sound–letter correspondences and of regularities within written words. These connections or links are built up through a rapid and efficient memory storage system so that direct links exist between a written word and its pronunciation. Finally, the child emerges into the morphemic stage during which there is the adoption of strategies based on units of meaning.

Ehri's (1992) model of reading development describes links between children's phonological skills and their connection with memory storage systems. In the next chapter we shall consider in more detail, memory processes involved in beginning reading.

Summary

- Phonological awareness refers to children's appreciation of, and ability to process and manipulate, the speech sound segments of words.
- Phonological awareness begins to emerge before children start to learn to read, and is a powerful predictor of reading achievement, both in the short and long term.
- An even more powerful predictor of beginning reading development is children's ease of learning the letter identities.
- When children combine their phoneme awareness with their knowledge of sound-to-letter relationships, they acquire the alphabetic principle; to quote from Byrne again, this describes 'the usable knowledge of the fact that phonemes can be represented by letters, such that whenever a particular phoneme occurs in a word, and in whatever position, it can be represented by the same letter' (Byrne and Fielding-Barnsley, 1989, p. 313).
- Acquisition of the alphabetic principle forms the foundation for children's rapid expansion of their reading vocabulary.

CHAPTER 3

Reading, verbal memory and naming skills

Verbal working memory

It seems obvious that learning to read will involve memory processes in one form or another. Parents and teachers talk a great deal about children's ability to remember new words they have learnt in their reading books or for their spelling lists. Memorizing is a complex skill with many subcomponents. The particular aspect we shall look at in some detail is that of phonological working memory, which has been implicated, both in normal reading development and also as a contributory cause of reading failure.

'Working memory' refers to a set of systems responsible for the temporary storage of information during the performance of cognitive tasks. A widely accepted model of working memory is that formulated by Baddeley and Hitch (1974). These authors conceptualized working memory as a complex of stores and systems within which information is processed during the performance of a cognitive task. It consists of a limited capacity central executive that interacts with two slave subsystems; the phonological or speech-based articulatory loop and the visuo-spatial scratch pad (Figure 3.1).

The 'central executive' is the controlling and co-ordinating system for memory processes; it controls the manipulation and flow of information, retrieves relevant information from other parts of the memory system and

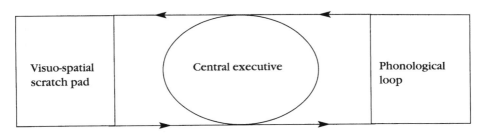

Figure 3.1 The memory system and the articulatory loop. (Source: Baddeley and Hitch, 1974.)

39

forms associations and relationships between items in memory. The visuo-spatial scratch pad is concerned with visual short-term memory, whereas the articulatory loop is concerned with verbal short-term memory. It is the articulatory loop that plays a crucial role in ongoing reading processes. Only a small amount of speech-based information can be retained in the articulatory loop, with the capacity of the loop estimated at between 1.5 and 2 seconds (Baddeley, Thomson and Buchanan, 1975). Because the memory traces in the loop decay rapidly, they can be maintained only through rehearsal. An example of the articulatory loop in operation is when one is given a telephone number to remember; it will remain in the loop for only a few seconds at most and will, therefore, very rapidly be forgotten. However, it is possible to retain it for much longer periods of time by reciting it out loud or more typically rehearsing it subvocally — in this way, the memory trace is constantly being refreshed.

It is fair to state that the role of verbal short-term memory in early reading development is not fully understood. It is well documented in the scientific literature that short-term verbal memory is closely related to level of reading skill, whether the materials to be remembered are digits and letters (Katz, Healy and Shankweiler, 1983), words (Brady, Shankweiler and Mann, 1983) or sentences (Mann, Liberman and Shankweiler, 1980). Children who have great difficulty learning to read are often found to have limited short-term verbal memory spans. JM (the dyslexic boy studied by Snowling and colleagues throughout his school years; Snowling, 2000) could remember only four digits forward even as an adolescent, in spite of being a highly intelligent individual. We know that it is short-term verbal (not visual) memory that is implicated in the reading process because poor readers are not disadvantaged when the material to be remembered is not phonetic, for instance nonsense shapes or unfamiliar faces (Katz, Shankweiler and Liberman, 1981).

Whether verbal memory span is an important predictor of reading skill independent of, and separate from, children's phonological abilities is not entirely clear. Hansen and Bowey (1994) found in their correlational study of 7-year-olds that both phonological analysis and verbal working memory contributed separately and uniquely to three reading measures. However, other studies have found that short-term verbal memory does not significantly predict reading skills after controlling for the children's level of phonological skill (Wagner, Torgesen and Rashotte, 1994; Rohl and Pratt, 1995). Snowling (1998) suggested that short-term verbal memory tasks may essentially be tapping the completeness or intactness of the child's phonological representations. Wagner, Torgesen and Rashotte (1994) would agree with this view; they propose that various phonological processing tasks, including those of short-term verbal or working memory, are tapping the quality of underlying phonological representation and it is the quality of these represen-tations that, in turn, affects children's ability to learn to read. With words only coarsely represented at the phonological level, there is a restriction on the number of verbal items that can be retained in memory. Another way of looking at this is to suggest that children who are able to process phonetic information slowly and inefficiently cause a constriction in their working memory system. Slow phonological processing might result in a bottleneck that impedes transfer of information to higher levels of processing within the system (Shankweiler et al., 1992). The interactive relationship between phonology and short-term verbal memory that is embodied in these two views may explain why, in some studies, short-term verbal memory does not uniquely predict reading skill once phonological abilities have been accounted for. Both perspectives see the core problem for poor readers being that of phonological processing, whether quality of underlying representa-tions or slow processing speed, which then affects short-term verbal memory.

Non-word repetition as a working memory measure

Gathercole and Baddeley (1989) conceptualized non-word repetition tasks as measures of phonological working memory that may relate to reading skill. In a non-word repetition task, children are asked to listen to and repeat a nonsense word spoken by an examiner or on an audiotape. Examples of non-words of two to five syllables used in their experimental studies, and which now constitute items on a standardized test, the Children's Non-word Repetition Test (CNRep) (Gathercole and Baddeley, 1996) are: 'glistow', 'trumpetine', 'contramponist' and 'defermication'.

In their first major study, Gathercole and Baddeley (1989) looked at the relationship between children's non-word repetition scores and the develop-ment of their spoken vocabulary knowledge. In a two-year longitudinal study of more than 100 4-year-old children, Gathercole and Baddeley gave a test of non-word repetition and a measure of vocabulary knowledge. They demon-strated that performance on a non-word repetition task predicted the children's vocabulary scores one year later, after taking account of the effects of variation in the children's ages and in their IQ levels. They went on to hypothesize that non-word repetition skill and, therefore, phonological working memory might also play a role in early reading development.

Gathercole, Baddeley and Willis (1991) conducted a three-year longitu-dinal study of children, originally selected as pre-readers, and looked at the changes in the contribution of phonological working memory to reading achievement over time. In fact, these workers failed to uncover a relationship between non-word repetition and reading ability in the first year at school. However, the correlation between these skills was statistically significant by year 2. Gathercole, Baddeley and Willis postulated that phonological working memory makes its greatest contribution to reading as the child enters the alphabetic stage of reading development. In their longitudinal study, Muter and Snowling (1998) found a significant relationship between children's non-word repetition scores at ages 5 and 6 and their reading accuracy skill at age 9. Moreover, two subgroups (designated good and poor readers) were selected from the 9-year-olds; the 13 good readers scored in the top 25 per cent of the sample on a prose reading test, whereas the seven poor readers scored in the bottom 25 per cent. A statistical procedure called 'discriminant function analysis' that allows the prediction of group membership from a set of predict-ors was carried out, in order to determine which set of predictor measures, taken at ages 5 and 6, would best discriminate the good from poor readers up to four years later. The best long-term predictor set consisted of the children's phoneme deletion and non-word repetition scores at ages 5 and 6, with a successful classification rate of 80 per cent. In other words, for this group of 20 children, knowing their phoneme deletion and non-word repetition scores at ages 5 and 6 enabled us to predict with 80 per cent accuracy whether they would be good or poor readers three to four years later.

However, Snowling, Chiat and Hulme (1991) challenged the assumption that a test of non-word repetition is a pure and direct measure of phonological memory. These workers argued that non-word repetition tasks are complex measures that certainly contain a memory component, but which also tap into children's phonological segmentation skills and their ability to articulate sequences of speech sounds. If non-word repetition tasks are pure measures of memory, we should expect to find a systematic increase in difficulty of repetition as the length of the non-word increases. However, Snowling, Chiat and Hulme did not find this relationship to be straightforward. In fact, in the study by these authors, ease of repetition was as strongly related to the non-word's phonological or morphemic similarity to real words. Snowling, Chiat and Hulme (1991) further point out that even the effects of length of the non-word cannot simply be attributed to the influence of memory. Longer words are not only harder to remember, but they also place greater demands on other phonological processes and on the motor skills required to articulate the sound sequence of a non-word. Metsala (1999) would agree with this view; in cross-sectional studies of children aged 3 to 5 years, she found that both short-term memory span and phonemic awareness contributed to children's performance on a non-word repetition task.

An important point to appreciate is that it may be very difficult to separate phonological memory mechanisms meaningfully from other phonological processes, such as segmentation skill (Hulme and Mackenzie, 1992). It is evident that some phonological awareness measures contain a sizeable working memory component (Bradley and Bryant's rhyme oddity task for instance). Similarly, purported measures of phonological working memory may simultaneously tap other phonological processes (as in non-word repetition tasks). To what extent phonological skills and working memory processes are inextricably linked and to what extent they may be demonstrated to function independently is an issue for further research.

Naming speed

Naming speed ability (sometimes referred to as 'rapid automatized naming'; RAN) involves asking children to name highly familiar objects or symbols under speeded conditions. This task, developed by Denkla and Rudel in 1976, requires the child to name series of letters, digits, coloured patches or common objects while being strictly timed with a stopwatch. It has emerged that there is a strong relationship between naming speed and reading skill, demonstrable in normal readers and, in particular, in poor readers who have been shown to be inordinately slow at naming a wide range of familiar objects and symbols. Figures 3.2 a and b shows instructions from the Digit Naming Speed and some items from the Object Naming Speed tasks from the standardized Phonological Assessment Battery (PhAB) (Frederickson, Frith and Reason, 1997). In each task the child must name the individual digit or object items in the series as fast as he or she can while the examiner records with a stopwatch how long it takes the child in seconds to complete the activity.

Digit Naming Card 1

'Now I'd like you to read this line of numbers as fast as possible.'

Read each number separately. For example, the first number is two, the next number is three and so on
(Point to the first two numbers as you say each number).

'Read from left to right'.

Sweep your hand across the row, from left to right, as you say 'left to right'.

'Don't stop between these groups of numbers'.

(Contd)

Figure 3.2a Instructions from the Phonological Assessment Battery (PhAB) Digit Naming Speed Test. (Source: Frederick, Frith and Reason, 1997). Reproduced by permission of nfer-Nelson Publishing Co.

Point to the first three groups after you say this.

'Just read the whole line of numbers straight through without stopping. Read them as quickly as you can and I'll time you with this stop watch.

Try not to make any mistakes. If you make a mistake you can put it right, but carry on quickly.

Do you have any questions?'
Answer questions.

'Remember, read as fast as possible. You may begin when I say "start"'.

Pause for about two seconds before proceeding.

'Ready...start'.
Begin timing as you say *'start'.*

Stop timing as the child names the last digit.

Praise the child's efforts.

Allow the child 30 seconds rest before turning over to reveal Digit Naming Card 2.

Figure 3.2a (Contd).

Figure 3.2b Object Naming items from the Phonological Assessment Battery (PhAB). (Source: Frederickson, Frith and Reason, 1997.) Reproduced by permission of nfer-Nelson Publishing Co.

A large body of evidence has demonstrated a strong predictive relationship between rapid automatized naming and later reading skill (see Wolf and O'Brien, 2001, for a recent review).

What are the main features of this relationship? First, naming speed with digits or letters is thought to be more predictive than with pictures (Badian, 2000). In a recent study by Clarke, Snowing and Hulme (2001) of 8- to 11-year-old normal readers, digit naming speed and letter naming speed correlated highly with an exception (irregular) word reading task (0.54 and 0.47, respectively), whereas picture naming speed exhibited a rather lower correlation of 0.39. This is not a surprising finding given that letters and numbers are symbolic in nature and more obviously related to reading than are colours and pictures. Also, naming speed predicts word recognition in reading rather than reading comprehension (Wolf, 1997). Finally, there is some evidence for the view that naming speed may have a stronger association with poor reading than with good reading (Wolf and O'Brien, 2001).

Wagner et al. (1997) found that individual differences in naming speed influenced subsequent individual differences in word-level reading initially, but that these influences faded with development. Thus, the association between naming speed and reading is not as consistent or as robust in normal populations as is the association between phonological segmentation and reading skill. In contrast, deficits in naming speed are purported to be a major characteristic of severely impaired readers across the life span (Wolf, 1997). One study by Wolf (1982) investigated the relationship between naming speed and reading in 64 children aged 6 to 11 years (32 average readers and 32 severely impaired readers). The naming speed tasks differentiated average from impaired readers throughout the elementary school years; indeed, the naming speed tasks proved to be the best predictor of poor reading group membership.

What is a naming speed task essentially measuring and by what mechanisms does it affect reading? There are currently two views of how naming speed might affect reading development. First, it could be that naming speed is just another indicator of the quality and discreteness of the child's phonological representations. It is harder and takes longer to 'find' a word in long-term memory during a naming speed task if it is represented in a 'fuzzy' or incomplete way. Expressed more technically, naming speed tasks appear to tap into children's ability to access their phonological representations in long-term memory; incomplete or coarsened phonological representations are more difficult to access so that a child's speed of recalling even these highly familiar names is impaired. In this view, the relationship between reading and naming skill is similar to that between reading and other phonological processes. Of course, this conceptualization of naming speed tasks makes it hard to explain why a number of studies have demonstrated separate and independent contributions from phonological segmentation and naming tasks to reading skill, including those of Wolf and colleagues.

The alternative account views rapid naming deficits as the consequence of an impairment of a timing mechanism (Wolf and Bowers, 1999) which is independent of the phonological skills children bring to bear on the reading process. Indeed, Wolf (1997, p. 85) has suggested that naming speed is 'appropriately depicted as a complex, rapid integration of many cognitive, perceptual and linguistic processes'. If a child is slow to name highly familiar symbols like letters and digits then he or she will be slow to automate their reading processes and ultimately this will affect fluency of reading.

An interesting line of evidence which contrasts the roles of phonological segmentation skill and naming speed in reading comes from cross-linguistic studies which compare and contrast the skills children need for reading in different orthographies. In English orthography, because it is phonologically opaque or in common vernacular 'irregularly spelled', the demands on the children's phonological and decoding skills are very great. In German orthography, which is much more phonologically transparent, these demands are far fewer; indeed, German-speaking poor readers have fewer difficulties in carrying out phonological segmentation tasks or in reading non-words than do English-speaking children (Wimmer, 1993). However, German-speaking dyslexic children do have considerable difficulties in performing naming speed tasks. These children have persisting problems in reading speedily and automatically, which not only affects their fluency but also their reading comprehension — in spite of their having relatively good phonological segmentation and decoding skills. In fact, it has been shown that digit naming speed is the best predictor of reading differences among German-speaking normally achieving and dyslexic children (Wimmer, 1993). By way of contrast, phonological segmentation tasks tend to be more powerful and robust predictors of both good and poor reading in English-speaking children than naming speed tasks.

The distinction between phonological segmentation and naming speed tasks and their differential effect on reading skills led Wolf and Bowers (1999) to propose a dual deficit hypothesis of reading impairment. These workers suggest that children's reading problems may arise from a phonological segmentation difficulty or a naming speed deficit or, if they are especially unlucky, both. We shall return to the dual deficit hypothesis in more depth in a later chapter when we consider the difficulties experienced by dyslexic children.

Most recently, Manis, Seidenberg and Doi (1999) have attempted to disentangle the relationships between naming speed, phonological awareness and reading. These authors carried out a longitudinal study of 85 children from grade 1 to grade 2. When the children were in grade 1 they were given a test of vocabulary knowledge as a control for verbal ability, together with two naming speed tests (for digits and letters) and a test of phonological segmentation (specifically, a phoneme deletion task). The children were seen a year later when they were in grade 2 and given a range of reading tests that tapped into the following different components of reading skill:

- single-word reading in order to look at their word recognition
- non-word reading in order to assess phonic-based word attack strategies
- exception-word reading to look at their ability to recognize irregularly constructed words (for example, *said, island, stomach*)
- reading comprehension to assess their understanding and recall of what they had read.

Finally, the children were given two measures of what is referred to as 'orthographic skill'. This reading-related skill encapsulates children's knowledge and appreciation of spelling conventions. One task, developed by Olson et al. (1989), 'orthographic choice', was designed to assess children's knowledge of word-specific spellings. Children had to decide which of three spellings was correct; the spellings were all phonologically similar but orthographically dissimilar, for example 'tite', 'tight', 'tiet' (the correct choice was of course *tight*). In the second orthographic test, the 'Word Likeness Test' (adapted from Stanovich and Siegel, 1994), children were shown pairs of nonsense words, and then asked to circle which looked more like a word, for example 'beff–ffeb', 'nist–niir', 'celp–cepl'. The correct responses were 'beff', 'nist' and 'celp', respectively, because these words conform to the conventions of English orthography, whereas 'ffeb', 'niir' and 'cepl' clearly do not.

Manis, Seidenberg and Doi (1999) examined the contributions of phonological awareness skill and rapid naming in grade 1 to the various components of reading in grade 2 (after controlling for the effects of verbal ability and children's earlier reading levels). Naming speed made a unique contribution to later word recognition, the orthographic tasks and the exception words, but not to non-word reading. By contrast, phoneme deletion in grade 1 contributed to later word recognition, non-word reading and reading comprehension, but not to the orthographic tasks. These findings were replicated in a correlational study conducted by Clarke, Snowling and Hulme (2001). These workers found, like Manis, Seidenberg and Doi (1999), that naming speed and phonological awareness tasks tapped separable aspects of phonological processing. Naming speed uniquely predicted exception word reading (but not non-word reading) after controlling for the effects of phonological awareness skill. In contrast, only the children's score on a phoneme deletion task contributed to non-word reading.

Manis, Seidenberg and Doi (1999) developed a model of reading which proposes that naming speed tasks make a unique contribution to reading when compared to phoneme awareness because naming speed involves arbitrary associations between print and sound, whereas phoneme awareness is more related to the learning of systematic spelling–sound correspondences. Learning arbitrary associations (between sounds and letters) probably plays a central role in the development of early reading skill, whereas knowledge of segmental phonology (tapped by phonological awareness tasks) is relevant to both the earlier and later phases of learning to read. This suggestion fits in with the observations of Wagner and colleagues, who maintain that naming speed tasks contribute transitorily to the early stages of learning to read but then drop out of the picture as predictors. In contrast, phonological awareness has both a powerful and long-term bearing on reading progress and outcome. It might be hypothesized that naming speed is one of the predictors or determiners, alongside phonological awareness, of letter knowledge acquisition in young children — although this has yet to be tested. If, as claimed by Manis, Seidenberg and Doi (1999), naming speed tasks tap into the acquisition of arbitrary associations between sounds and letters then it might be expected that children who are slow namers have difficulty in learning the connections between specific sounds and letters when they first encounter the alphabet. Similarly, children who have naming speed problems and who find learning arbitrary phoneme–grapheme relations difficult would be expected to have difficulty learning irregular and exception words and variations in spelling patterns in English. We shall return to the Manis, Seidenberg and Doi (1991) model later on when we look at the evidence for there being different subtypes of dyslexia.

Speech rate, memory and reading

A model of memory that implicated the efficiency of the phonological loop in reading development was discussed at the beginning of this chapter. Hulme and colleagues explored the relationship between short-term memory and phonological processing by examining speech rate. This refers to the speed with which a specified word or words can be spoken. The Phonological Abilities Test (PAT) (Muter, Hulme and Snowling, 1997) includes a speech rate task which requires children to recite the word *buttercup* over and over as fast as they can. The amount of time taken by the child to say *buttercup* 10 times is recorded with a stopwatch and a words-per-second measure derived. Speech rate is thought to provide a measure of rate of processing within the phonological loop (see Hulme and Roodenrys, 1995, for a review). Bearing in mind the limited capacity of the loop, the more quickly words can be coded and rehearsed, the longer the sequence of items that can be remembered.

Hulme and colleagues have gathered evidence from developmental studies that demonstrates a close relationship between changes in speech rate and increases in memory span. With regard to reading, McDougall et al. (1994) studied the relationship between memory span, speech rate and phonological awareness in good, average and poor readers. Sixty-nine children aged between $7^{1}/_{2}$ and $9^{1}/_{2}$ were assessed on tests of single-word reading, memory span (for one-, two- and three-letter words), speech rate, memory span for abstract forms, and phonological awareness (a rhyme oddity task and a phoneme deletion task). They were also given a shortened version of an IQ test as a control for ability level. The sample was divided into three reading ability groups on the basis of their scores on the single-word reading test. There were 23 children in each of the low, average and high ability groups, and they were well matched on age.

McDougall et al. (1994) found that there were no differences between the different reading ability groups in their memory for abstract shapes; this is in accord with the results of other studies showing that visual memory for non-letter-like forms has no bearing on reading skill. However, there were large differences between the groups in memory span for words. The authors went on to demonstrate that the differences in memory span among the groups was roughly proportional to the children's speech rate for those same words. Furthermore, after accounting for speech rate, memory span made no contribution to reading skill. Conversely, however, speech rate did predict reading skill even after controlling for the effects of memory span. Thus, differences in reading ability are associated with differences in the efficiency of the speech-based rehearsal component of short-term memory span as measured by a speech rate task. Children's scores on the test of speech rate made a significant contribution to reading skill independently of that made by the two measures of phonological awareness. So, it appears that it is the efficiency and speed of the rehearsal process (tapped by speech rate) rather than the size of the memory span per se that is the critical factor in influencing reading skill.

Consistent with the findings of McDougall et al. (1994), Muter and Snowling (1998) found speech rate was a better predictor of reading skill than a verbal (word span) memory task. Moreover, Muter and Snowling found that speech rate made a contribution to reading additional to that made by measures of phonological awareness (in this case a phoneme deletion task) and of grammatical awareness.

Hulme and colleagues suggest that speech rate provides an index of the speed and efficiency with which phonological representations of words in long-term memory can be activated, and that this is a skill separate from the phonological processes tapped by measures of phonological awareness. In a sense, this notion is not dissimilar to the explanation put forward by Wagner and colleagues to explain how naming speed tasks relate to reading skill. It would be interesting to explore the relationship between phonological working memory, naming speed, speech rate and reading. It could well be the case that these measures load on the same factor reflecting speed and efficiency of phonological access — and they are consequently different ways of measuring essentially the same underlying skill.

To what extent phonological analysis ability and phonological memory skills are inextricably linked within the reading process and to what extent they function independently remains an issue in need of some clarification. It seems to me that it may be a question of whether one looks at the phonology–memory association from a structural or processing perspective. From a structural viewpoint, tests of phonological awareness, verbal memory, naming speed and speech rate are seen to be tapping the specificity of underlying phonological representations, and it is the quality or 'fine-grainedness' of these representations that, in turn, affects children's ability to learn to read. From a more process-oriented view, naming speed, measures of working memory and speech rate may be seen as tapping speed and efficiency of access, which is separate from phonological analysis skill, though still within the phonological domain.

Paired associate learning

There has been a recent renewal of interest in paired associate learning tasks. It seems obvious that learning an orthography is a specific instance of visual–verbal paired associate learning in which the printed (visual) attributes of words are associated with their phonological (verbal) forms. At an even more fundamental level for the beginning reader, paired associate learning is required to establish letter–sound and letter–name knowledge.

In a recent study, Windfuhr and Snowling (2001) set out to explore the interrelationship between paired associate learning, phonological segmentation skill and reading in normal ability readers from 7 to 11 years. These workers' paired associate learning task required the pairing of two-dimensional visual shapes with spoken non-words. Windfuhr and Snowling (2001) assessed the children's phonological segmentation ability through administering a phoneme deletion task (after McDougall et al., 1994). Children's performance on these measures was then related to their concurrent reading ability, in the form of both single-word recognition and decoding (non-word reading). Windfuhr and Snowling found that both paired associate learning and phonological segmentation skill made separate contributions to reading skill in normally developing children. Furthermore, phonological segmentation ability was a strong predictor of paired associate learning. Importantly, paired associate learning made a significant contribution to both non-word and real word reading, although the predictive relationship between paired associate learning and non-word reading was not as strong as between phonological segmentation skill and non-word reading. The fact that paired associate learning contributed to word recognition skill, even when performance in non-word reading was controlled, suggested that paired associate learning has a distinct role to play in establishing connections between words and their pronunciations. However, it was not possible to say from this study which component of paired associate learning depends on phonological sensitivity. Clearly, when carrying out a paired associate learning task, children must learn the abstract visual shapes and the new phonological forms of the non-words whilst establishing a link between their memorial representations.

Memory and sight-word reading

Before leaving the consideration of verbal memory and related processes, it would be helpful to draw again on the model of sight-word reading proposed by Ehri (1992). This pulls together an explanation of how phonological skills may link with memory processes as children establish an early sight vocabulary.

Sight-word reading is often posited as the method of choice for reading irregularly constructed words, of which the English orthography has many; consider words such as *island, busy, yacht, heights, rhythm*. However, sight-word reading need not be restricted to oddly spelled, difficult to decode words. Given sufficient practice, all words become sight words. In Ehri's (1992) model of sight-word reading, the process involved is not a pure memory-based visual one at all. In children's initial reading attempts, they form important connections between sounds and letters that are maintained even after words achieve sight-word status. Ehri (1992) suggests that children retain an awareness of the letter–sound relations within a word after it has been learnt so that these links can participate in a reading by memory operation. Specific connections between visual cues within the word (sequences of letters, not phonemes) and its pronunciation in memory are set up. These connections are formed out of the reader's knowledge of sound–letter correspondences and of orthographic regularities. This process is different from, and faster than, a decoding route because it omits the intermediate stage of applying sound-to-letter correspondence rules. This slower route is likely to be used when a new word is encountered. But once it has been seen and decoded in this fashion several times, the sound–letter translation drops out, leaving direct links between the spelling and its pronunciation. When sight words are known well enough, readers can recognize their pronunciations and meanings automatically.

Evidence for this model of sight word acquisition comes from a study by Ehri and Wilce (1985). These workers taught kindergarten children to read two kinds of word by sight — systematically spelled words in which letters corresponded to some sounds in words, for example 'msk' for *mask*, 'jrf' for *giraffe*, and arbitrarily spelled words exhibiting no sound–letter relations, for example 'uhe' for *mask*, 'wbc' for *giraffe*. The children were given several trials to learn to read six words of each type, each set taught on a different day. Ehri and Wilce found that word learning was not the same for the two types of words. Whether kindergarten children learnt to read the systematic or arbitrary spellings more easily depended on their existing reading skills and letter knowledge. Non-readers with no letter knowledge learnt to read the arbitrary spellings more readily than the systematic phonetic spellings. In contrast, beginning readers who had complete letter knowledge learnt the systematic spellings more readily than the arbitrary spellings. It was not the case that the beginning readers read systematic phonetic spellings better because they could decode the words; the words had to be read from memory because they lacked letters for all the sounds. The reason the non-readers did not learn systematic spellings as easily as arbitrary spellings is that they lacked the letter–sound knowledge to form visual–phonological connections in memory. The reason beginning readers learned systematic spellings better than arbitrary spellings is that they possessed and used their letter–sound knowledge to form systematic connections in memory.

Very young children develop a core sight vocabulary of commonplace words even when they have been at school for a very short period of time. The 100 most common words in written English, which make up about half of all the words we read and write, would be well established in the sight word lexicons of most 7-year-olds (Figure 3.3).

Of the 32 most common words of the English language that make up a third of all the words we read and write (taken from Figure 3.3), nine (about

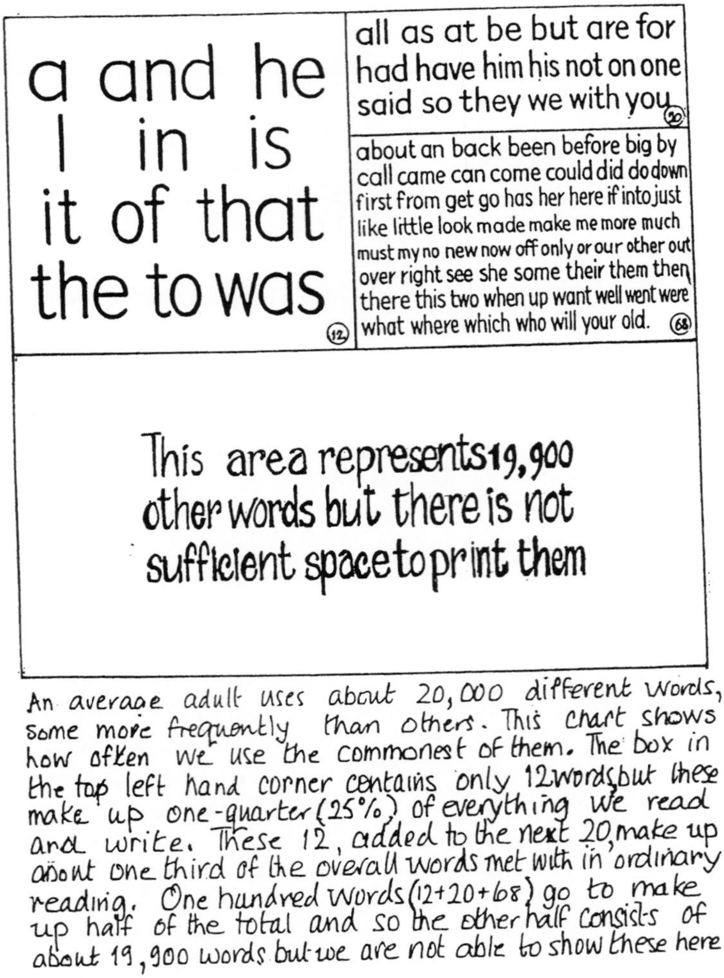

a and he
I in is
it of that
the to was ⑫

all as at be but are for had have him his not on one said so they we with you ㉚

about an back been before big by call came can come could did do down first from get go has her here if into just like little look made make me more much must my no new now off only or our other out over right see she some their them then there this two when up want well went were what where which who will your old. ㉖⑧

This area represents 19,900 other words but there is not sufficient space to print them

An average adult uses about 20,000 different words, some more frequently than others. This chart shows how often we use the commonest of them. The box in the top left hand corner contains only 12 words but these make up one-quarter (25%) of everything we read and write. These 12, added to the next 20, make up about one third of the overall words met with in ordinary reading. One hundred words (12+20+68) go to make up half of the total and so the other half consists of about 19,900 words but we are not able to show these here

Figure 3.3 The most common words in the English language. (Source: Doyle, 1996.)

30 per cent) are irregularly constructed, that is, *the, to, was, all, are, have, one, said, you*. Ehri (1992) proposed that the connections formed are essentially the same for regular words and irregular words. As Ehri points out, most of the letters in irregular words conform to phoneme–grapheme conventions, for example all but the *s* in *island*, all but the *w* in *sword*. When remembering letters that do not conform to phonemes, readers may remember them as extra visual forms, or flag them as 'silent' in memory, or remember a special pronunciation that includes the silent letter, for example remembering *listen* as *lis-ten*. In essence, spellings are like maps that lay out the phonological forms of words visually. Even young readers soon become rapidly skilled at computing these mappings. It is the knowledge of sound-to-letter relations that provides this powerful mnemonic system that bonds the written forms of specific words to their pronunciation in memory.

The next chapter provides an illustrative example of how the phonological and related skills we have discussed in this and the previous chapter relate to reading progress in a child who was studied during the course of the original longitudinal study by Muter et al. (1998).

Summary

- Tests of short-term verbal working memory (including non-word repetition measures) and more recently naming speed and speech rate tasks, have been shown to have a predictive relationship to early reading development.
- Whether these tasks are merely another indicator (alongside phonological awareness) of the intactness of the child's underlying phonological representations, or whether they are tapping a qualitatively different reading-related ability, such as a timing mechanism, is an issue of some controversy.
- The model developed by Manis, Seidenberg and Doi (1999) proposes that phonological awareness contributes to the development of phonemic decoding skills while, in contrast, naming speed contributes to orthographic skills, including the ability to learn and memorize exception words.
- In Ehri's (1992) model of reading development, memory processes play a role in the acquisition of a sight-word vocabulary; specific connections between visual cues within the word (sequences of letters) and its pronunciation in memory are formed out of the child's knowledge of sound–letter relationships and of orthographic regularities.

Chapter 4

Phonological difficulties and reading failure — a case study

In the previous chapter, we saw that phonological abilities assessed even in very young children are highly predictive of their ease of learning to read, both in the short and long term. To demonstrate the salience and robustness of phonological tests and their applicability to children's reading difficulties during the elementary school years, the case of Nicholas (Muter et al., 1998; Muter and Snowling, 1998) is now presented.

Nicholas as a pre-schooler

Nicholas was selected at random (along with 37 other children) for a longitudinal study of early literacy development. There was no indication at the outset of the study that he would turn out to be severely dyslexic. When first seen, Nicholas was 4½ years old and in his last term at a London state nursery school. Like his classmates, he was a non-reader. Nicholas was given a test of intelligence, the Wechsler Pre-school and Primary Scale of Intelligence (WPPSI) (Wechsler 1967). He achieved a full scale or overall IQ of 110. His verbal IQ, which was based on measures of vocabulary and verbal reasoning, was 115 ('bright' range). His performance or non-verbal IQ, which was based on measures of visual learning such as spatial ability and visual perception, was 103 ('average' range).

Nicholas's oral language skills were well developed. He was given a test of grammatical knowledge, the Illinois Test of Psycholinguistic Abilities (ITPA) (Kirk, McCarthy and Kirk, 1968). Nicholas was required to supply a word with the correct inflection ending for unfinished sentences that were spoken by the examiner and accompanied by appropriate pictorial representations; for instance, 'Here is a dog; here are two ... [dogs]', 'This man is painting the fence — he is a ... [painter]'. Nicholas was able to appreciate both regular and irregular grammatical inflections; he knew about irregular as well as regular plural endings and verb tenses. His average sentence length was normal for his age, about eight to 10 words, as was his ability to convey information expressively when asked to recite to the examiner a story that had been read to him (Bus Story; Renfrew, 1969). In fact, on these measures, he scored at between the $4^{1}/_{2}$ and 6-year levels. Nicholas was, therefore, presenting as a child of normal intelligence with good language development. He was a friendly, eager to please little boy, always smiling, who got on well with his teachers and classmates, and who had no behavioural or social difficulties. This was evident not only from working with him and observing him in the classroom and playground but also from questionnaires completed by parents and teachers. There was nothing untoward about his learning and language profile before he commenced formal schooling.

During Nicholas's last term at nursery, he and the other children in the study were given tests of phonological segmentation ability and letter knowledge. These have already been described in Chapter 2. Recall that one test tapped simple or implicit phonological segmentation skill; when shown a picture of a common object, for example *ship*, Nicholas had to supply the final phoneme of the word, /p/. The second phonological test assessed the more complex level of segmentation skill, namely the ability to manipulate phonemes within words (explicit segmentation). Nicholas was required to delete the initial phoneme of a single-syllable word, for example *cat* without the /c/ says 'at'. Nicholas's performance on these two tasks and on a letter knowledge test at age 4, and during the subsequent two years of the longitudinal study, is summarized in Table 4.1; the scores in parentheses represent the average scores of the 38 children in the study. There was nothing striking in Nicholas's profile at age 4 that would have led to a prediction that he might go on to have severe reading problems. True, he had not developed any meaningful phonological segmentation skills, but then neither had most of his classmates. He could identify one letter of the alphabet, whereas the group of 38 achieved a slightly higher average score of four.

Table 4.1 Nicholas's phonological and letter knowledge scores at ages 4, 5 and 6, relative to the mean scores for the group as a whole (in parentheses)

	Age 4	Age 5	Age 6
Phoneme completion /8	0 (2)	0 (3)	5 (6)
Phoneme deletion /10	0 (0)	1 (3)	0 (5)
Letter knowledge /26	1 (4)	5 (12)	5 (19)

Nicholas at age 5

Nicholas and the other 37 children in the study were seen again one year later; he was now aged 5 and in his last term of reception class. He and his classmates had been receiving formal reading instruction for almost a full school year. There was now emerging evidence of a widening gap between Nicholas and his peers, specifically in respect of his phonological segmentation skills and his letter knowledge. Inspection of Table 4.1 reveals that Nicholas was making very slow, if any, progress in his phonological and letter knowledge skills while his peers were beginning to move from the 'floor' or lower limits of the tests. Nicholas was still unable to score at all on the test of implicit phonological segmentation, and it was suspected that his achieving one correct response on the phoneme deletion task was attributable to a lucky guess. His ability to blend sounds to form words was in advance of his segmentation abilities. On the ITPA Sound Blending Test (Kirk et al., 1968) given to the children at age 5, Nicholas scored 10/32 while the average for the group as a whole was only four points higher than this.

Despite having poor phonological segmentation skills and letter knowledge Nicholas was able to read at a level that was not worryingly different from his peers. He could read four words correctly from the single-word reading test of the British Abilities Scales (BAS) (Elliot, Murray and Pearson, 1983); the average for the group as a whole was also four. Nicholas read surprisingly well in context. The number of words the children could read correctly was scored from the first two (simplest) passages of the prose reading test, the Neale Analysis of Reading Ability (NARA) (Neale, 1989); Nicholas read 28 words correctly, whereas the average score for the group was nine.

How did Nicholas make a relatively promising start in reading in the absence of even very basic phonological segmentation skills and with such limited letter knowledge? One possible explanation comes from the finding in the previous year that Nicholas was an able little boy with good language skills; he had a verbal IQ of 115. Perhaps his good oral ability helped him to read in context, as he was required to do on the NARA. In effect, Nicholas had used his good grammatical and vocabulary knowledge in order to take advantage of surrounding prose context, so 'guessing' correctly at words according to their position in the sentence and his appreciation of the content of the story.

Another possible explanation for Nicholas making a reasonable start in reading comes from his relatively competent visual memory. The children were given a test of visual memory which involved memorizing sequences of letter-like forms (specifically, Greek letters) (Goulandris, 1989). Nicholas scored 14/24 on this test, two points higher than the group as a whole. It seemed that Nicholas was a reasonably successful logographic reader at age 5; he could use visual cues to recognize and remember words and he made appropriate use of language-based context cues. Few of the children had spelling skills at age 5, and Nicholas was no exception; he could not score at all on the Schonell Spelling Test (Schonell and Goodacre, 1971), but then his classmates managed an average score of only 1.5. His efforts at writing individual letters from their names or sounds are shown in Figure 4.1.

Figure 4.1 Nicholas's attempts at writing letters at age 5.

Nicholas at age 6

By the time Nicholas was seen again at age 6, having now completed almost two years of formal schooling, his poor phonological skills and weak letter knowledge were beginning to have a significant effect on his literacy development. Inspection of Table 4.1 revealed that Nicholas had finally established implicit phonological segmentation ability (5/8 on the phoneme completion task). However, he had not yet achieved the more advanced and, as it turns out, critical skill of phoneme manipulation; he scored 0/10 on the beginning phoneme deletion test, whereas the group as a whole scored 5/10. His sound blending had not improved at all during his second year at school. He still scored only 10/32, whereas his classmates had increased their average score to 18/32. What was particularly striking was that Nicholas's letter knowledge score remained stagnant at 5/26, whereas the letter knowledge average for the group was beginning to edge closer to ceiling.

With these limited phonological awareness and letter knowledge skills, would Nicholas be able to make the transition from the limited logographic stage of learning to read to the next important alphabetic stage? His performance on a range of reading tests revealed that he had not been able to make this transition. He read five words correctly from the BAS reading test (the group as a whole read an average of 17). He had failed to progress as well as his peers on the prose reading task (NARA), being able to read 34 words correctly from the first two passages, in contrast to the average score of 58 for the group. An experimentally based non-word reading test was introduced at this stage that required the children to read 10 three- and four-letter non-words, such as 'tig' and 'blem'. Nicholas achieved a score of zero in contrast to the average for the group of 3.5. Nicholas's delayed development of his reading vocabulary, and his total inability to read even very simple non-words, indicated that he had failed to move from logographic to alphabetic reading. This was in contrast to his peers, who were steadily improving their phonological and letter knowledge; in turn, they were then able to use these skills to develop some simple decoding strategies that characterize the child's emergence into the alphabetic stage. Nicholas was unable to spell correctly any words from the spelling test (see Figure 4.2), whereas the score for the group as a whole was eight. However, his written arithmetic skills at age 6 were well up to the standard of the rest of the sample; in an adapted version of the Basic Number Screening Test (Gillham and Hesse, 1976), Nicholas scored 12/27, only four points lower than the average for the group as a whole. Thus, Nicholas was not uniformly weak across the full range of educational subjects. Indeed, his problems seemed to be restricted to reading and spelling.

Nicholas at age 10

Nicholas's teachers were alerted to his being 'at risk' of having significant reading delay and he did receive some special needs support over the following years. The children in the longitudinal study were reassessed when they were 9–10 years of age, during their penultimate year at elementary school. By then Nicholas was aged 10 years and 2 months. The phonological tests that had been administered when he was younger were not appropriate to a child nearing the end of elementary school, so experimentally based measures better suited to the older child were introduced at this stage. The phonological segmentation task used, which had been developed by McDougall et al. (1994), was a challenging phoneme deletion task. This has already been described in some detail in Chapter 2 when discussing details of the long-term follow-up. The reader may recall that the children were asked to delete either a beginning, middle or end phoneme from a non-word in

Can

Sat

Yes

Net

Figure 4.2 Nicholas's spelling at age 6.

order to produce a real word. They were also given a speech rate test that, as seen in the previous chapter, was designed to assess their efficiency in accessing their phonological representations in long-term memory. The children were asked to repeat each of eight single-syllable words (for example, *leaf, doll*) as quickly as they could; the time taken to repeat a given word 10 times was recorded to the nearest 0.1 of a second and the mean time taken in words per second was then calculated. As a measure of decoding, the children were given the Graded Nonword Reading Test (Snowling, Stothard and Maclean, 1996) which comprises 10 single-syllable and 10 two-syllable non-words, for example 'kisp' and 'nolcrid'.

Nicholas's scores on these three measures are given in Table 4.2, alongside the average scores for the group of 34. As can be seen, Nicholas had severely underdeveloped phonological segmentation ability. Although his speech rate score did not seem to be markedly different from the group as a whole, the variation of scores within the group for this measure was exceedingly small, so that his score was actually well below the average for the group. Nicholas had very limited decoding ability; he even made errors in decoding the demonstration items consisting of three-letter consonant–vowel–consonant (C–V–C) non-words; he read 'kib' as 'kip', 'fep' as 'feb'. As shall be seen in subsequent chapters, difficulties with phonological processing and phonemic decoding ability characterize the profile of the child with dyslexia.

Not unexpectedly, Nicholas proved to be a very poor reader, writer and speller. On the NARA, he scored at the second centile; in other words, 98% of the children in the follow-up study achieved a higher reading score than he did. Nicholas disliked reading intensely. He completed a reading habits questionnaire (given orally) and responded to questions such as *'What sort of things do you like to read?'* with the answer *'None'* and *'Can you name two or three of your favourite authors?'* with *'Don't know any'*. Nicholas scored at the eighth centile for spelling on the British Abilities Scale (BAS) test (Elliot, Murray and Pearson 1983). His spelling attempts are shown in Figure 4.3. Finally, the children were given five minutes to write the story of 'Goldilocks and the Three Bears' in their own words. Nicholas's attempt at prose writing is given in Figure 4.4.

Table 4.2 Nicholas's scores on the phonological segmentation, speech rate and phoneme decoding tests at age 10, relative to the mean scores for the group of 34

	Nicholas	Whole group
Phoneme deletion /24	4	17
Speech rate: words per second	3.4	4.8
Non-word reading /20	2	14.6

Words spelled correctly		Words spelled incorrectly	
Play	Play	*firend*	Friend
are	Are	*LN*	Leave
home	Home	*no*	Know
eat	Eat	*brith*	Bridge
come	Come	*ell*	Ill
back	Back	*bavl*	Blue
nev	New	*wack*	Walk
down	Down	*moring*	Morning
bird	Bird	*soll*	Soil
Pie	Pie	*egth*	Eight

Figure 4.3 Nicholas's spelling at age 10.

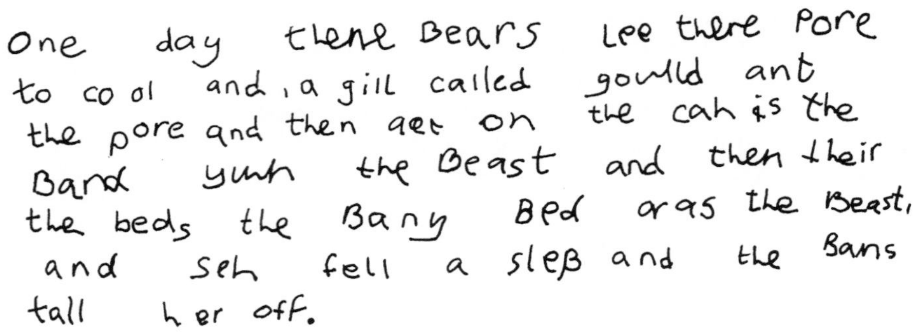

One day thene Bears Lee there Pore
to cool and a gill called gould ant
the pore and then aet on the cah is the
Bard yuh the Beast and then their
the beds the Bany Bed aras the Beast,
and seh fell a sleß and the Bans
tall h er off.

Figure 4.4 Nicholas's attempt at writing the story of 'Goldilocks and the Three Bears'. The examiner's interpretation of what Nicholas had written is as follows:

> One day three bears left their porridge to cool ... and a girl called Goldilocks ate the porridge and then ... on the chair ... the beds the baby bed was the best, and she fell asleep and the bears told her off.

Nicholas's mathematical skills, although not advanced, were within normal limits for his age (39th centile on the BAS number skills test; Elliot, Murray and Pearson, 1983) and certainly superior to his reading, writing and spelling skills. His educational failure continued to be specific to the literacy-based subjects.

By the age of 10, Nicholas's frustration over his severe and persisting reading failure was beginning to affect his behavioural adjustment. At that time, his parents completed a behaviour rating scale, the Achenbach Child Behavior Checklist (Achenbach, 1991). Nicholas's scores on the 'anxious/depressed' and 'attention problem' scales of the checklist fell within the clinical problem range. This was in contrast to his excellent behavioural and social adjustment when younger.

Summary

Nicholas's story provides a clear picture of a child of normal, indeed above-average, intelligence, who having had a relatively happy and uneventful nursery school career, had encountered enormous problems in learning to read and spell. By the time he was approaching the end of primary schooling he was failing within the educational system and was seemingly ill-prepared for the impending move to secondary school. Additionally, the motivated well-adjusted little boy observed at ages 4 and 5 had been replaced by a rather anxious, defensive 10-year-old whose motivation was low and who had very negative attitudes towards school work. Yet, it is evident that the warning signs that Nicholas was at risk for significant reading problems were emerging quite clearly by the age of 5 years, though interestingly not at age 4. It would seem that the administration of a few simple measures of phonological processing skill and of letter knowledge shortly after children begin formal schooling might form a reliable basis for identifying at-risk children like Nicholas. If we can identify, target and intervene early enough, the long-term educational failure and the behavioural sequaelae experienced by such children might be avoided, or at any rate reduced. On a note of caution, Nicholas's case could be seen to provide an argument against screening too early, say in children as young as 4 years; it may be difficult to detect reliable differences between at-risk and normal readers in children who are at the very early stages of developing phoneme and letter awareness. In Chapter 8, we shall look at early reading screening measures that can be used to identify at-risk children at ages 5 and 6.

CHAPTER 5

Risk factors, protective influences and compensatory strategies

The previous chapters have highlighted the importance of measures of phonological processing ability, short-term verbal memory and letter knowledge in the prediction of literacy success or failure. Indeed, weaknesses in phonological skill are thought to be the single most common cause of early reading failure. However, that is not to say that there are not other cognitive, psychological and environmental variables that affect the process of learning to read. For some children with phonological difficulties these additional variables may come to function as further risk factors or perhaps even as protective and compensatory factors. These important terms are defined briefly below.

A 'risk factor' increases the probability that a child will present with a given difficulty. Consequently, a child with poor fine motor skills will be at risk of having poor handwriting, though this outcome is by no means inevitable. Some children with poor fine motor control go on to develop perfectly acceptable handwriting. This is in contrast, for instance, to a child who is born with Down's syndrome. Having this syndrome does not place the child 'at risk' of learning difficulties; it is certain (that is, the probability is 100%) that a child born with this syndrome will have learning problems. A risk factor embodies within it the concept of elevated probability, but not of certainty of a given outcome.

A 'protective influence' is most usually an environmental or experiential factor that improves the outcome for a child with a given difficulty. The case could be argued for early identification and intervention being powerful and positive influences over outcome in the young child with an at-risk reading profile. However, in this chaper the focus is on certain other experience-based protective (and risk) influences, such as social factors and print exposure, that can affect children's early literacy development.

A 'compensatory resource' refers to a skill or ability that a child is able to draw on in order to lessen the impact of a given deficit. In this chapter, particular attention is paid to poor readers' ability to use other language skills (for instance, awareness of syntax and semantics) as a compensatory resource when their phonological skills are weak.

Increasing attention has been paid of late to non-phonological language skills, including syntax and semantics, that might have a bearing on how easily children learn to read. Whitehurst and Lonigan (1998) referred to phonological and letter knowledge skills as 'inside in' processes that determine children's knowledge of the rules for translating the written words into sounds. In contrast, syntax and semantic abilities, constitute 'outside in' processes that relate to children's understanding of the context in which they are reading. Both these processes constitute 'within child' factors that affect early reading development. There are also non-cognitive experiential and environmental factors that may play a role. In this chapter we shall look at both 'outside in' factors (specifically semantic and syntactic influences), and at environmental and experiential factors that may have a bearing on young children's early progress in learning to read.

Syntax, semantics and learning to read

Tunmer (1989) was one of the first researchers to emphasize the importance of syntactic awareness as an independent contributor to early reading skill. Syntactic awareness refers to children's knowledge of, and ability to manipulate, the structural features of sentences, most typically word order. In a longitudinal study, Tunmer (1989) administered tests of verbal ability, phonological awareness, syntactic awareness and reading to 100 children at the end of the first grade and again one year later. The verbal test was a measure of vocabulary that employed pictures. The phonological awareness task required the children to tap out the number of phonemes in single-syllable non-words containing up to five phonemes. The measure of syntax required the children to correct ungrammatical sentences. Sentences of between three and six words were presented orally to the child with the words in incorrect, and therefore ungrammatical, order. The child needed to reflect on the word order and then say the sentence back to the examiner having changed the word order so it 'sounded right'. For instance, the examiner would ask the child to correct the sentence 'Made biscuits mum' to which the child with good syntactic awareness would respond 'Mum made biscuits'. The results clearly demonstrated that both phonological and syntactic awareness influenced both reading comprehension and phonological recoding (as measured by a non-word reading test); this was true even after controlling for the effects of verbal ability. It seems that children use their phonological skills in combination with their syntactic ability to read words and to understand and recall what they have read.

Bowey (1986) also found that performance on a syntactic awareness task was correlated with measures of reading comprehension and comprehension monitoring, even after controlling for the effects of general verbal ability. 'Comprehension monitoring' is a term used to describe how children keep track of whether they are comprehending what they are reading and taking remedial action if necessary. A comprehension monitoring strategy that syntactically aware children are able to use is to check that the meanings they assign to words they have read conform to the surrounding grammatical context.

It is not difficult to see why syntactic awareness and, in particular, semantics (the appreciation of the meaning of words) might influence children's understanding of what they have read. But why should a grammatical ability such as syntactic awareness influence word recognition and decoding? Tunmer and Chapman (1998) suggested that young readers often combine incomplete phoneme–grapheme information with their knowledge of sentence constraints in order to identify unfamiliar words. This, in turn, increases their word-specific knowledge (including irregular words) and their knowledge of grapheme–phoneme correspondences. The ability to use contextual information allows young readers to monitor their reading accuracy by providing them with immediate feedback when their attempted readings of unfamiliar words fail to conform to the surrounding grammatical context. They can then make the necessary adjustments to their subsequent attempts at reading the unfamiliar word up to the point where their response satisfies both the phoneme–grapheme relations within the word and its surrounding sentence constraints. For instance, a young child might be reading a story in which the sentence 'The ball hit him in the stomach' occurs. Supposing the child does not know how to read the word *stomach* but has some rudimentary decoding ability which enables him or her to 'sound out' the letters *s, t, o* and *m*. He or she might try to decode the first part of the word and then draw on the sentence structure in which the unfamiliar word is embedded to decide that its most likely pronunciation is stomach; certainly, it would be hard to think of any other part of the body a ball could hit that contained the letters *s, t, o* and *m*.

There are other ways in which syntactic and semantic awareness might influence reading development. Children with good syntactic or grammatic awareness might try out different pronunciations of words in which a single letter sequence is associated with more than one pronunciation; these are what are referred to as 'homographic letter patterns'. The letter sequence 'ough' is pronounced differently in the words *cough, rough* and *dough*. Children can combine their knowledge of the varying pronunciations of a given letter sequence with grammatical and semantic cues contained in surrounding prose in order to determine which pronunciation best fits the word and its context. In this way, children come to learn about complex relationships between orthographic patterns and pronunciations. Finally, children can use context to help them to learn about and to recognize exception words such as *pint* and *yacht*. Even an exception word like *yacht* shows some phonemic regularity if only in respect of the initial and final letters /y/ and /t/. So again, children can apply their knowledge of sound to letter relationships to produce a reading attempt sufficiently close to the correct form to enable sentence context cues to 'fill the gaps', with the result that the child eventually arrives at the correct reading of the word. For instance, in a sentence such as 'The sailor guided his *yacht* into the harbour', identifying the letters /y/ and /t/ in *yacht* and then noting key context words, such as *sailor* and *harbour* will cue the child into realizing that the word he or she is looking for is a boat or similar object. The child with good verbal skills should be able to generate boat-related words that might well include *yacht* which ties in well with his or her partial decoding attempt of this difficult-to-decode irregular word.

Further support for the combined phonology–context view of reading comes from a recent study (Muter and Snowling, 1998) in which an important concurrent predictor of reading accuracy at age 9 (alongside that of phonological segmentation ability) was found to be grammatical awareness. In this study, children were given a task that tapped their knowledge of grammatical rules, mainly inflection endings of words. This was the Grammatic Closure subtest from the ITPA (Kirk, McCarthy and Kirk, 1968). Recall from the previous chapter that this task required the child to supply the final word of a sentence given orally by the examiner, for example 'Here is a foot, here are two ... [feet]'; 'The girl plants the trees — here is the tree she ... [planted]'. The phonological awareness task was a phoneme deletion task using non-words. In this study, grammatical awareness was found to be a predictor of reading accuracy in context, as measured by a prose reading test, but not of a pure measure of decoding skill, namely non-word reading. This finding was rather different from that of Tunmer (1989) who found that his measure of syntactic awareness predicted non-word reading. It may be that the two different aspects of grammar, that is, syntax versus knowledge of inflectional endings, influence reading in somewhat different ways. It is nonetheless clear that grammatical knowledge interacts with decoding ability to increase word identification skills. This may be particularly true of children who have moved beyond single-word decoding of simple text towards an increasing appreciation of the value of context and content cues contained in more complex reading materials.

Consistent with this idea, Nation and Snowling (1998) found that the extent to which children can use a spoken sentence context to facilitate decoding depends on their verbal skills. These authors presented children with a printed word, either in isolation or following a spoken context. Words such as *aunt* and *hymn* were shown to children on a computer screen, either as individual words or preceded by a spoken sentence frame, for example 'I went shopping with my mother and my ...'; 'We end our assembly with a ...', respectively. The children's speed and accuracy of reading the words was noted. Not surprisingly, the children's reading accuracy increased when context was made available to them. However, what was of particular interest was that the children who benefited most were those with poor phonological skills but good verbal ability, whereas the children who benefited least were those with relatively weak verbal skills.

Clearly, children with poor phonological but good verbal skills could use the information from the sentence frame to bring their pronunciations of target words in line with the context — which is very similar to the argument that was put forward by Tunmer and Chapman (1998). Nation and Snowling (1998) then carried out a further study of over 90 children that showed that the size of this 'contextual facilitation effect' was related to children's semantic processing skills. These workers asked children to carry out two semantic tasks, one requiring them to judge whether two words had the same meaning, and the other requiring them to generate lists of words that had the same or similar meanings. Children who did well on these tasks were those who benefited most from context. Nation and Snowling (1998) suggest that semantic skills might come to act as a compensatory resource for children with poor phonological skills.

The developmental stage at which children begin to draw on their grammatical and syntactical awareness in order to assist word identification and reading comprehension is not clear. Willows and Ryan (1986) suggested that children become increasingly sensitive to semantic and syntactic features in reading tasks during their elementary school years. Thus, syntactic and semantic abilities may gather in predictive importance as children proceed from early single-word decoding to the mastery of more complex text. In a study of grammatical awareness and reading Muter and Snowling (1998) were able to demonstrate that grammatical awareness plays a significant role in word identification in context-based reading by the age of 9. However, it may not be so important a predictor in children as young as 5 or 6 years of age. A longitudinal study of French-speaking children (Casalis and Louis-Alexandre, 2000) found that phonological awareness accounted for the major part of the variance in reading skill at age $6^1/2$. However, by the time the children were aged $7^1/2$, both phonological and grammatical awareness made significant independent contributions to reading accuracy.

More recently, the interrelationship between grammatical awareness, phoneme awareness, and reading accuracy and comprehension has been observed in a longitudinal study of 4- to 6-year-old children (Muter et al., submitted). Composite scores were used that reflected the children's level of phoneme and grammatical awareness when they were 4 and 5 years of age. Their predictive relationship to reading accuracy in a prose reading test and to reading comprehension, Neale Analysis of Reading Ability II (NARA II), (Neale, 1997), was then assessed. The composite phoneme awareness measure consisted of the children's beginning and end phoneme deletion scores at ages 4 and 5. The composite grammatical awareness measure consisted of their scores on two separate tasks at age 5. One of these was a measure of the children's awareness of inflectional endings of words (similar to the ITPA measure described earlier). The second grammatical awareness test was the word order correction task that Tunmer employed in his 1989 study. The relationships between these measures are depicted in the (simplified) path diagrams shown in Figure 5.1.

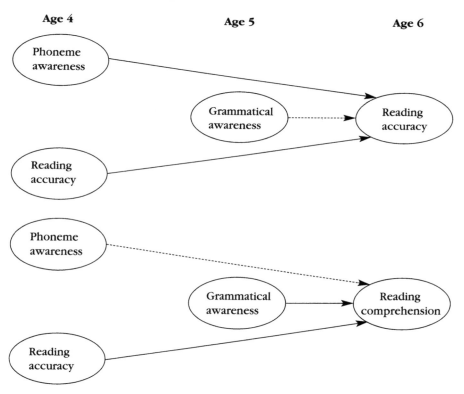

Figure 5.1 Path diagrams depicting the predictive relationships between early phoneme and grammatical awareness, and later reading accuracy and comprehension. A solid arrow line indicates a significant causal pathway, whereas a broken arrow line indicates a non-significant pathway.

What can clearly be seen in these diagrams is that early phoneme awareness is an important predictor of reading accuracy at age 6, whereas
grammatical awareness is not. Thus, word identification at age 6 is determined by the child's ability to manipulate phonemes in words, combined
with the reading skills he or she has already established. It seems likely that
grammatical awareness does not begin to play a role in word identification
until children are rather older; the earlier study by Muter and Snowling,
(1998) suggested that the association between grammatical awareness and
word identification is established by the age of 9 years (Muter and Snowling,
1998). In contrast, reading comprehension from the earliest age is driven not
by children's phoneme awareness skills, but by their established reading
accuracy, in interaction with their awareness of the grammatical and syntactical structures of language.

Another way of viewing the interaction of semantic and phonological
information in the development of reading skill is to draw on computer-
simulated connectionist models of reading. A recent model by Plaut et al.
(1996) introduced a semantic mechanism in order to simulate the reading
process. There are two pathways by which orthographic information can
influence phonological information: a phonological pathway and a semantic
pathway. Thus, from this connectionist perspective, the task when learning
to read is to acquire mappings between the representations of written words
(orthographic units), spoken words (phonological units) and their meanings
(semantic units) — see Figure 5.2. As the training proceeds, the semantic

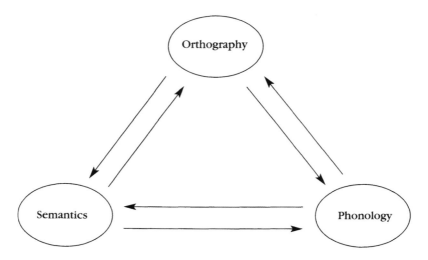

Figure 5.2 Schematic representation of the semantic and phonological pathways
proposed in the model by Plaut et al. (1996).

pathway becomes increasingly specialized for the pronunciation of exception words, whereas the phonological pathway becomes more specialized for the pronunciation of words with consistent spelling patterns. Children with reading problems may have difficulty in establishing the orthography–phonology mappings that comprise the phonological pathway. However, there is evidence that the exception-word reading of many reading-disabled children is relatively unimpaired (Snowling, Hulme and Goulandris, 1994); this suggests that they are able to establish orthography–semantic mappings more easily. These children are able to use semantic support to 'bootstrap' word recognition processes, thus enabling the orthography–semantic pathway to function as a compensatory resource.

Non-cognitive predictors of early reading skill

Thus far, only cognitive predictors of early reading success have been considered. However, there are also non-cognitive determinants of children's early progress in reading that enable us to put together a more complete picture of how children learn to read within an environmental context. In Chapter 1 we saw that epidemiological studies have shown that reading underachievement prevalence rates are effectively doubled in deprived inner city areas as opposed to outer town or rural communities (Rutter and Yule, 1975). This finding points to environmental, in particular social, factors playing a role in the expression and persistence of reading difficulties. It has also been suggested that the home environment may be a likely source of experiences that can enhance the development of both oral and written language skills. We shall consider the contribution of social and family factors in turn.

Social factors, phonological awareness and learning to read

It is well documented that young children's level of language proficiency and their reading skill are closely correlated with the socio-economic status of their parents. In general, children from middle class families attain higher levels of language and literacy than their lower-income peers (Feagans and Farran, 1982; White, 1982). Of particular relevance to this perspective of reading is the relationship between socio-economic status, reading progress and phonological sensitivity. Raz and Bryant (1990) and Bowey (1995) have suggested that socio-economic status differences in word-level reading in young children are mediated mainly through pre-existing differences in phonological sensitivity.

Raz and Bryant (1990) reported strong socio-economic status differences in their young children's reading performance, even when they controlled for the effects of general IQ. Furthermore, when the children's scores on a test of phonological awareness were taken into account, differences in socio-economic status were no longer significant in the tests of reading accuracy. This suggests that socio-economic status differences in phonological sensitivity may mediate the observed socio-economic status differences in reading achievement.

Bowey (1995) conducted a longitudinal study of 5-year-old children differing in socio-economic status (specifically, parental occupation) during their first year of learning to read. Marked differences on a wide variety of measures emerged when the children were grouped according to high or low socio-economic status. The children from high socio-economic status backgrounds obtained higher scores on measures of vocabulary and short-term verbal memory as well as on tests of phonological awareness (that included measures of phoneme identity and rhyme oddity). Most of these differences remained when performance or non-verbal IQ was controlled. More critically, when verbal ability effects were controlled, differences in phonological sensitivity and word-level reading remained.

The studies of Raz and Bryant (1990) and Bowey (1995) support the view that social class differences in word-level reading can largely be accounted for by levels of general intelligence and phonological awareness. A recent longitudinal study by Hecht et al. (2000) extended this previous work in two ways. First, Hecht and colleagues extended the range of measures used to include print knowledge (mainly letter knowledge) and rate of access (naming speed tasks). Second, they extended the age range of the study up to fourth grade (10 years of age). In this study, social class differences in word-level reading skill were substantially accounted for by beginning (kindergarten) levels of reading-related skills. However, these early predictors did not account for quite as much variance in social class differences in reading outcome as in the studies of Raz and Bryant (1990) and of Bowey (1995). This leaves open the question as to whether social class might influence reading through additional factors, beyond those of phonological ability and print awareness, particularly as children get older. Having said that, Hecht et al. found early levels of print knowledge to be the single most important mediator of social class difference in children's reading skill right up to fourth grade.

It seems that many children from lower socio-economic groups may be arriving at school with underdeveloped phonological awareness and limited print knowledge, which then seriously disadvantages them in acquiring early reading skills. It may be particularly important to target children from low socio-economic status groups in respect of screening for phonological difficulties, and to expose them to activities that foster both their awareness of the sound structure of words and their knowledge of sound-to-letter relationships.

Social factors, print exposure and learning to read

An important environmental factor is that which is usually termed 'print exposure'. Print exposure refers to the amount of exposure children have to text, whether in the form of alphabet books, storybooks, comics or magazines. It appears that this is quite strongly related to socio-economic status. A small study of 10 pre-schoolers whose middle-class parents were avid story book readers found that these parents read an average of four books a day to their children, usually at bedtime (Phillips and McNaughton, 1990). The parents visited the library often and reported that they possessed in their homes an average of 300 children's books. It would be reasonable to assume that when they get to school children such as these know a great deal about what stories are like, what print is for and how books work. In contrast to the experiences of middle-class children, children from low-income families have very different early literacy experiences.

Teale (1986) studied 24 pre-schoolers from low-income families and found that they were read to on average only five times per year. A larger-scale study of 102 children directly compared the reading experiences of kindergarten children in geographical areas where scholastic achievement was good with those where the scholastic standards were low (Feitelson and Goldstein, 1986). Sixty per cent of children in the low achievement area did not own any books and were not read to at all. In contrast, children from the high achievement area had an average of 54 books at home and were being read to, on average, for half an hour per day.

What effect does print exposure have on children's early reading experiences and how could we measure it? One way to quantify the amount of exposure children have to text materials is to measure their familiarity with book titles or authors' names. Title and author recognition tasks of this sort have been developed by Stanovich and West (1989). In the title recognition task, children are shown a list of book titles (half of which are real and half of which are fictitious). The children must tick which titles they recognize as real books. The author recognition task is similar but uses authors' names as opposed to book titles. Table 5.1 depicts extracts from tests of print exposure devised for a UK sample of 15–16-year-olds.

A study by Cunningham and Stanovich (1998) looked at the relationship between phonological awareness, print exposure and reading skill in 26 first-grade children. The children were given a number of tasks that measured phonological awareness, including phoneme deletion and phoneme transposition tasks. They also completed a title recognition task, along with standardized tests of reading and spelling, and a measure of orthographic processing. The latter required the children to circle which of two printed words looked most like it could be a real word, for example 'beff' as opposed to 'ffeb'. The children's performance on the title recognition task contributed to their

Table 5.1 Extracts from tests of print exposure devised for a UK sample of 15–16-year-olds. The task is to tick (a) the correct author names, (b) the correct book titles

Author recognition task

Dean Koontz	Michael Harshorne
A.C. Leach	Stephen King
Paul Dobson	John Steinbeck
Anthony Lunch	Enid Blyton
Dick King-Smith	Charles Dickens
Betsy Byars	Carolyn Young
Judy Blume	Rosie Gunning

Title recognition task

Space Brownie	Forever
BFG	Great Expectations
Animal Farm	Lord of the Rings
Pride and Prejudice	MacBeth
Without Wishes	Reasons for Trying
Squashed Bananas	Dreams of New York
1984	The Babysitters' Club

performance on the measures of reading, spelling and orthographic processing, even after controlling for the contribution made by the phonological measures to the literacy tasks. These findings were confirmed longitudinally when the authors studied the children from grade 1 to grade 3. Not surprisingly, print exposure affects reading comprehension as well as word recognition and orthographic knowledge. Cipielewski and Stanovich (1992) showed that exposure to print is implicated in comprehension growth over a period of two years. This study was conducted with rather older children who were in grade 3 at the outset and who were followed up until grade 5. The authors demonstrated that print exposure contributed to reading comprehension in grade 5, even after controlling for the effect of decoding skill and earlier comprehension levels.

Print exposure interacts with reading skill in what is essentially a cumulative fashion. Children who are exposed to text from an early age clearly have a reading advantage. Because they read well, they will gain success and enjoyment from reading and want to read all the more. The more they read the better their reading becomes — a case of the rich getting richer. In contrast, children who have limited early exposure to text will be disadvantaged at the beginning stages of being taught to read. Because they may perceive reading as difficult and experience little success, they avoid what is for them an aversive experience. They read less and so make slower progress in terms of expanding their reading vocabulary — so, in effect, the poor get poorer. The problem for these children is likely to be made all the worse if they also have limited phonological skills. It seems likely that pre-schoolers in this unfortunate position might benefit from early screening and intervention programmes that focus on language activities that foster children's sensitivity to sound patterns in words and which link these to their experience of print in terms of alphabet and story books.

Do parents who read to their pre-schoolers help to promote their literacy development?

A further relevant factor, clearly strongly related to print exposure, is how often parents read to their pre-school children. Scarborough and Dobrich (1994) reviewed 31 studies that looked at the effect of parents' reading to their pre-school children on the children's oral language and literacy development. Twenty of these studies were correlational in methodology; they looked at the relationship between measures such as the amount of time spent reading to children or the frequency of story book reading, and outcome measures such as oral language proficiency, phonological awareness and emerging literacy skill. The remaining 11 studies were intervention programmes, which meant that parents in an experimental group were given instruction and guidance in how to read to their children. The effect of this intervention on their children's language and reading was then compared to that of a control group who had not had the benefit of specific instruction and support.

Scarbrough and Dobrich (1994) found that the results from one study to another varied a great deal, even when similar kinds of language or reading outcome measures were used. However, they were able to draw some general conclusions. First, it appeared that frequency of reading to pre-school children seemed to be the important predictor factor; the quality of shared reading was understandably more difficult to assess. This may explain why there was little indication that improved quality of parental reading affected children's language or reading skills. Second, the correlational studies showed that frequency of reading was most usually associated with growth in spoken vocabulary knowledge, semantic content of language and developing literacy (but not growth in syntactic or phonological structures). In the intervention studies, more positive results emerged for oral language than for literacy outcome. Third, although there appears to be a significant association between parent–pre-school child reading and language/literacy outcome in the correlational studies, this is of modest proportions. Most correlations were at or less than 0.28, accounting for no more than about 8 per cent of the overall variance in language or reading achievement. Lastly, intervention studies that altered the frequency and/or quality of parent–pre-school child reading showed that modifying parents' shared reading practices could bring about short-term, and in some instances even lasting, growth in at least some literacy-related abilities.

A recent study by Senechal et al. (1998) contrasted frequency of story book reading and frequency of parents teaching the reading and writing of words in their effect on children's oral and written language skills. Children from middle-class schools were studied whilst in kindergarten and grade 1. Senechal et al. found that story book exposure significantly contributed to the children's oral language skills, though not to their written language. This was true even after controlling for differences in the parent's print exposure (measured by an author recognition task) and the children's IQ. In contrast, parent teaching of reading made a unique contribution to the children's written language skills, but not to their oral language. These authors conclude that their findings are consistent with the hypothesis that story-book exposure may enhance children's oral language skills, whereas additional support in the form of reading teaching may be necessary to promote written language development.

It is possible that shared reading experiences may affect children's subsequent reading skills in a number of ways. First, shared reading with parents means that children learn a lot about print convention and may, in fact, start school with a much greater appreciation of the function and structure of books. Second, exposure to print, whether in the form of alphabet books or story-books, may well give them a head start in terms of learning sound-to-print rules. Third, shared reading promotes semantic skills and vocabulary knowledge which, as we saw in the earlier part of this chapter, contribute significantly to both word-level reading and reading comprehension.

There seems to be little evidence that parent–pre-school child story book experiences have a direct effect on children's reading via the promotion of their phonological skills; Lonigan, Anthony and Dyer (1996) showed that growth in phonological sensitivity was not linked to shared reading experience. However, a number of the studies reviewed by Scarborough and Dobrich (1994) suggested that early shared story book experiences at home may enhance children's vocabulary development, which is thought by some to be an important precursor of emerging phonological segmentation skill (Fowler, 1991; Walley, 1993). Consequently, there might be an arguable case for story book reading having an indirect effect on phonological skill, this being mediated through the effect that shared reading has on earlier established language skills.

Does the language of instruction make a difference?

Much of the research into early reading development and its associated language and phonological abilities has been carried out in English. English is a much more difficult language to learn to read (and, in particular, to spell) than say Spanish, Italian or even German. We have seen that English has a complex morpho-phonological orthography which can make it hard for children to learn the sound-to-letter consistencies, and in particular to cope with the many exceptions and homophones. Languages such as Spanish or German are phonologically transparent and consequently show greater consistency in respect of spelling patterns. It is proposed, therefore, that the language in which the child is learning to read is an environmental factor that can affect ease of literacy acquisition, in particular in children who might be predisposed to reading problems in the first place.

Faster rates of reading acquisition have been observed among readers of Italian (Cossu et al., 1988), German (Frith, Wimmer and Landerl, 1998) and Greek (Nikolopoulos, 1999) than in English-language children. The position is similar for spelling. Wimmer and Landerl (1998) found that German-speaking children in grade 2 to grade 4 performed better on a single-word spelling task than English-speaking children of comparable age.

Of especial interest is the finding that phonological awareness develops more quickly in children who are learning a transparent orthography, such as Italian (Cossu, 1999). In relation to reading problems, we shall see in the next chapter that children who are described as dyslexic have deficits in phonological skill and non-word reading. However, some authors have suggested that this observation relates mainly to children learning written English. Wimmer and colleagues (Wimmer, Mayringer and Landerl, 1998) argued that children with a predisposition towards dyslexia who are being educated in German, for instance, tend to do relatively well on tasks of phonological segmentation and non-word reading. Their difficulties may be evident, though, on speed-oriented measures, such as rapid naming tasks, or on measures of short-term verbal memory. Such children are likely to read quite accurately but they will be slow and laborious readers.

However, some recent research has suggested that the differences between dyslexic subjects operating in a transparent as opposed to an opaque (usually a morpho-phonological) orthography may be overstated. Caravolas and Volin (2001) found that Czech-speaking dyslexic children who are acquiring a transparent orthography have persistent difficulties in phonological segmentation and decoding skills that are similar to, though not as severe as, those seen in English-speaking children. These authors have suggested that exposure to a transparent orthography, in conjunction with phonic-based teaching methods, may not be sufficient to enable dyslexic children to compensate for their difficulties.

So far, this book has concentrated mainly on the factors that influence reading development in normally developing 4- to 7-year-olds. The emphasis is now shifted to look at the characteristics of 5 to 8 per cent of our young child population that has unexpected difficulty in learning to read, that is, children we describe as 'dyslexic'. The next two chapters will describe the specific difficulties experienced by young dyslexic children and the probable causes of their literacy problems. The remaining chapters will address practitioner issues, including screening and early identification, assessment, prevention and intervention in the young dyslexic child.

Summary

- Children's awareness of grammar, in combination with their semantic knowledge, has been shown to influence their word-level reading, as well as their comprehension of what they read.
- Verbally able poor readers, with limited phonological skills, may be able to take advantage of their good semantic skills as a compensatory resource to aid their word recognition.
- Children from low-income families tend to have poorer reading skills than those from high-income families, a discrepancy that has been shown to be largely attributed to their weaker phonological awareness and print awareness as pre-schoolers; these children form an at-risk group that may be appropriately targeted for early screening and phonological training.
- Children's exposure to print influences their reading development from an early age.
- In particular, parents reading to children has a role to play in determining later reading ability; shared reading not only provides early print exposure but also promotes the development of semantic skills and vocabulary knowledge which, in turn, contribute to word-level reading and reading comprehension.
- Children exposed to a transparent orthography, such as Italian or German, are at an advantage in learning to read and spell when compared to children who must acquire an opaque orthography, such as English or French.

CHAPTER 6
Phonological deficits in dyslexia

So far, a strong and persuasive case has been argued for the powerful role that is played by phonological abilities in early reading development. In particular, it is argued that it is the status of the child's underlying phonological representations that critically determines the ease with which he or she learns to read. Given that that is true of children occupying a wide range of reading skills and abilities, does this apply also to children who are recognized as dyslexic? Since 1980 there have been many studies that point to language difficulties in the dyslexic child, in particular at the level of phonology. We shall shortly see that dyslexic children typically tend to perform poorly on a wide range of measures of phonological awareness, verbal short-term memory, rapid naming and speech perception tasks which essentially tap children's representation of, access to, and recall of, phonological information.

Defining dyslexia

Before embarking on a review of the phonological deficits in this group of children let us consider what we mean by the term 'dyslexia'. Its definition has been fraught with controversy. Indeed, some specialists in the field of reading disability believe that we should avoid the use of such a medical sounding term to describe what is, in essence, both a cognitive and an educational deficit. Instead, they prefer to use more descriptively oriented terms such as 'specific learning difficulty', 'specific reading retardation', 'specific written language problems' and so on. In addition, there is the controversy over whether the term should be adopted only for children who show a specifically prescribed pattern of language, in particular phonological, difficulty that affects their literacy development.The alternative view is that the term should be adopted rather more generically to describe children who, in spite of having normal intelligence and appropriate schooling experiences, fail to learn to read — irrespective of the nature of their underlying deficit.

Some years ago I attended a one-day conference of psychologists in London; the aim was to discuss and explore what is meant by 'dyslexia' and possibly to arrive at an agreed definition. After several hours of debate, sometimes quite heated, no consensus could be reached on what is meant by the term and how it should be used to describe the difficulties and educational needs of individual children. We have come a little further since those days, both in terms of the research progress that has been made and, in particular, in relation to the development of specific assessment and teaching techniques for use with children who fail to develop literacy skills as they should. Nonetheless a meeting of research and practitioner psychologists held today would probably still result in heated debate and a lot of disagreement on at least the finer points of the definition of this much-used term.

Until recently, the term dyslexia has been, in effect, a definition by exclusion. Dyslexia is frequently defined as 'inordinate difficulty learning to read in the absence of low IQ, sensory deficits or adverse schooling and environmental factors'. However, we are moving away from this rather unhelpful definition; it is all very well to know what *does not* cause dyslexia but in order to help children we need to know what *does* cause it. A more recent definition of dyslexia has been offered by Stein (2001, p. 12), who describes dyslexia as a learning disability in which 'reading is significantly behind that expected from IQ, in the presence of other symptoms — inco-ordination, left–right confusion, poor sequencing — that characterise it as a neurological syndrome'. However, Stein's (2001) definition fails to specify the core deficit in dyslexia that would help us in its identification, measurement and management. Additionally neurologists (and those in allied professions) might take issue with the view of dyslexia as a 'neurological syndrome'. In a recent book on dyslexia, Snowling (2000) attempted a working definition of dyslexia that is specific and focused, and yet which takes into account the heterogeneity of expression of this difficulty:

> Dyslexia is a specific form of language impairment that affects the way in which the brain encodes the phonological features of spoken words. The core deficit is in phonological processing and stems from poorly specified phonological representations. Dyslexia specifically affects the development of reading and spelling skills but its effects can be modified through development leading to a variety of behavioural manifestations. (Snowling, 2000, pp 213–14).

There are two important features of Snowling's definition of dyslexia. First, it is very specific in terms of indicating the underlying cause of dyslexia. This specificity points to ways in which we might assess the difficulties and needs of the dyslexic child, and also directs us to specific teaching practices that might help them overcome, or at the very least, ameliorate their difficulties. These issues are followed up in detail in Chapters 10 and 11. Second, the definition enables us to account for the considerable variability seen among dyslexic children. These individual differences may be partly explained by the severity of the dyslexic difficulty. What is argued here is that dyslexia is not an all-or-none learning disability but one that occupies a continuum from the very mild to the very severe. Recall that Wolf and Bowers (1999) attempted to explain severity in terms of single deficit versus dual deficit phonological dyslexia, with the degree of reading disability being related to whether a child has a deficit in phonological segmentation or phonological processing, or both.

Although dyslexia is a lifelong difficulty, its manifestation can change with maturation and through experiential factors. Cognitive and educational expressions of dyslexia that are evident at one point in development may not be present at another. Individuals also respond to teaching intervention that may resolve, or at any rate ameliorate, some of the deficits. Similarly, compensatory strategies may develop in the individual in response not only to teaching and experiential factors but also the availability of specific cognitive strengths. For instance, as seen in the previous chapter, reading-disabled children who are particularly verbally able may be able to compensate for their phonological and decoding deficiencies by paying attention to context cues within prose reading (Nation and Snowling, 1998). They combine their good vocabularies and grammatical skills with their fragmented phonological/phonic knowledge, permitting them to arrive at the correct reading of a given word, which they might not have been able to achieve on the basis of their incomplete decoding abilities alone.

How dyslexia is defined may depend on the level of description being focused upon. Frith (1997) attempted to define dyslexia within the framework of a model that acknowledges three different levels in the causal chain: the biological; the cognitive; and the behavioural. Moreover, this model shows how environmental factors influence the causal pathway. Frith's (1997) model is represented in Figure 6.1.

At the uppermost level of this framework is the biological basis of dyslexia, which is explored in some detail in the next chapter. We know that there is a genetic predisposition towards dyslexia and that this is evident both from genetic research studies and from those that have addressed brain abnormality and dysfunction in dyslexic subjects. The genetic brain abnormality results at the next level (that is, the cognitive level) in a phonological deficit. This, in turn, interacts with other cognitive skills, which together influence the behavioural expression of dyslexia, namely that of delay in learning to read and spell. There are also environmental factors that affect the causal pathway; these might take the form of schooling and family factors, and even the writing system to which the child is exposed. In effect, the behavioural manifestation of the core phonological deficit will depend on its

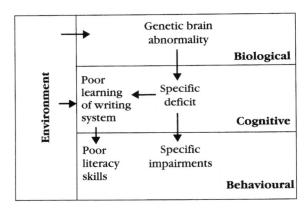

Figure 6.1 A causal model of dyslexia. (Source: Frith, 1997.)

interaction both with environmental influences and the availability of compensatory strategies.

Evidence for phonological deficits in dyslexic children

The phonological deficits of dyslexic children have been widely studied over the past 20 years. Early research typically compared the language and phonological skills of dyslexic children with children of the same age who were not dyslexic; this is referred to as the 'chronological-age-matched research design'. However, this approach presents a major methodological problem that can make it difficult to interpret the results of such comparisons. In the chronological-age-matched design, the two groups of children are, of necessity, reading at very different levels. Bearing in mind that there is a two-way influence between phonological skills and reading ability, it becomes very difficult to be sure that the problems dyslexic children experience in phonological tasks arise from a fundamental core deficit or whether they are a direct consequence of their poor reading levels.

The way out of this conundrum is to employ a 'reading-age-matched research design' in which the two groups are matched not on chronological age but on reading age. Consequently, an experimenter might compare a group of dyslexic children aged approximately 9 years, but with a reading age of 7 years, with a group of 7-year-olds, reading at their age-appropriate standard. It is the aim of the experimenter to demonstrate that the control group of normally reading 7-year-olds is able to perform better than the older dyslexic group on phonological or other-reading relevant tasks. If this proves to be the case, the experimenter has provided a very stringent test for the presence of a fundamental core deficit in the dyslexic children that cannot be accounted for by their reading level or experience.

The reading-age-matched design is a highly conservative one, and is not without its flaws. A particular problem is that, of necessity, the dyslexic children may be three to four years older than the reading-age-matched control group; maturational factors within the children and remedial teaching factors might act to obscure differences between the two groups, which can then be difficult to interpret. Some studies have, therefore, employed two control groups — a chronological-age-matched control group and a reading-age-matched group.

Bearing in mind these methodological issues, let us go on to review the evidence for phonological and related deficits in dyslexia. The focus is on key studies in a number of different task paradigms, but for a fuller discussion of these, the reader is directed to the review by Snowling (2000).

Not surprisingly, there has been extensive research on phonological awareness skills in dyslexic children. The variety of ways one can assess phonological awareness and the effect that phonological segmentation ability, in particular, has on subsequent reading development in normally developing children has already been examined in Chapter 2. Not unexpectedly, dyslexic children perform poorly on tasks that require them to blend, analyse, segment or to manipulate speech segments in words, whether syllables, onsets and rimes or phonemes. Of late, studies have begun to address the important issue of which level of phonological awareness is particularly affected in dyslexic children. For instance, Swan and Goswami (1997) compared the ability of dyslexic children on tasks of syllable, rime and phoneme segmentation with that of chronological-age- and reading-age-matched control subjects. Although the dyslexic children were disadvantaged relative to the chronological-age-matched control subjects on all three levels of segmentation task, they were impaired relative to the reading age-matched-control subjects only on the phoneme segmentation task. This suggests that phonological segmentation tasks may be more powerful predictors of reading than onset-rime tasks in dyslexic children, as well as in normally developing readers.

Verbal short-term memory deficits have long been a documented feature of dyslexic children. Dyslexic children typically have no problem remembering visual information but have enormous difficulty in remembering verbal materials. So, young dyslexic children might be expected to have difficulty in repeating number or word sequences, lengthy sentences, and so on. As we saw in Chapter 3, there is a lot of evidence that verbal material is held in short-term memory in the form of a speech- or phonetically based-code. It may be that dyslexic children's impaired representation of the phonological forms of words results in a restriction in the number of verbal items they can retain in memory.

Consequently, many dyslexic children have difficulty in remembering lengthy verbal instructions and in carrying out mental calculations. We saw in Chapter 3 that poor readers have been shown to have slow speech rates (McDougall et al., 1994). It has been suggested that this is due to their difficulty in retrieving verbal information from long-term memory. The efficient retrieval of verbal information from the long-term store is necessary for the reconstruction of a memory trace as it begins to fade from short-term memory (Hulme et al., 1997). As the memory trace for a specific word item begins to fade, the system attempts to 'fill in' the missing phonetic information by drawing upon knowledge of phonologically similar words in long-term memory. It seems likely that dyslexic children have difficulty with this process, which is sometimes referred to as 'redintegration'. Because the memory trace of the word is fading so much faster in dyslexic children, their ability to blend sounds together during the decoding of a word is much reduced.

We have already seen in Chapter 3 that naming-speed tasks are good predictors of early reading skill in normally developing children. As a corollary to this, slowness in carrying out naming-speed tasks is a characteristic of many dyslexic children (Wolf, 1997; Wolf and Bowers, 1999). Not unrelated to the naming-speed deficit is the frequent clinical observation that dyslexic children have difficulties in retrieving verbal labels that may take the form of 'word finding' difficulty, that is, children who cannot find the word that they are looking for and so resort to circumlocutions such as 'thinigummy', 'what's it', etc.

Snowling, van Wagtendonk and Stafford (1988) showed pictures of common objects to 11-year-old dyslexic children and asked them to name them. The items included words such as *accordion, monkey, aquarium*. Each dyslexic child was matched with a normal reader according to his or her performance on a task of word definitions. Although well-matched for vocabulary knowledge, the dyslexic children were significantly impaired on the picture-naming task relative to the matched control subjects. Thus, dyslexic children have difficulty in retrieving the names of objects with which they are, in fact, familiar. Their memory representations are adequately specified in terms of their semantic features, otherwise the dyslexic children would have had difficulty with the word definition task. Rather, it is the phonological representation of the word that is either poorly specified or else inaccessible. In a reading-age-matched study conducted by Swan and Goswami (1997), dyslexic children could define many words they could not name. So, for instance, a dyslexic child might look at a picture of an accordion and respond 'You play it with your fingers, it makes music', but be unable to come up with the name *accordion*. Again, this evidence suggests that semantic representations are intact in dyslexic subjects but that phonological representations are impaired.

Clinical evaluations of dyslexic children have often highlighted problems in pronouncing polysyllabic words. Such difficulties provide evidence for dyslexic children having 'verbal repetition difficulties'. In a very early study by Snowling (1981), dyslexic children were found to have no difficulty (relative to reading-age-matched control subjects) in repeating polysyllabic real words (for example, *pedestrian* and *magnificent*), but they had marked problems in repeating polysyllabic non-words that were similar in phonological structure ('kebestrian', 'bagmivishent'). Again, this fits in well with the evidence described in Chapter 3 that pointed to non-word repetition tasks being good predictors of later reading skills in normal children. It is important to note that dyslexic children do not have any particular difficulty at the level of discriminating non-words. So, when dyslexic children are asked to decide if two presented non-words are similar or different they do not have any especial problem when their performance is compared to that of matched control subjects (Snowling, 1981). Thus, the difficulty for dyslexic children appears to be at the level of speech production, not speech discrimination. Why should dyslexic children have particular problems repeating non-words as opposed to real words? Snowling (1981) explains this by hypothesizing that dyslexic readers may have particular difficulty in analysing and segmenting the word prior to the assembly of the motor programme for its articulation. Real words may be more readily analysed and segmented because they are already likely to have a representation in long-term memory, as opposed to non-words, which do not have such an existing representation, so placing a greater load on the dyslexic child's deficient segmentation skills.

We saw in Chapter 3 that children's ability to learn to associate pairs of items ('paired associate learning') may play a role in establishing connections between words and their pronunciations. Windfuhr (1998) compared the paired associate learning performance of adolescent dyslexic readers with that of both chronological age- and younger 8-year-old reading-age-matched control subjects. The chronological-age-matched control subjects performed better than both the reading-age-matched control subjects and dyslexic groups. There was also a trend towards the dyslexic children struggling more than the reading-age control subjects. Within the dyslexic group, there was a markedly discrepant performance between paired associate learning and phonological awareness for many of the children. Windfuhr (1998) suggests that this dissociation might reflect different subtypes of dyslexia. Some dyslexic children have a single deficit in phonological awareness, whereas others have a dual deficit that encompasses problems of both phonological awareness and association learning. Thus, children with both phonological awareness and paired associate learning deficits would have difficulty, not only in phonological decoding but also in 'hooking up' orthography and phonology, a skill that forms the basis for creating word-specific associations.

The evidence addressed to date has very much concentrated on dyslexic children having difficulties in 'output phonology' (that is, at the level of speech production), but not in respect of 'input phonology' (that is, at the level of speech perception). However, there are some studies of speech perception in dyslexic readers that suggest that at least some children may have difficulty in accurately perceiving the difference between speech sounds that differ in respect of a single phonetic feature, for example discriminating between the words *bath* and *path*. Manis and colleagues (Manis et al., 1997) carried out such a task with dyslexic children and compared their performance with reading-age- and chronological-age-matched control subjects. Fewer than one-third of the dyslexic children showed speech perception abnormalities, although this reflected a far higher incidence of perceptual difficulties than in either of the two control groups. The dyslexic children who were most likely to show problems of speech perception were those who had obtained the lowest scores on a test of phoneme awareness. The findings of speech perception studies have been somewhat equivocal for the following reasons. First, the findings may have been affected by the attentional demands of some speech perception tasks, so they may prove particularly difficult for those dyslexic children who have concentration problems. Second, there is the possibility that some dyslexic children may adopt compensatory strategies or alternative processing methods (such as verbal labelling) that might obscure the results.

Do the phonological deficits of dyslexic children stem from a fundamental sensory deficit?

The above findings provide converging evidence for the core deficit in dyslexia being a phonological deficit. Having said that, recent research into neurophysiological bases of dyslexia has resulted in an emerging body of evidence suggesting that the phonological and reading difficulties experienced by dyslexic readers might be traced back to more fundamental sensory deficits. It is this evidence that may ultimately provide the link between the genetic–biological basis of dyslexia and its cognitive–educational expression shown in the Frith (1997) model.

One of the first sensory-based hypotheses claimed that dyslexic children are impaired in their auditory temporal processing. This view stems from work conducted by Tallal and her colleagues who have mainly studied, not dyslexic children, but those with specific language impairment. Children with specific language impairment have normal non-verbal ability but have great difficulty in acquiring spoken language skills. The specific language impaired children in Tallal's studies were required to carry out a temporal order judgement task in which the stimuli were high or low tones (Tallal and Piercey, 1974). The children listened to sequences of tones and then pressed one of two keys in order to indicate the order in which they heard the high and low tones presented. The specific language impaired children had no particular difficulty in carrying out this task (in contrast to control subjects) when the time interval between the tones was long. However, when the time intervals were shortened the performance of the specific language impaired children was far poorer than that of the control subjects.

On the basis of this evidence, Tallal proposed that an auditory temporal processing deficit was the underlying problem in children with specific language impairment. She then went on to attempt to extend this model to dyslexic children by relating the difficulty with temporal ordering to problems of phonological processing (Tallal, 1980). However, Heath, Hogben and Clark (1999) found that problems of auditory temporal processing could be replicated only for children with specific language impairment and were not evident in children with reading difficulties who did not have accompanying oral language problems. In a recent study by Marshall, Snowling and Bailey (2001), there was no clear-cut relationship between phonological difficulties in dyslexic children and their performance on an auditory processing task. Although some dyslexic children with severe phonological impairments performed poorly on the auditory processing task, others with similarly severe phonological problems performed normally on the auditory processing task. Moreover, in this study reading ability was better predicted by the children's scores on phonological tasks than by their scores on the auditory processing task.

A very considerable problem for Tallal's work, which sees her out of step with many of her contemporaries in the area of language development, is her assumption that the processes required for processing non-speech sounds (tones, music, etc.) are the same as those involved in speech processing. Mody, Studdert-Kennedy and Brady (1997) demonstrated that dyslexic children perform like normal readers on tasks that require the processing of non-speech auditory stimuli (in this case sine waves) while they have marked problems in speech processing tasks. Tallal's work has had a significant impact on the treatment of children with specific language impairment, since the publication of a computerized therapeutic instrument, FastForward, which purports to train children to process auditory information more rapidly and efficiently. The improvements in the children's comprehension and use of language quoted in their training studies have been dramatic. However, there is a need to replicate these findings by independent bodies. Notwithstanding the findings of Tallal, the general consensus at present is that it is speech-related skills, not generalized auditory processing, that predict reading ability and that it is an impairment in these abilities that causes the reading problems of dyslexic children.

A visual sensory-based hypothesis is that proposed by Lovegrove and colleagues who have used psychophysical methods to study low-level visual impairments they believe are characteristic of many dyslexic children (Lovegrove, Martin and Slaghuis, 1986). The visual system in man has two parallel operating systems: the transient system, which detects moving stimuli, and which is fast-acting but has poor acuity; and the sustained system, in which information is transmitted slowly but at a high level of acuity. The efficiency of the transient system may be assessed by use of a test of sensitivity to flickering patterns; dyslexic children have been found to be less sensitive to flicker effects, in particular as the rate or temporal frequency of the flicker increases. However, they seem not to have problems with tasks that assess the functioning of the sustained visual system, the efficiency of which can be measured by use of non-flickering spatial tasks. The transient system is thought to be important in reading for extracting forthcoming information to the right of fixation — in effect, scanning ahead.

It is the visual magnocellular structures in the brain that are responsible for the operation of the transient system in man, and it is therefore assumed that these structures are in some way deficient in dyslexic subjects. Stein (2001) has studied this magnocellular hypothesis by developing a computerized procedure that tests children's sensitivity to the visual motion of arrays of dots (see Stein, 2001, for a review); it is claimed that children whose reading is significantly behind that expected from their age and IQ have poorer motion sensitivity than control subjects matched for age and IQ. Visual motion signals are thought to be important in achieving visual perceptual stability. Because visual stability is binocular, visual confusion results from the two eyes presenting different and competing versions of where letters are situated on the page. Stein (2001) goes on to suggest that reading with one eye blanked with a patch might improve reading in dyslexic individuals. This treatment technique of 'monocular occlusion' will be considered again in Chapter 11.

The magnocellular hypothesis is not without its problems in explaining the difficulties dyslexic children have when reading. As Hulme (1988) pointed out, if the transient system is impaired in dyslexic children then they should have far greater difficulty in reading prose than single words. In fact, this is not the case; indeed, the reverse seems to be true (Frith and Snowling, 1983). Additionally, there has been a general failure to replicate the findings of those researching low-level visual impairments in dyslexia. Lastly, Frith and Frith (1996) suggested that perhaps these subtle transient system deficits are biological markers of dyslexia but are unrelated to the cognitive level and, therefore, may be irrelevant to the reading problems of dyslexic children.

The investigation of more fundamental sensory deficits in dyslexia, whether visual or auditory, is still in its infancy. It has been fraught with methodological problems and a general failure to replicate findings. It is clear, though, that further research needs to be conducted in this field, important as it is to clarifying the nature of the links between the biological basis of dyslexia and its cognitive/educational expression.

How do phonological deficits in dyslexic children manifest themselves in reading failure?

We saw in Chapter 2 that phonological abilities interact with letter knowledge to enable young readers to acquire the alphabetic principle, that is, the realization that particular speech sounds are systematically associated with printed letters. Byrne (1998) specified three conditions that need to be met for children to acquire the alphabetic principle and to emerge from the logographic stage of learning to read into the alphabetic stage. First, children need to know the letters of the alphabet. Second, they require a minimal level of phonological segmentation skill that enables them to split words into sounds. Third, children need to connect or link their emerging speech sound sensitivity with their experience of print — what Hatcher et al. (1994) refer to as 'phonological linkage'.

In dyslexic children, these three conditions for the emergence of the alphabetic stage are slow to develop, with the result that the child soon falls far behind his or her peers in reading. Put in terms of Frith's (1997) stage theory of reading, it is hypothesized that dyslexic children's failure to acquire the alphabetic principle means that they are effectively 'arrested within the logographic stage of reading', expanding their reading lexicon only through the addition of sight words. Thus, young dyslexic children who have failed to progress to alphabetic reading are likely to have difficulty in learning to read phonetically. They are therefore forced to base their attempts at word identification on visual features, such as word shape and length, and isolated or partial phonic cues (for instance, guessing at the word on the basis of a single letter, usually at the beginning or end of a word).

It is agreed that the vast majority of dyslexic children have problems in mapping alphabetic symbols to speech sounds: 83 per cent in Vellutino and Scanlon's (1991) analysis of hundreds of impaired readers. This inability to abstract letter–sound correspondences from experience with printed words results in a failure to develop phonic reading strategies. One direct way of tapping the level of phonic reading skill is to ask children to attempt to read nonsense words that cannot be recognized from previous experience, nor accessed through semantic clues. These words can be read only if the child is able to apply sound-to-letter correspondence rules in a systematic way. Indeed, there is a great deal of evidence that dyslexic children have considerable difficulty in reading non-words such as 'fup', 'tweps' and 'soltip'.

The non-word reading deficit in dyslexia is thought to be a consequence of other essentially phonological limitations within the system. An extensive review of studies that assessed the non-word reading deficit in dyslexia was conducted by Rack, Snowling and Olson (1992). All the studies they evaluated showed that dyslexic children were impaired in non-word reading relative to chronological-age-matched control subjects. However, not all the studies were able to demonstrate a non-word reading impairment in the dyslexic group relative to reading-age-matched control subjects. Thus, it was not entirely clear whether the non-word reading deficit could pass the stringent task of being a fundamental and core deficit. This dilemma was clarified further in another review paper by van Ijzendoorn and Bus (1994). Studies of clinical populations are often handicapped by necessarily small sample sizes that can make it very hard to detect real differences between the groups. Van Ijzendoorn and Bus (1994) ameliorated this problem by pooling the results of a number of non-word reading studies so as to increase the statistical power of the measure. These authors then carried out a large-scale statistical analysis that provided compelling evidence for the non-word reading deficit being a very real one. As we shall see later, the use of non-word reading tests as an assessment technique is of enormous value in diagnosing dyslexia and in quantifying the severity of the phonological decoding deficit in the individual child.

The reading difficulties of dyslexic children may also be conceptualized within a connectionist framework. In order to simulate problems with alphabetic reading in a computerized model, it is necessary to constrain or restrict the mappings that are established between orthography and phonology during training. In line with the extensive research on the contribution of phonological processing to reading, the most obvious modification to the training procedure would be somehow to underspecify the units in the phonological store. For instance, Harm and Seidenberg (1999) simulated dyslexia by reducing the network's capacity to represent phonological information. A severe impairment of phonological representation was achieved by severing connections within the phonological layer. This dyslexic model had difficulty reading non-words, reflecting the decoding problems one expects to see in the dyslexic child or adult. Harm and Seidenberg's (1999) simulations also showed that the more severe the phonological deficit, the more the network had to draw upon other processing resources such as visual memory or semantic skills. So, computer models (and indeed dyslexic children) can make use of resources or strengths they might have in visual memory or semantics to compensate for their phonological deficiencies.

If we accept that the majority of severely disabled readers have problems in mapping alphabetic symbols to sounds then this 'underspecified phonological representation' view seems to be the most plausible way of representing dyslexia within a connectionist model. However, Snowling (1998) suggested two other strategies that might be used to interfere with the normal 'running' of a connectionist model. One would be to decrease the number of hidden units so that the activation between the phonological and orthographic units is 'lost', perhaps by limitations in verbal short-term memory. Alternatively, the connectionist framework could be compromised due to insufficiencies in the coding of the orthographic representations. This might result from a visual perceptual problem, a view that might go some way to reconciling the recent findings on low-level visual processing problems in some dyslexic individuals. Thus, short-term memory limitations or visual processing deficits might account for the problems of a minority of reading-disabled children whose phonological representations are relatively unimpaired. This raises the issue as to whether it is feasible to classify dyslexic children into subtypes. We might accept that the majority of reading-disabled children would fall into what might be termed a 'phonological dyslexia' subgroup, that is, children whose reading difficulty arises from a phonological processing deficit that impairs their ability to develop decoding skills. Nonetheless, there may be smaller subgroups of children whose reading difficulty is related not so much to phonological difficulties but to other underlying problems of the sort just raised, that is, difficulties in short-term memory or visual processing.

Are there different subtypes of dyslexia?

Early attempts at classifying dyslexic children into clinically and educationally meaningful subtypes were not very successful. Even with a sufficiently large sample of poor readers, it is hard to establish distinct and internally homogeneous subgroups. Indeed, many studies were left with as many as 20–50 per cent of their sample of poor readers described as 'unclassifiable'. One early approach to classification that might be regarded as clinically and educationally relevant was that taken by Boder (1971, 1973) who studied the word attack strategies and spelling errors of a sample of poor readers. This author went on to use this information to classify children into three subtypes. The largest subgroup, accounting for about 60 per cent of the sample, was defined as the 'dysphonetic subtype'; these children had very limited reading and spelling vocabularies, they had poor word attack skills, including problems of phonological analysis and synthesis, and they made non-phonetic spelling errors. A second subgroup, constituting about 10 per cent of the sample, sounded out words laboriously in reading, made phonetic

spelling errors and found it hard to memorize word 'shapes'; these children
formed the 'dyseidectic subtype'. The last group, comprising 22 per cent of
the sample, had the greatest difficulties of all in reading, and exhibited word
attack features and spelling errors typical of both the dysphonetic and dyseidectic groups.

A large-scale attempt at subtyping children with reading difficulties was
conducted at the Yale Center for the Study of Disorders of Learning and
Attention (Shaywitz, Shaywitz and Fletcher, 1992b). These workers made an
initial assumption that dyslexia is more than a reading disorder and that
children's problems should be considered within a multivariate context.
What the latter means, in effect, is that a core phonological deficit that may
be seen in most dyslexic children needs to be considered in the context of
their other cognitive skills. Bearing these considerations in mind, these
authors administered a wide range of cognitive and educational measures to
378 children aged 7^1/$_2$ to 9^1/$_2$ years. The majority were low achievers (in
reading or maths, or both) though some could be described as 'contrast'
group children who were either not learning-disabled at all, or who had low
IQs, or who had been diagnosed with attention deficit with hyperactivity
disorder (ADHD). The measures were selected in accord with a hypothetical
model of the relationship between language and reading skills. They
included tasks of phonological segmentation, verbal short-term memory,
rapid naming, lexical (vocabulary) knowledge, speech production,
visual–spatial ability, visual attention and non-verbal short-term memory.

The statistics involved in generating the subtypes and in carrying out
internal and external validity checks is necessarily complex and is beyond
the scope of this book. Suffice to say that the Shaywitz, Shaywitz and
Fletcher (1992b) conducted rigorous statistical tests to ensure that the nine
subtypes generated were valid and psychologically meaningful. Of the nine
subtypes, two did not contain children who were specifically disabled in
reading. One was labelled 'global deficit' and had an essentially flat profile
consistent with that seen in low-IQ children. Another (labelled 'global
language') consisted of children who had difficulties with spoken and
written language but did better on the visual processing tasks. Of particular
interest were the five 'specific' subtypes of reading-disabled children. Four
of these exhibited weaknesses in phonological segmentation skill, along
with other variable co-occurring deficits:

- The 'phonology–verbal STM subgroup' comprised 43 children who had
  specific deficits in phoneme segmentation and verbal short-term memory.
- The 18 children in the 'phonology–rate group' had weaknesses in phonological segmentation and naming speed (rather like Wolf and Bowers's
  (1999) dual deficit dyslexic subjects).

- The 'phonology–VSTM–lexical group' was occupied by 15 children who showed deficits in phonological segmentation and verbal short-term memory along with some problems in lexical or vocabulary knowledge.
- The 'phonology–VSTM–non-verbal group' consisted of 31 children who showed a relative strength in rapid naming, but had deficits in phonological segmentation, verbal short-term memory and in spatial ability.
- The final subtype, labelled the 'rate deficit group', was not impaired in phonological segmentation but had difficulty with a wide range of tasks requiring rapid and/or sequential responses, for example rapid naming, speech production and visual attention (15 children occupied this subtype).

The Yale subtyping system clearly points to a core phonological deficit in dyslexic children, but also indicates that this may co-occur alongside other deficits that may alter, or at any rate modify, the educational expression of the child's difficulties. This may go some way to explaining the individual differences seen among dyslexic children. It also raises the possibility that the subtypes will respond differentially to reading interventions.

More recently, Castles and Coltheart (1993) adopted what is usually termed a 'regression approach' to the classification of diagnosed dyslexic children. These workers studied a sample of 53 dyslexic children and based their classification on the children's relative ability to read non-words and exception (irregularly constructed) words. Their approach involved identifying children whose reading of either the non-words or the exception words fell outside the expected range for their age. By use of this method, Castles and Coltheart (1993) identified subgroups of children whom they described as 'phonological dyslexics' (having a non-word reading deficit) and 'surface dyslexics' (having a specific deficit in exception-word reading). The numbers in each group depended on where the authors set their cut-off points and whether or not they included in the subtype children who had difficulties with both word types, but more with one than the other. By use of a 'soft' subtyping that allowed children to have problems with both non-words and exception words to a lesser or greater degree, Castles and Coltheart (1993) eventually classified 55 per cent of their sample as phonological dyslexics and 30 per cent as surface dyslexics. However, a limitation of this study was that it used chronological-age-matched control subjects, not reading-age-matched control subjects. In effect, the authors were extrapolating from the reading patterns of children at a higher level of reading to those at a much lower level. As Snowling, Bryant and Hulme (1996) pointed out, this approach was inappropriate to the defining of abnormal reading patterns.

Manis et al. (1996) resolved this problem by use of Castles and Coltheart's (1993) regression approach, but using a reading-age-matched study design.

With reading age controlled, it proved very difficult to identify children who showed clear dissociations between non-word and exception-word reading. Indeed, 75 per cent of the sample showed normal patterns of reading, whereas the number of surface dyslexic children identified was virtually nil.

Where does this leave us in relation to subtyping of dyslexia? The classification of dyslexia into phonological and surface subtypes has become more popular of late, but there is disagreement as to whether one is looking at two distinct subtypes or merely the same underlying problem but at differing degrees of severity.

Some authors prefer to think of phonological and surface dyslexics as two discrete subtypes, with phonological dyslexia being the more commonplace and the more severe, with deviant and persistent reading problems ensuing. Surface dyslexias are thought to be rarer, milder and are more likely to result in a delay rather than a persisting deviance. Further to this school of thought, Manis, Seidenberg and Doi (1999) proposed that, consistent with their connectionist model of word recognition, a deficit in rapid naming may be the critical predictive measure of reading for individuals who have 'surface dyslexia'. These children would be expected to exhibit a delay in the development of word recognition skills and problems in reading exception-words, but with lesser impairment in phonological skill. In contrast, naming speed tasks may be less predictive than phonological segmentation tasks of the reading difficulties experienced by children with phonological dyslexia. Recall that Wolf and Bowers (1999) described children who have both phonological awareness and naming-speed deficits as having in effect a dual deficit that makes their reading (including comprehension) problems more severe than if only one of these skills was affected; the literacy outcome for such children is further worsened by the fact that they also have fewer compensatory mechanisms on which they can draw. Although the subtyping approaches of both Wolf and Bowers (1999) and of Manis, Seidenberg and Doi (1999) differ quite substantially, nonetheless both teams of researchers place the emphasis firmly on the phonological nature of the reading problem.

An alternative perspective on phonological versus surface dyslexia is that provided by Snowling (2000), who prefers to view these two rather different presentations as an issue of severity, rather than constituting qualitatively discrete subtypes. In essence, Snowling (2000) argues that all dyslexic individuals have a phonological deficit but that this varies in terms of severity — with phonological dyslexias at the severe end of the continuum and surface dyslexias at the milder end. Thus, the form of the literacy problem will depend critically on the severity of the underlying phonological impairment. Snowling (2000) argues for a unitary definition of dyslexia with phonological impairment at its core. Children who have milder deficits in phonological processing can acquire the use of phonological reading and spelling strategies, although at a rate slower than their peers. These children will present as having surface dyslexia. Children with more severe underlying phonological deficits may well find it hard, even in the very long term, to acquire phonetic decoding strategies; these are phonologically dyslexic children whose use of decoding strategies may be permanently deviant.

In addition, it is acknowledged that how dyslexia manifests itself in terms of reading level and skill will depend on a number of environmental factors and contingencies. First, there is the interaction of the child's phonological system with his or her other cognitive (including visual and semantic) systems. The child with a strong visual memory may be able to use visual imagery to recall spellings, whereas the child who has highly developed semantic skills may be able to compensate for his or her poor phonological skills by taking advantage of contextual facilitation effects possible in the reading of prose materials. Also, the child's phonological difficulty interacts with important experiential factors; for instance, Stanovich, Siegel and Gottardo (1997) suggested that low levels of exposure to print may be a potential cause of the surface dyslexic pattern, since the development of word recognition skill is dependent on how much reading exposure the child has had. Very importantly, the child's access to appropriate learning support may have a significant effect on the expression of the dyslexic difficulty. Eventually, the child with initially poor phonological skills may improve with explicit phonological awareness and phonic decoding training. In effect, after successful training, the child who appears to be phonologically dyslexic pre-treatment may become surface dyslexic post-treatment.

The case of Annabel — a phonological or surface dyslexic?

The following case study highlights some of the issues concerning the classification of dyslexic children into subtypes. It also demonstrates how a child's profile and hence classification might change over time in response to experiential factors and the availability of compensatory resources.

Annabel presented for assessment at age $6^1/_2$ years, with a referral from the school that she was attending just outside London. She was described by her parents and teachers as a very able and articulate little girl who was doing well in maths. However, she was making slow progress in reading. Annabel herself was becoming aware of being behind her classmates and this was already beginning to set the scene for avoidance of reading activities. She was attending small informal extra reading groups held in the context of the classroom. Annabel's early developmental history was worthy of note. She was one of a set of twins. Her brother had a significant expressive language disorder and received extensive speech and language therapy and specialist learning support. Annabel was noted to be a little delayed in the development of her speech sound system, but this resolved itself without the necessity for a speech assessment or intervention. Both parents described themselves as 'late readers' and, even as an adult, her father did not view himself as a strong speller.

Annabel worked very well during a lengthy test session and certainly showed no evidence of having attentional or motivational problems that might be expected to affect her progress within the classroom. She was given a comprehensive intelligence test (Wechsler Intelligence Scale for Children III) (WISC III) (Wechsler, 1992), a measure of general cognitive ability whose use and applicability will be described in more detail in a later chapter. This was given in order to determine whether Annabel's learning difficulties were specific to reading and related skills, or whether her slowness in achieving basic literacy was part of more global learning or language problems. The WISC III comprises a series of individually administered subtests, half of which are language-based and half of which depend on non-verbal or visual abilities. A child's abilities are usually expressed as intelligence quotients or IQ scores, typically a Verbal IQ, a Performance IQ and sometimes a Full-Scale IQ, which is a composite figure based on all the verbal and performance subtests put together.

Annabel's Verbal IQ was 140, far in advance of the national average of 100; indeed, her Verbal IQ lay within what is accepted to be the 'gifted' range. This finding very much confirmed the impression of her parents and teachers that Annabel was a highly articulate girl. Her Performance IQ was a significantly lower, although nonetheless good-average, 109. There is good reason to believe that it is the child's Verbal IQ that is the better predictor of academic achievement and outcome than is his or her Performance IQ. Thus far, there was clear evidence that Annabel was a very bright and highly articulate little girl with good academic potential. Certainly, a child of her age and ability level would be expected to be an above-average student in terms of educational attainments.

But was Annabel achieving her educational potential? She certainly seemed to be in respect of her pencil and paper number skills. She scored at almost the 8-year level on a standardized arithmetic test, the Numerical Operations test from the Wechsler Objective Numerical Dimensions (WOND) (Rust, 1996).

Annabel's single-word reading and spelling scores were at the 6 years 3 months to 6^1/$_2$ years level (Wechsler Objective Reading Dimensions) (WORD) (Rust, Golombok and Trickey, 1993) — in keeping with her chronological age but behind her number skill level, and also well below the level to be expected for a child of her considerable verbal abilities. Annabel had a small sight vocabulary that included words such as *then, up, said*. She showed evidence of still being very much a logographic reader. Her reading errors suggested that she was recognizing and remembering words according to visual cues, a characteristic of the logographic stage. Specifically, Annabel would identify the initial letter of the word and then guess at its overall reading; so, she read *shut* as *so, know* as *keep* and *because* as *bunk*.

Although Annabel was able to identify all 26 letters of the alphabet when these were presented to her in random order, she was unable to use this knowledge to decode unfamiliar words phonically. Recall that it was said earlier that dyslexic children often fail to do well on non-word reading tasks. Annabel was given the Graded Nonword Reading Test (Snowling, Stothard and Maclean, 1996) on which she read only one (out of 20) non-words correctly; this placed her at under the 6-year level for decoding ability. Note that Annabel's non-word reading level was below her real-word reading — the gap we expect to see in dyslexic children who are unable to develop a phonological underpinning for their word recognition skills.

Further testing that focused on Annabel's phonological abilities very much confirmed that her difficulties in decoding were associated with fundamental phonological problems. She was given a short-term verbal memory task that required her to repeat increasingly lengthy digit strings (the Digit Span test from the WISC III; Wechsler, 1992); she scored at barely the 6^1/$_2$ year level, a relatively poor score for a verbally gifted child. Incidentally, Annabel exhibited no visual memory problems. She scored at a significantly above average level on a picture memory test from the British Abilities Scale (BAS) (Elliott, Murray and Pearson, 1983). Annabel was found to have phonological segmentation difficulties. She scored only 1/16 on a set of items that required her to attempt to delete either the initial or end phoneme of a single syllable word (Phoneme Deletion task from the Phonological Abilities Test (PAT); Muter, Hulme and Snowling, 1997). This is the level of performance one would expect to see in a 4- to 5-year-old child. It seemed very clear indeed that Annabel had a significant phonological dyslexia.

After the assessment, Annabel went on to receive a great deal of individual specialist learning support. She attended one-to-one lessons on a twice-weekly basis, some at school, some outside school, for a period of nearly four years. Annabel was reassessed when she was aged 10^1/$_2$ years, prior to her moving on to secondary school. She had retained her excellent language abilities, recording a WISC III Verbal IQ of 138, only two points different from that obtained at the earlier evaluation. Annabel continued to be a very strong mathematician, scoring at the 14-year-level on a mathematics test, the Mathematics Reasoning test from the WOND (Rust, 1996). She had greatly improved in her reading; she achieved a reading age of 11 to 11^1/$_2$ years

(WORD; Rust, Golombok and Trickey, 1993), a full year above her chronological age and reflecting a gain of five years in her reading age over the four years that had elapsed since the previous assessment. Annabel was now reading correctly words as challenging as *abrupt, governmental, ideally*, though she remained a somewhat slow reader. Her phonemic decoding skills had also substantially improved; she was now able to score 17/20 ($10^{1}/_{2}$ to 11-year-old level) on the Graded Nonword Reading Test (Snowling, Stothard and MacLean, 1996) on which she had achieved a score of only 1/20 four years earlier. Progress in spelling had been slower but her spelling level was about age-appropriate. When Annabel was assessed at age 6, she had exhibited severe problems in respect of her phonological segmentation skills, scoring at barely the five-year level on a simple phoneme deletion task. On a more advanced phoneme deletion task (after McDougall et al., 1994) given at follow-up, she scored 20/24 which placed her at around the 10–11-year level. At age 10, Annabel was also given a naming-speed test, Digit Naming Speed from the Phonological Assessment Battery (PhAB) (Frederickson, Frith and Reason, 1997), on which she achieved an above-average standard score of 120.

How do we now view Annabel's literacy difficulties in the light of her achievements at age 10, but bearing in mind how she presented as a 6-year-old? It is evident that she continued to have some literacy difficulties, mainly in respect of speed of reading and spelling, although these looked to be fairly mild by the time she had reached her last year at primary school. Her phonemic decoding strategies and her phonological segmentation skills had most definitely improved since her original assessment at age 6. Snowling's (2000) conceptualization of dyslexia in terms of a severity hypothesis would place Annabel's current difficulties at the 'surface' end of the continuum. However, there is no doubt that she looked to be a phonological dyslexic at age 6 when she was having marked problems with phonological segmentation and with decoding.

It appears that Annabel had shifted from having a more severe phonological dyslexia to a milder surface dyslexia during the course of her primary schooling. The idea that a single child might be able to shift between subtypes does tend to fit better with a severity hypothesis, such as that proposed by Snowling (2000) than a system of distinct and independent subtypes of the sort expounded by Castles and Coltheart (1993). How might this shift from phonological to surface dyslexia have come about? There are two factors that enabled this transition to take place. First, Annabel had received four years of twice-weekly individual specialist teaching intervention that directly and specifically addressed her core phonological and decoding problems. In a later chapter it will be seen that phonological awareness skills (such as segmentation ability) and phonemic decoding strategies are demonstrably 'trainable'. Because Annabel had been explicitly taught how to break words into sounds and how to decode printed words, she had improved in these core skills and this had in turn reaped benefits for her general reading levels. Second, it seemed likely that Annabel had developed compensatory strategies, made possible by her exceptionally high levels of language skill. She was very able in respect of her oral language capabilities and would consequently have been able to draw on these to achieve what was referred to earlier as a 'verbal contextual facilitation' effect. When confronted by an unfamiliar word, Annabel might attempt to decode it insofar as she was able, and then supplement her partial decoding with knowledge derived from her excellent verbal abilities so that she could best estimate or predict the pronunciation of the word.

Wolf and Bowers (1999) might well conceptualize Annabel's difficulties rather differently from Snowling (2000), describing her as having, not a surface dyslexia, but a single deficit phonological dyslexia, that is, one that is associated with either a phonological segmentation or a naming speed deficit. In Annabel's case, she exhibited phonological segmentation, but not naming speed, deficits. Thus, hers was a milder learning difficulty than that seen in children with dual deficit dyslexia, in which both segmentation and naming speed skills are compromised. Wolf and Bowers (1999) would suggest that Annabel's relatively mild single deficit dyslexia had responded well to learning support and to the availability of compensatory resources, so that her educational underachievement had lessened over time.

Recall that Annabel came from a family with a strong history of language and literacy difficulties. Both parents were late readers, her father was a poor speller even as an adult, and her brother had an expressive language disorder. A high level of familiality is commonplace in developmental disorders such as dyslexia, and points to there being a biological basis for many cases of reading failure. Indeed, considering Annabel's family history of reading failure and her own early difficulty with speech sound production, it would have been safe to conclude that she was 'at risk' for reading problems even before she started school. In the next chapter we shall look at the biological and genetic bases of reading failure.

Summary

- Dyslexia is a specific language difficulty that has as its core deficit an impairment in phonological processing; indeed, dyslexic children have been shown to perform poorly on a wide range of phonologically sensitive measures, such as verbal memory span tasks, naming speed tasks and phonological awareness tasks.
- The phonological deficit that dyslexic children experience makes it hard for them to develop phonic decoding skills that characterize alphabetic

reading strategies — the child's level of phonic reading skill may be tapped by asking him or her to attempt to read nonsense words.

- The manifestation of the phonological deficit can be modified through the child's development of compensatory strategies and through successful teaching.
- There has been a recent move towards characterizing reading-disabled children as having either phonological or surface dyslexia — whether these constitute qualitatively discrete subtypes or whether they merely reflect the severity of the core phonological deficit is an area of some disagreement.

CHAPTER 7

Children at risk of dyslexia

Genetic research and dyslexia

It has long been recognized that dyslexia is a learning difficulty that 'runs in families'. Thus, when a child is referred for assessment of a reading difficulty, it is usual to explore whether other family members have been similarly affected. If a dyslexic individual becomes a parent, the chance that his or her son will also be dyslexic is approximately 35–40 per cent. Daughters face a lesser risk, but nonetheless the chance of a girl becoming dyslexic if either of her parents has this learning difficulty is a moderately high 20 per cent (Gilger, Pennington and DeFries, 1991). There is thus compelling evidence to suggest that dyslexia is an inherited condition.

Looking at whether dyslexia occurs at elevated levels in a particular family does not, however, provide unequivocal evidence for a purely inherited trait because families share not only genes but also similar environments. In order to tease out the relative contributions of genes versus environment to dyslexia, it is usual to carry out twin studies. These studies typically compare incidence rates of dyslexia in identical (monozygotic) and non-identical or fraternal (dizygotic) twin pairs. Identical twins share 100 per cent of their genes, together with a large proportion of their environment. Non-identical twins share 50 per cent of their genes and also a large proportion of their environment. Research studies have consistently shown that there is a far higher probability of both twins being dyslexic if they are identical than if they are fraternal — which points to a likely significant genetic contribution to dyslexia (DeFries, Fulker and LaBuda, 1987; Stevenson et al., 1987).

The statistics of twin research are very complicated and are beyond the scope of this book. Estimates of the genetic contribution to reading are usually expressed in heritability values that range from zero to one; a value of one would indicate that all the variance between the twins on the reading measures is due to genetic factors, whereas zero would indicate that the trait under study is not influenced by genetic factors. Estimates of heritability vary somewhat from study to study and are dependent on which literacy subskills are being evaluated as well as other factors, such as age and even socio-economic status. But in general, they are in the region between 0.4 and 0.7 (DeFries, Alarcon and Olson, 1997), a figure that indicates a relatively high level of heritability. There is some evidence that genetic influences may decrease as children get older, presumably because environmental factors, including teaching influences, begin to play a bigger part (Stevenson et al., 1987). Also, if children from lower socio-economic groups are included in the study sample, this tends to result in lower heritability estimates, again because the contribution from environmental influences is likely to be comparatively greater.

Further studies by the Colorado research group (DeFries, Alarcon and Olson, 1997) suggest that the genetic contribution to phonological and orthographic skills is far higher than to reading comprehension. In studies conducted in the 1980s and 1990s, these authors typically assessed phono-logical decoding by use of a non-word reading test. Orthographic skills were evaluated by asking children to decide which of two phonologically similar letter strings was a real word, for example *stain–stane, froun–frown*. Lastly, underlying phonological skills were assessed by use of a variety of phono-logical awareness tasks that required the manipulation of speech sounds in words.

Heritability estimates of phonological decoding and orthographic skills were typically recorded at approximately the 0.55–0.60 level, whereas estimates for reading comprehension were much lower. Since phonological skills underpin the development of orthography, it is suggested that what is inherited is phonological processing ability, which contributes to the devel-opment of both phonological decoding and orthographic skill. Further evidence for this comes from a recent twin study conducted by Gayan and Olson (1999); heritability of phonological awareness was estimated at 0.89, significantly higher than for other components of the reading process (word recognition 0.68, phonic decoding 0.77, and orthographic decoding 0.76). In contrast, other aspects of reading, such as comprehension, seemed to be less constrained by genetic factors.

Environmental influences may play a bigger role for some dyslexic individ-uals than others. One genetic study that attempted to evaluate the relative contribution of genetic versus environmental factors to different subtypes of dyslexia was conducted by Castles et al. (1999). The concept of phonological and surface dyslexia is, as we have already seen, a controversial one and it is not entirely clear whether we are looking at two qualitatively different types of reading problem or at similar difficulties varying along a continuum of severity. Despite this theoretical controversy, it is illuminating to look at the findings of this genetic study in which large numbers of dyslexic twins were assessed on measures of exception-word reading and phonological decoding (non-word reading). The children's scores on these two measures were standardized and subtracted one from the other so that each child's relative standing on exception-word versus non-word reading was expressed as a single measure.

Two relatively extreme subgroups, constituting two-thirds of the children in the original sample, were classified. Children whose score indicated that they performed far better on the exception words than the non-words were classified as 'phonological dyslexics', whereas those whose score showed that they did better on the non-word than exception-word reading were classified as 'surface dyslexics'. The heritability estimates for reading were then obtained for the two subtypes. The heritability estimate for the phonological dyslexic subjects was 0.67, with the environmental variance estimate being only 0.27. In contrast, the surface dyslexic subjects showed a lower heritability estimate of 0.31 but a relatively higher estimate of environmental variance of 0.63. Therefore, there seems to be a strong genetic component to phonological dyslexia. Although the nature of surface dyslexia remains less clear than that of its phonological counterpart, environmental factors such as print exposure may play a far greater role in surface dyslexia.

With emerging evidence for dyslexia being an inherited trait, there have been attempts to isolate the genes that are responsible for reading skill development and to determine which markers for dyslexia could be transmitted from one generation to the next. Gene research in the field of reading and dyslexia is still in its infancy, but some important clues as to the genetic source of dyslexia have been found in studies that have looked at the structure of the chromosomes taken from affected members in dyslexic families. Although some inherited simple traits in man are determined by a single gene (for instance, eye colour), this is unlikely to be the case for a complex learning difficulty like dyslexia. Indeed, most cognitive abilities in man are regarded as determined by multiple genes in interaction with each other.

We have seen that, in the case of reading, there are several skill components, including phonological and orthographic coding as well as reading comprehension. A complex inherited trait such as this has five distinguishing characteristics. First, there is no clear mode of 'transmission of inheritance'. Second, there is 'genetic heterogeneity' which means that different families may provide conflicting mapping data; in other words, different genes may be involved in different families of dyslexic subjects. Third, complex traits are characterized by 'oligogenic inheritance'. What this means is that several different genes interact within a single family to produce the dyslexic outcome. Fourth, there is 'decreased penetrance', so that an individual with predisposing genes need not manifest the dyslexic difficulty, because of modifying influences either from other genes or from the environment.

Lastly, there is the phenomenon of 'phenocopy' which means that a person who is not genetically at risk of dyslexia may still go on to develop this condition. Many practitioner psychologists and teachers will have assessed or worked with children who are clearly dyslexic but for whom no other dyslexic family member can be identified. These features of complex traits do present quite a challenge to behavioural geneticists because it is very hard to know exactly which genes to look at in a given dyslexic family. What is clear though, is that we must expect to find multiple gene loci when studying a trait as complex as dyslexia.

The most usual method of gene study is that of model-based linkage analysis of known dyslexic families. The procedure involves identifying very large families with many affected dyslexic members. Deoxyribonucleic acid (or DNA) sequences of selected chromosomes that can function as markers are stained. The isolated chromosomal regions derived from a large pedigree can then be tested on a wide range of dyslexic families in order to determine whether this locus specific to the original family also plays a role in other dyslexic subjects. The linkage analysis method targets only a small portion of the human genome. Consequently, it is not possible to state with any certainty that the genes implicated so far are the only ones likely to be involved. Until the entire human genome has been scanned for dyslexic markers, we simply cannot say how many, and indeed which, chromosomes play a part.

The first study to isolate gene markers in dyslexia by use of linkage analysis located these on chromosome 15 (Smith et al., 1983). These genes are thought to be implicated in approximately 30 per cent of dyslexic families (Grigorenko et al., 1997; Schulke-Korne et al., 1997). Gene markers have also been identified on the short arm of chromosome 6 (most recently by Grigorenko et al., 1997 and by Fisher et al., 1999), with one report of a translocation on chromosome 1 (Rabin et al., 1993).

It is likely that more genes associated with dyslexia will be found in future studies and it may even be possible to implicate specific genes with particular deficits in dyslexic children. Different gene combinations might be implicated in cases of severe versus mild dyslexia, or in phonological versus surface dyslexia. In fact, there is evidence emerging from very recent studies, some still ongoing, that point to other chromosomes beyond the now well-established chromosome 6 and chromosome 15 being implicated. Technological advances over the past few years have permitted the specification of the entire human genome. It is now possible to conduct a complete genome-wide scan of all the chromosomes in a set. A study such as that conducted by Fisher and colleagues (Fisher et al., 2002), with large samples of dyslexic families from the UK and the USA, has implicated dyslexia marker loci on chromosomes 2, 4, 6, 9, 13 and 18. Preliminary analyses from this study (Fisher et al., 2002) suggest that it may even be possible to link specific genes with particular deficits shown by the dyslexic families who were given a wide range of phonological and other reading-related tasks. There was, for instance, evidence of a linkage for single-word reading at a specific locus on chromosome 18 (defined as 18p11.2 linkage). Measures related to phonological and orthographic processing also showed linkage to this locus. Fisher and colleagues (2002) then went on to replicate linkage to 18p11.2 in an independent sample in which the strongest evidence came from a phoneme awareness measure. A combined analysis of all the UK families confirmed that this 18p quantitative-trait locus is probably a general risk factor for dyslexia, influencing a number of word-level processes in reading.

Dyslexia and brain function

In parallel with the genetic studies of dyslexia, there have been recent attempts to relate the difficulties experienced by dyslexic people to specifics of brain function. Early studies looked at anatomical differences in the brains of deceased dyslexic individuals during post-mortem examinations. Before considering the findings of these studies of brain structure, it is appropriate to embark on a necessarily brief tutorial on the basics of human brain anatomy. The brain is composed of two hemispheres, left and right, connected by a large band of fibres called the 'corpus callosum' which allows for transmission of information from one hemisphere to the other. In the adult human, the hemispheres are considered to function in a domain-specific way; the right hemisphere is largely specialized for visuo-spatial and other non-verbal cognitive functions, whereas the left hemisphere is specialized for the processing of speech and language.

Within the left hemisphere, there are two particular areas known to be heavily involved in language processing in the temporal lobe. The two areas are separated by the Sylvian Fissure, a deep fold in the left hemisphere; Wernicke's area, which lies below this fissure, is thought to be intimately involved in language comprehension, while Broca's area, lying above the fissure, is specialized for speech production (Figure 7.1). The phonological processing skills essential to reading development are thought to be associated with these temporal brain regions. It has been well documented that, as a rule, these left temporal regions are larger in volume than those homologous areas in the right temporal lobe. However, when the temporal lobes of dyslexic individuals were studied at post-mortem, it was found that this characteristic asymmetry favouring the left hemisphere structures was absent (Geschwind and Levitsky, 1968). In particular, the planum temporale that lies just behind the Sylvian Fissure was symmetric for both the left and right hemispheres in dyslexic subjects. This is in contrast to that seen in

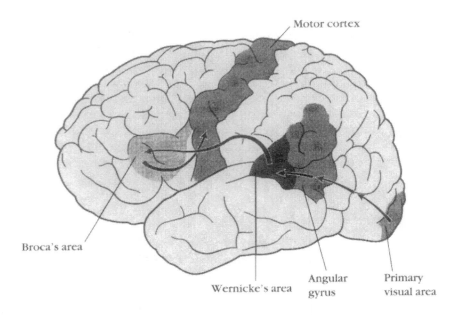

Figure 7.1 Figure showing the left hemisphere of the brain, including Broca's and Wernicke's areas.

normal brains, in which the left planum temporale is significantly larger than its right equivalent. It is reasonable to infer that these differences in brain structure are controlled by genetic factors.

The problem with postmortem evidence is that one is never really sure that the deceased individuals were truly dyslexic; evidence for their dyslexic status was often sketchy and frequently based on family opinion or anecdote. Fortunately, non-invasive imaging techniques such as magnetic resonance imaging (MRI) are now available that allow the scanning of brain sections in order to study their structures in individuals whose dyslexic status can be verified empirically. The results of MRI studies have confirmed that the symmetry of the planum temporale that is a feature of the majority of dyslexic subjects is not commonly observed in normal control groups (Hynd and Hiemenz, 1997).

Clearly, this phenomenon of planum symmetry in dyslexia is an important finding, but how does it relate to the specific phonologically based reading difficulties experienced by dyslexic individuals? A study that attempted to answer this question was carried out by Larsen and colleagues in 1990. These authors studied 19 15-year-old dyslexic children who were individually matched to control subjects for age, gender, IQ, socio-economic class and educational environment. MRI scans revealed symmetry of the planum for the majority of the dyslexic children, whereas asymmetry was evident for the majority of the control subjects. The dyslexic children were then classified into subgroups of 'pure phonological', 'pure orthographic' and 'mixed phonological–orthographic'. Needless to say, with such a small sample — and bearing in mind the difficulties of classifying poor readers into subtypes — there was a degree of overlap between the groups. But, if we accept this crude classification, the results make interesting reading. All five of the 'pure phonological' dyslexic children and seven of the nine 'mixed phonological–orthographic' dyslexic children showed symmetry of the planum. One child who had a 'pure orthographic' profile and three of the four who were deemed 'unclassifiable' showed the normal pattern of asymmetry.

A more recent MRI study (Pennington et al., 1999) looked at a wider set of brain structures in a much larger sample of dyslexic adolescents. The MRI scans of 75 reading-disabled youngsters were compared with those of 22 control subjects who did not have reading problems. All the participants were single members of a twin pair, and the two groups were matched on age, gender and handedness. However, the two groups differed in IQ, with the dyslexic children having a lower mean IQ than the control subjects (though all the subjects were of average-to-above ability). The volumes of major cortical and subcortical structures were measured blind from magnetic resonance images (that is, the technicians reading the scans did not know from which group of subjects each scan came). After controlling for age, gender and IQ, Pennington et al. found that there were differences between the groups in the volume of certain cortical, but not subcortical, structures. Although most brain structures did not differ in size in the reading-disabled group, some components of cortical development were subtly altered. Specifically, the anterior superior neocortex and insula were smaller in the reading-disabled group, whereas the retrocallosal cortex was larger. The former structures are considered to be language-related areas, whereas the retrocallosal cortex has been implicated in non-language functions. This suggests that there may be some developmental trade-offs or compensations that are evident even in the brain structure of reading-disabled children (see below for a fuller discussion of this issue).

Recent technological advances have now made it possible not only to study the precise structure of the brain but also to analyse its activity and functioning during ongoing cognitive processing. This is a burgeoning area of brain research; a description of the techniques involved and the complexities of analysis are not issues that are appropriately addressed in a book that is aimed at a broad readership. Therefore, the focus here is on only two recent studies that are of relevance to this discussion of the phonology–reading connection and its relationship to brain function.

There are many others, and readers who wish to pursue this field in more depth are directed to a recent excellent and comprehensive review article by Grigorenko (2001).

Paulesu et al. (1996) used the technique of positron emission tomography (PET) to study the ongoing phonological functioning of five adults with well-documented histories of significant childhood dyslexia. In this study, subjects were given two phonological tasks: a rhyme judgement task and a test of verbal short-term memory. Parallel visual-based control tasks were also devised so that the performance of the dyslexic individuals on these types of tasks could be compared and contrasted. In fact, the dyslexic individuals performed the phonological and visual tasks as well as the matched control subjects. In terms of brain function, Broca's area was activated when making rhyme judgements, whereas Wernicke's area was activated during the short-term memory task. The areas activated were the same for the dyslexic individuals and the matched control subjects. But the extent of the activation was less in the dyslexic individuals' scans and the two areas were not activated in concert; in other words, major sites of the phonologically based reading system could be activated in dyslexic individuals separately but not together (as they were in the control subjects). The area that showed least activation in the dyslexic individuals was a region known as the 'insula' that connects Wernicke's and Broca's regions.

Paulesu et al. (1996) point out that a rhyme judgement task requires the use of segmental codes, that is, a representation in which the word is segmented into sublexical units (in this case onsets and rimes), whereas a short-term verbal memory task also has a phonological representation but does not use segmented codes. The authors go on to propose that the left insula may be responsible for converting between segmented and unsegmented codes. To carry out a complex phonological task it is usually necessary to hold segmented and unsegmented codes simultaneously in working memory. Because of the failure of the insula in dyslexic individuals, these codes are not activated at the same time and the result is the inefficient execution of the phonological task. What we may have here in effect is a sort of disconnection syndrome, caused by the lack of an activated left insula that fails to link the different phonological codes.

Brunswick et al. (1999) conducted a PET scan study of six dyslexic adults that concentrated on reading per se as opposed to the underlying phonological system. These workers found that when dyslexic individuals read real or non-words they showed decreased activation (when compared to matched control subjects) in the following areas: the left posterior inferior temporal cortex (also known as Broca's area 37, BA37); the left and midline cerebellum; the left thalamus; and the medial extrastriate cortex. It has been found that BA37 is critical in the specification and retrieval of phonological information. In fact, it may function as a sort to thesaurus for Wernicke's area, that is, a mental lexicon (or dictionary) that provides an access facility to the names of words. Of course, it is extensively documented that dyslexic individuals have specific difficulty in retrieving phonological codes that correspond to the items to be named. In keeping with the findings of Paulesu et al. (1996), Brunswick et al. (1999) proposed that no single component of the phonological reading system may be defective per se, but that the system malfunctions as a whole because the components do not work in concert.

Thus there is converging evidence from twin and family studies, and from brain research, to suggest that the phonological deficits that cause reading difficulties in the majority of those diagnosed as dyslexic are attributable to genetic factors. These, in turn, result in neuro-anatomical and physiological differences in specific regions of the left hemisphere, in particular those areas that are implicated in speech perception and production. In addition, there is an emerging viewpoint that suggests that in dyslexic subjects additional brain areas not normally implicated in reading may be recruited to take over the function of those regions that are devoted to phonological processing in normal individuals, but which in dyslexic individuals may be dysfunctional.

Grigorenko (2001) concluded her extensive review of the genetic and neurological basis of dyslexia by pointing out that, although studies have pointed to reduced activity in some regions of the brain in dyslexic individuals (most usually left-temporal areas), this has not infrequently been accompanied by enhancement of activity in other brain regions. Converging evidence suggests that phonological processing, which is core to a dyslexic difficulty, is rooted in the left temporal gyrus of the brain. However, environmental influences and even self-reorganization of cognitive systems can result in other regions of the brain being 'pulled in'. These recruited regions might attempt to take over the phonological processing of the left temporal regions, although they may do this far less well because they have not been specifically designed to carry out these tasks. Alternatively, newly recruited areas might be involved in a compensatory process that involves using non-phonological skills to access print; for instance, visual routes to word recognition or the adoption of other verbal mechanisms to aid word identification, such as verbal memorization or forming semantic links. Further brain regions, that might normally be recruited for reading, are dropped, either because their function is incompatible with the newly built cognitive compensatory system, or because they may function less efficiently as a result of initial dyslexia-related damage. Needless to say, this creates a pattern of brain activation and deactivation in the dyslexic child that involves a number of distinct brain regions that interact in a complex fashion that might even vary from one dyslexic individual to another.

Is gender an 'at risk' factor?

It is well documented that boys are more likely to be dyslexic than girls. Most epidemiological studies find that boys far outnumber girls among reading underachievers. Does this mean that boys are genetically more at risk of dyslexia or are they simply more disposed to kicking a football than reading a book? In other words, can the gender factor be explained by environmentally based print exposure rather than genetic influences?

In a sample of over 200 kindergarten children, Byrne and Fielding-Barnsley (1993) were able to study gender differences on a range of early reading-related measures. They found that girls had far more sophisticated concepts of print and were able to identify significantly more letters of the alphabet than boys. In addition, the girls did better on a decoding measure. However, there was no gender difference in respect of phoneme awareness; boys and girls performed equally well on a phoneme identity test. It seemed very likely that the girls' superiority in reading and decoding was mediated through their head start in terms of letter knowledge acquisition and familiarity with print conventions. These latter aspects of reading are much more likely to be culturally than genetically determined. In this sample, the gender differences were short lived. There were no gender differences in any aspect of reading after the kindergarten level.

It is certainly the case that evidence for gender differences after kindergarten is at best equivocal. It has been suggested that boys take a more persistently phonic approach to reading than girls (Baron, 1979). In this study, 9- to 10-year-olds were asked to read lists of regular words, exception words and non-words. The boys were slower to read the list of exception words, presumably because their preference towards decoding resulted in an assembled phonology that was in conflict with the word's actual pronunciation. However, Treiman (1984) found no evidence of a gender difference in a study of 9-year-olds when she used similar materials.

Of course, the research on gender differences in normally developing readers does not explain why boys are over-represented in the dyslexic population. At any rate, the studies conducted to date have not resulted in a robust pattern of differences between boys and girls, except to say that there may be some differences that can be accounted for by print exposure factors early in development. It is worth bearing in mind that boys are more vulnerable than girls to all sorts of developmental disorders, especially those in which language functioning is an integral part. This suggests that that there may be some genetic basis for the higher incidence of dyslexia in boys than girls but the reasons for this await further multidisciplinary research.

Children from dyslexic families

Studies of children with known dyslexic problems have their limitations. We saw earlier that the relationship between phonological skills and reading is a reciprocal one; phonological skills affect reading, whereas reading can promote phonological awareness. It follows, therefore, that the phonological deficits observed in dyslexic readers could have been influenced by the reading impairment itself. To circumvent this problem, and to complement retrospective studies, some researchers have concentrated on looking at young children who are highly at risk of developing dyslexia. Genetic research on dyslexia clearly indicates that this condition shows a tendency to run in families. One way of identifying children at risk of dyslexia before they have had the opportunity to learn to read is to select children from families where there is high incidence of dyslexia. These children's performance on language tasks is then contrasted with that of children from families in which there is no dyslexia. This approach allows for the very detailed study of the child's language development and difficulties before he or she actually exhibits any reading problems.

A classic pioneering study of this type was conducted by Scarborough (1990, 1991), who compared the performance of reading-disabled and non-reading-disabled children from dyslexic families with that of normal-reading children from non-dyslexic families, all of whom had been recruited for the study at the age of 2 years. The children were given a range of language, phonological and preliteracy measures at several different ages. There were 34 children in the genetically at-risk group, of whom 65 per cent were diagnosed as dyslexic by the age of 8 years. The language skills of the children who turned out to be dyslexic were then compared with those of the children in the high-risk group who did not develop dyslexia and with the children from the non-dyslexic families, essentially providing two control groups. The dyslexic children were significantly poorer than those in the control groups on tests of expressive syntax and sentence comprehension at ages 30–48 months, and on tests of phonological awareness, letter–sound knowledge, letter identification and object naming at 60 months. Scarborough (1990, 1991) suggested that dyslexic children have a broader language disorder that is not simply reflected in phonological problems or reading failure. This disorder is expressed as different observable weaknesses at different ages; first, syntax problems, then weaknesses in phonological awareness, naming and other preliteracy skills and, lastly, difficulties with reading and spelling during the school years. Deficits in language skill at ages 2 to 4 years may reflect underlying problems in the linguistic precursors of phonological awareness. The fact that different cognitive skills have differing predictive power according to the age at which they are assessed is an important consideration when devising predictor and early assessment instruments. A series of tests relevant for 3-year-olds may have a very different language content, beyond that of difficulty level, to that devised for 5-year-olds.

More recent studies of children at risk of dyslexia have also highlighted differences between high-risk and low-risk children in respect of phonological awareness tasks and letter knowledge/identification. The findings of these studies have proved remarkably robust across different continents and even across different orthographies. Lefly and Pennington (1996) found that 73 high-risk American kindergarten children could be differentiated from 57 low-risk children on measures of letter knowledge, detection of initial consonant differences, rime oddity, rapid naming and later on phonemic awareness. Byrne et al. (1997) studied a group of approximately 50 4-year-old Australian high-risk children and found that they performed poorly relative to control subjects on measures of phoneme identity, knowledge of print conventions and letter knowledge. Similar results were obtained for a sample of Danish children for whom the 'risk factors' in those from dyslexic families proved to be performance on measures of phoneme identity, letter naming and the precision with which they could articulate words (Elbro, Borstrom and Petersen, 1998).

Gallagher, Frith and Snowling (2000) looked at reading outcome at age 6 from language scores obtained at 45 months of age in a group of reading 'at risk' children. Half the children were delayed in their early literacy development (at age 6) when compared with low-risk children. The two groups could not be differentiated on the basis of a non-verbal intelligence test that was administered when the children were aged 3 years. Gallagher, Frith and Snowling found that the strongest predictor of early reading progress was letter knowledge. The children at risk of delayed literacy were also subject to mild delays in all aspects of spoken language, semantic and syntactic as well as phonological.

This finding of early quite pervasive language immaturities is consistent with that of Scarborough (1990, 1991). The involvement of semantic and syntactic, as well as phonological, skills in these children fits in well with the view that semantic skills may help to determine the acquisition of an initial sight vocabulary. In contrast, phonological skills become increasingly important in setting up a set of mappings or links between orthography and phonology (Snowling, 1998). The literacy-delayed children in the study by Gallagher, Frith and Snowling (2000) who were making the best progress were those with better vocabulary and expressive language skills. Thus, eventual success in overcoming early reading delay may depend not only on the status of the children's phonological deficit but also upon how successfully they can use syntactic and semantic skills to compensate for their likely decoding inadequacies. As these authors point out, studies of early reading skill and at-risk status need to address two critical issues. First, they need to focus on the core cognitive deficiencies that give rise to the reading problem. Second, and just as important, they need to look at the availability and integrity of complementary cognitive (certainly syntactic and semantic, but maybe also visual) resources that the child is able to bring to the reading task by way of compensation.

The observation of vocabulary and other language deficits, beyond those of phonology, in very young high-risk children, does take us a little away from the view of early reading and dyslexia as being driven purely phonologically. However, it is important to recognize that there is likely to be a two-way inter-active process between phonological development and other linguistic processes. We saw in Chapter 2 that there is some evidence that vocabulary growth is a factor that drives the development of phonological skills — so children who are delayed in their vocabulary development may experience subsequent phonological difficulties. However, there is also some evidence for the reciprocal effect. Gathercole and Baddeley (1990) and Frith and Happe (1998) have suggested that phonological deficits affect the growth of receptive and expressive vocabulary. It may be the case that children at risk of dyslexia exhibit a range of language impairments in their pre-school years, some of which may be causally related to, or a consequence of, their core phonological deficit. It is probable, though, that many of these children show resolution of their non-phonological difficulties with maturation. If this is the case, one would not necessarily expect to see language problems that extend beyond those of phonology in older dyslexic children.

A Norwegian study by Hagtvet (2000) went some way to clarifying the relations between broader language variables and reading in a group of 70 randomly selected children who were followed longitudinally from age 4 to age 9 years. One test that was administered at age 4 was a Norwegian version of the Reynell Developmental Language Scales (RDLS) (Reynell, 1977) that provided measures of children's oral receptive and expressive language skills. Hagtvet (2000) found that semantically loaded reading tasks at age 9 were positively related to Reynell scores at age 4, whereas reading tasks that demanded accurate decoding were less strongly related. In fact, the children's Reynell scores at age 4 accounted for 13 per cent of the variance in text reading comprehension at age 9, whereas the Reynell scores predicted only 4 per cent of the variance in word reading at age 9. Thus, the contribution of early linguistic and phonological skills depends critically on what reading outcome measure is being studied. Phonological abilities relate strongly to word-level reading and decoding skills, whereas broader language measures, such as expressive vocabulary or syntax, may have much more to do with text comprehension.

One further point made by Hagtvet (2000) is that the age at which children's language skills are assessed may have an effect on the predictive power they carry, a view that follows also from the findings of Scarborough's original pioneering study (Scarborough, 1990, 1991). Few predictor studies, other than those of high-risk groups, have studied children younger than 5 years of age. It may well be the case that semantic and syntactic measures obtained at ages 3 and 4 are better predictors of later reading abilities in both high-risk and normal groups than those obtained at ages 5 and 6; at these latter ages, the variance in early reading is mopped up by letter and phonemic identification, which is likely to wipe out any effects of broader linguistic measures. Relevant to this point is a longitudinal study by Bishop and Adams (1990) of 83 children who had been identified as significantly language-impaired at age 4 years. The best single predictor of their reading at age 8 was their 'mean length of utterance' (MLU) at 4 years (that is, the average number of words per sentence uttered by the child). In contrast, the children's phonological skills at age 4 showed only weak correlations with their later reading and spelling ability, although the correlation became stronger when the children were seen at age $5^{1}/_{2}$ years. Many early predictor studies have tended to neglect to measure semantic and syntactic skills, preferring instead to concentrate on phonological and related measures. In the absence of broader language measures, it is hard to compare the relative efficacy of the various linguistic measures to later reading development. Hagtvet (2000) makes a plea for not overemphasizing phonological- and word-level reading to the exclusion of broader language measures and text comprehension outcome measures.

So far in this book, we have covered a lot of ground, both theoretical and empirical, that has led us to an understanding of how young children begin to learn to read, and indeed what can happen when this process is disrupted. The remaining chapters draw on this, by now extensive, backdrop of knowledge in order to address practitioner issues that concentrate on screening, assessment and teaching of reading at the beginning stages. We know a lot about how young children learn to read and why some children have difficulties. In practical terms, what can we do about it? Can we identify, through simple cost-effective screening methods, at-risk children even before they have begun formally to learn to read? Can we reliably assess dyslexic children who are as young as 5 and 6 years of age, and if so how? What is the best way to teach children to read in their classrooms during the first two years at school so they are less likely to have later reading problems? And, what is the best way to help already-identified young dyslexic children get off to a good start in reading? We could not have answered these questions with any degree of confidence as recently as 10 years ago. However, with the huge amount of reading research conducted during the past two decades, and the subsequent (and very recent) development and publication of specialist assessment and teaching methods, these questions are now beginning to be answered. The first of the following practitioner chapters focuses on early screening and identification of children at risk of reading problems. This draws on the longitudinal research studies explored in some depth in Chapter 2 and also on the findings of studies of at-risk dyslexic families covered in the present chapter.

Summary

- There is evidence for dyslexia being a strongly inherited trait, with heritability estimates in the moderately high 0.4–0.7 range; in a complex trait such as reading, multiple genes are implicated.
- Brain studies have shown that dyslexic individuals show symmetry of the planum temporale of the temporal region, in contrast to normal control subjects who show an asymmetric enlarged left planum temporale (a region known to be important to speech processing).
- Studies of brain function during the reading process have shown that the brain regions important in analysing phonological information may not be defective per se in dyslexic individuals, but may not work in a co-ordinated way.
- There is some evidence that girls make an earlier start in learning to read than boys, not because they have superior phonological skill, but because they seem to have a head start in acquiring letter knowledge and in becoming familiar with conventions of print.
- Studies of at-risk children from dyslexic families have shown that children identified early on show a broader language disorder (at ages 4 and 5 years) than may be evident after they have begun to learn to read.
- Language measures, such as average sentence length, assessed at age 4, may be better predictors of later reading than phonological skills assessed at the same age; in contrast, phonological skills become stronger predictors of later reading by the ages of 5 and 6 years.

CHAPTER 8

Screening for early reading failure

The finding that most reading problems (certainly dyslexic difficulties) have their origins in pre-school spoken language deficits means that early identification, intervention and even prevention have now become very real possibilities. Whether a disorder such as dyslexia manifests itself in a reading difficulty very much depends on the complex interaction of the at-risk child's deficient language processes with the learning environment to which he or she is exposed. So, being genetically at risk of dyslexia may not inevitably result in persistent reading difficulties or long-term educational failure, provided early identification and intervention take place.

How easy is it to develop an early screening instrument?

The goal of an early screening instrument is to identify children at risk of reading failure before they have proceeded too far along the reading route. One seemingly obvious way to do this might be to ask teachers to identify which children in their class seem to be 'getting off to a slow start'. This would seem to be a plausible, 'hands-on' and cost-effective means of identifying at-risk poor readers since it draws on the observations and knowledge of teachers who are already familiar with the children. Unfortunately, the prediction rates for this method are disappointingly low. In a review of teacher prediction rates conducted by Flynn (2000) these range from 15 per cent to 41 per cent. We shall shortly see that screening test prediction rates can be as high as 80–90 per cent.

Flynn (2000) discussed a number of reasons for low teacher prediction rates. First, teachers may be reluctant to predict failure in young children at a time of rapid and unpredictable growth spurts; with so much individual variation in children's rate of progress this is an understandable reservation. Second, many teachers lack knowledge in the theoretical and scientific underpinning of reading development. They may know very little about how speech maps on to print and as a result they are unprepared to look out for those skills that have relevance for how children learn to read. Lastly, many teachers may base their criteria of at-risk status on general developmental observations rather than research-validated predictors of reading success. If a teacher is predisposed to label a child as 'at risk' because he or she seems to be developmentally 'a little slower' than others in the class, this might result in inappropriate decision-making. For instance, it might be decided to hold a child back from formal school entry for a year, a policy that does not usually, as it turns out, improve educational progress in the long term (Flynn and Rahbar, 1993). Also, basing a child's 'at risk' status on an ill-defined impression of developmental slowness does not help teachers to devise a specific teaching strategy that might help to promote reading progress.

Although it might be tempting to simply eschew the use of teachers at all in early reading prediction, Flynn (2000) goes on to argue a case for the greater involvement of the class teacher. It is, after all, the teacher who will ultimately be the deliverer of intervention support programmes and who will have a great deal of say in the child's day-to-day educational management, which will significantly affect outcome. Before we consider how teachers might be helped to improve their ability to identify at-risk poor readers, let us look in more depth at the use of standardized, that is, norm-based screening instruments.

The earlier chapters of this book have highlighted the importance of prediction studies that tell us a great deal about the knowledge and skills young children bring to bear on the task of learning to read. In particular, we looked at the predictive relationship between children's early phonological abilities and their later progress in learning to read. We might propose, therefore, that phonological awareness measures, generated from sufficiently large samples of children, could provide norms for the purposes of screening young children, or against which individual 'slow starter' readers might be compared.

However, whether these research studies can suggest a strategy for reliably identifying those specific children who go on to have severe and persisting reading problems that necessitate special needs intervention is a rather complex issue. When considering individual children, it is not always possible to confidently conclude that the child who obtains a low score on a measure of phonological awareness will necessarily go on to have significant and persistent reading difficulties. Indeed, in terms of individual prediction, two errors are possible. First, there is the error of neglect which is a false negative, that is, failing to identify an at-risk child and therefore preventing the child having access to reading intervention which might prevent reading failure. In a review of studies that attempted to predict later reading status from phonological awareness skill in kindergarten children, Scarborough

(1998) found that, on average, 22 per cent of children who later developed a reading disability were not initially classified as 'at-risk' on the basis of their kindergarten phonological awareness scores. The converse is that of the error of identification (false positives) in which children are labelled as at risk, but then go on to have normal or above-average reading skills. This could be seen as 'stigmatizing' because of the expectation of parents and teachers that the child's development will be slow.

Scarborough (1998) found that, on average, 45 per cent of children meeting the at-risk criteria in terms of their phonological awareness scores in kindergarten did not become disabled readers. Bradley and Bryant (1985) suggested that a phonological awareness test on its own might not be a particularly effective way of predicting persisting reading problems. In these authors' longitudinal study of early readers, only 30 per cent of the children who initially produced good sound categorization scores went on to become exceptionally good readers. Of greater relevance to the early identification issue is the finding that just 28 per cent of those who initially produced poor sound categorization scores became exceptionally poor readers.

If a single phonological awareness measure is inadequate for predicting individual outcome in learning to read, can the sensitivity rating of a screening instrument (that is, the proportion of correctly identified poor readers) be increased if more than one predictor measure is used? More recent studies that have used a number of independent predictors have reported higher sensitivity ratings. Such studies have typically employed one or more phonological awareness measures, and have sometimes included measures of short-term verbal memory, rapid naming, or even both.

In a German predictor study conducted by Schneider and Naslund (1993) the sensitivity rating was reported as 48 per cent, based on a combination of phoneme awareness and rapid naming measures. Even more impressively, Badian (1994) used three reading-related measures to predict accurately the problems of 14 of 15 poor readers. These measures were: syllable counting; rapid object-naming; and a test of orthographic processing (the last task required children to match sequences of letters or numbers from an array of similar stimuli). However, a high sensitivity rating such as this may be at the cost of a relatively high number of false alarms or false positives, depending on where the cut-off point for group inclusion is placed. In the study by Badian (1994) 10 of 24 children did not develop later reading difficulties as predicted.

It is possible to improve prediction by including a large number of predictor measures that cover a wide range of potential contributors to reading skill. However, this practice of adopting a large number of predictors in order to achieve higher prediction rates also has its disadvantages. The use of a large number of independent predictors will provide an almost perfect or even a perfect prediction (Elbro, Borstrom and Petersen, 1998). Beyond the practical limitations of time and cost, this is not desirable, either theoretically or methodologically. From a statistical point of view, prediction is best when each measure is strongly correlated with the outcome measure of reading, but uncorrelated with the other measures (Tabachnick and Fidell, 1989). What this means is that each of the predictor measures should correlate highly with the reading outcome measure, but the predictor measures should have very low correlations with each other so that we can ensure that they are separate and independent, not redundant, measures. Thus, the goal of any screening instrument is to select the fewest independent measures necessary to provide a good prediction of reading outcome where each measure predicts a substantial and independent segment of the variability in reading outcome.

Screening instruments for identifying at-risk poor readers

There are a number of tests that have employed phonological awareness measures as screening instruments for children in kindergarten or grade 1. One of the first early screening tests was Sawyer's Test of Awareness of Language Segments (TALS) (Sawyer, 1987). This may be used as a screen for children at the kindergarten or grade 1 level, but is also recommended for use diagnostically and prescriptively for older children who are already exhibiting delay in learning to read. In this test, children are required to segment language, first from sentences-to-words, then words-to-syllables and finally from words-to-sounds. The Test of Phonological Awareness (TOPA) (Torgesen and Bryant, 1994) is a group-administered test in which children use pictorial material to demonstrate their ability to identify initial sounds (kindergarten version) or end sounds (elementary version) within words. Predictive validation studies have shown that the TALS or TOPA scores of kindergarten children significantly predict reading skill through to third grade (Sawyer, 1987; Torgersen and Bryant, 1994, respectively).

The above instruments have adopted one single measure of phonological skill to predict, and to screen, reading success or failure. This may be inadvisable, bearing in mind the observation of Bradley and Bryant (1985) and the error rate findings in Scarborough's (1998) review paper. However, at the other extreme, some authors have produced screening instruments that have a very large number of measures. Although these may well ensure long-term predictive validity, they fail to meet the criteria of parsimony and economy discussed earlier. The Dyslexia Early Screening Test (DEST) (Nicolson and Fawcett, 1996) aims to screen and to assess dyslexia from the age of 5. The

DEST consists of 10 subtests: bead threading; postural stability; digit span; phonological discrimination; shape copying; naming digits; naming letters; rhyme detection and alliteration; sound order; rapid naming of pictures. It is hard to see how such a broad and mixed array of tests can be seen to predict and assess specific reading problems. Having said that, with such a wide range of skills and abilities covered, it is possible that the DEST might identify children who have general developmental immaturities that could predispose them to educational (including literacy) failure.

Nicolson and Fawcett (1996) claim that, with an appropriate cut-off point, they have been able to predict, with 90 per cent accuracy, later reading failure in children given the tests at age 5 years. What these authors do not demonstrate in their predictive validation studies is which tests, or combination of tests, are accounting for that high success rate. As we shall see later, it is possible to achieve 90 per cent predictive accuracy in terms of determining which children eventually become good or poor readers, by the use of just two or three measures given at age 5. In a study of almost 100 5-year-olds (Muter et al., submitted) these were a letter knowledge test and one or two tests of phonological segmentation (for example, a phoneme deletion task). I would propose that the subtests within the DEST (Nicolson and Fawcett, 1996), which are carrying the greatest power in terms of predictive validity are those assessing letter knowledge and phonological skill, with possibly some assistance from naming speed and short-term verbal memory. Other tests that form part of this battery, and which assess more visuo-motor oriented skills, would not predict later reading skill — although they may detect either co-occurring difficulties in children failing to learn to read, or more generalized developmental problems.

Developing an effective multi-measure screening instrument

In 1997, Muter, Hulme and Snowling developed a multi-measure screening and early diagnostic instrument that met the objectives and criteria discussed in the earlier part of this chapter. One of the aims of this work was to move beyond the sensitivity limitations of a single measure screening instrument whilst avoiding the disadvantages of multi-measure tests that are excessively overinclusive and non-theoretically parsimonious. A second goal was to devise an instrument that would be simple and economic, and yet still provide good prediction. It was also very important that both the structure and content of the screening measure should reflect research findings on early reading development. Muter, Hulme and Snowling wanted to include phonological awareness tests that were representative of the skills young children bring to bear on their earliest reading experiences and which were consistent with the theoretical position on the relationship between phonological abilities and reading. Since phonological skills are the most stable and robust of the available predictors, and in view of their ability to predict independently reading attainment over long periods of time, it was reasoned that these should be given selection priority over more transitory predictors, such as vocabulary knowledge.

Two measures to assess children's ability to segment words into syllables or phonemes were selected — a test of syllable and phoneme completion, and a test of beginning and end phoneme deletion. Although Muter, Hulme and Snowling firmly believed that contemporaneous evidence favoured segmentation over rhyming as being the better predictor of beginning literacy, they did not want to exclude completely measures of onset-rime awareness. There is a well-documented view that rhyming skill may have a bearing on later stages of learning to read, and in particular on children's ability to adopt analogical strategies. There is increasingly strong evidence emerging as to the paramount importance of letter knowledge acquisition in early reading development. Thus, a test of letter knowledge as an indicator of the thoroughness and possibly ease with which the letter identities have been learned is a critical component of an early screening battery. Lastly, they wished to include a measure of children's phonological memory processes either through the adoption of a span test or, as more recent research had suggested, a test of speech rate.

The result was the Phonological Abilities Test (PAT) (Muter, Hulme, and Snowling, 1997). The PAT comprises four phonological awareness subtests (rhyme detection, rhyme production, word completion–syllables and phonemes, beginning and end phoneme deletion), a speech rate test (timed repetition of the word *buttercup*) and a test of letter knowledge (Figure 8.1).

The test was standardized on 826 children aged from 4 to 7 years, and norms provided in six-month age bands between 5 and 7 years (and in a 12-month age band for the 4-year-olds). When given in full, the PAT takes approximately 25–30 minutes to administer, with each subtest varying in administration time from approximately three minutes (letter knowledge and speech rate) up to eight minutes (beginning and end phoneme deletion). The individual subtests have been shown to demonstrate good internal and test–retest reliability.

A construct validation study was conducted to look at the extent to which the PAT is a valid measure of a psychological construct or trait. For this, principal components analyses were used. The results indicated that the PAT is tapping separate and independent subskills within the phonological domain. Factor 1, on which the word completion (syllable and phoneme) and the beginning and end phoneme deletion subtests loaded highly, was interpreted as a segmentation factor. Factor 2, on which only speech rate

Figure 8.1 Materials from the Phonological Abilities Test (PAT). (Source: Muter, Hulme and Snowling, 1997.)

loaded highly, was clearly measuring a different phonological skill, a finding consistent with the results of previous studies (McDougall et al., 1994; Muter and Snowling, 1998). Factor 3, on which the rhyme detection and production tests loaded highly, was interpreted as a rhyming factor, sensitive to children's awareness of the onset-rime structure of words.

In addition, a criterion-related validity study was performed that aimed to show that the PAT and its individual subtests have a strong concurrent and predictive relationship to reading. This was achieved by first demonstrating that the individual subtests correlate significantly with a standardized reading test (British Abilities Scales (BAS) reading test, Elliott, Murray and Pearson 1983) given concurrently. The correlations varied from 0.41 to 0.66; the measures that had the highest correlation with the reading test were the phoneme deletion and letter knowledge subtests. Multiple regression analyses were then conducted to demonstrate that the subtests were significant predictors of concurrent reading skill in the age range 5 to 7 years, with the best and most consistent predictor subtests being the phoneme deletion subtests and letter knowledge. Given to 4-year-olds, the PAT showed poor criterion-related validity, although few children in this age range had any measurable reading skill.

The predictive validity of PAT has been tested on a sample of almost 100 UK children studied longitudinally during their first two years at school

(Muter et al., submitted). Here the capacity of the PAT to predict reading skill into the future was looked at, a critical issue bearing in mind that the instrument was to be used for the purposes of prediction and early identification. The PAT was given to children of almost 5 years of age, who had had only very minimal exposure to formal reading instruction. The measures of letter knowledge, phoneme completion, and beginning and end phoneme deletion accounted for 55 per cent of the variance in the children's reading skills one year later. These measures together predicted, at a 90 per cent accuracy rate, whether the children could be categorized as good or poor readers one year later.

Not only is the PAT a reliable and valid measure of pre-reading ability, it is also an extremely robust screening measure. Evidence for this comes from the study described in Chapter 2, where the PAT was used as a screening instrument with 55 children from multilingual backgrounds who were being educated in English at an international school (Muter and Diethelm, 2001). Half the children in the sample had English as their mother tongue, whereas half were non-English mother tongue. The phoneme completion, phoneme deletion (beginning and end sounds) and letter knowledge subtests of the PAT proved to be excellent concurrent and longitudinal predictors of reading achievement for the sample as a whole, and also when split into language of origin (English mother tongue versus non-English mother tongue). Again, the accuracy of the PAT letter knowledge and phonological segmentation tests in predicting later good versus poor readers was in the region of 90 per cent. Indeed, the phonological and reading profiles of the children were strikingly similar, irrespective of their language of origin, and irrespective even of their oral proficiency in English.

In pedagogical terms, the findings of this study suggest that instruments such as the PAT, that have been developed with English mother tongue children, may nonetheless be equally good identifiers of at-risk poor readers among children from widely varying linguistic and cultural backgrounds. Administering measures of phonological segmentation and letter knowledge after non-English mother tongue children have had only minimal exposure to their new language of education may be viewed as a reliable and valid means of identifying, and consequently targeting, young children who might fail to learn to read. This is an important finding given that bilingual and multilingual education is a cultural and educational reality for large numbers of children in many parts of the world. Learning to read in a language that is not one's mother tongue is becoming an increasingly common challenge for many children by virtue of their immigrant status or simply as a consequence of greater global mobility. Educators need to be able to meet this challenge and to reassure parents and teachers that the instruments they develop meet the needs of children from many different backgrounds.

The PAT, like the TALS or the TOPA, may be used as a screening measure for children in the age range 4 to 7 years. If the test is given in its entirety it takes about 30 minutes to administer. Many teachers (both classroom and learning support teachers) have little time for activities beyond direct teaching, so 30 minutes' individual testing per child may not be realistic. There are two less time-consuming alternatives to whole-test administration. First, the test may be given in reduced form to the whole class; in which case, the recommended subtests are letter knowledge, phoneme completion and phoneme deletion, which together take about 15 minutes to administer, with resultant 90 per cent accurate prediction. Alternatively, the test may be given in whole or abridged form to targeted children, selected on the basis of their having made a slow start in, for instance, acquiring the alphabet or building up a word recognition vocabulary. This latter method does depend on the skill and experience of the teacher in the identification of 'slow starters' and may, therefore, be a reliable and realistic method only for the most experienced teachers, or for teachers with a special needs background.

Information from the screening procedure may be processed and used in a number of ways. A school may adopt a policy of selecting and focusing on an agreed percentage of the class (say 10–20 per cent) who achieve the lowest scores on the PAT measures. The children in this identified 'at risk' group might then be closely monitored for a period of one to two terms in order to see if they 'take off' or not. Those who go on to make improved progress may be discharged from the 'at risk' list, whereas those who continue to have problems would be targeted for learning support. The aim would then be to set up one-to-one or small group intervention lessons that would specifically train the skills that the screening procedure had identified as 'deficient'. The setting up and the efficacy of these 'prevention' training programmes are explored in the next chapter of this book.

Beyond its screening role, the PAT may also be given to selected older children who are already experiencing reading problems and for whom a diagnostic and prescriptive phonological profile is required. The PAT may be used diagnostically with children up to 7 or 8 years of age. Information from the PAT used in this way may help to determine, first, the level of phonological skill in norm-referenced terms; specifically, is the child's developmental level of phonological ability in keeping with his or her chronological age and the expectation of the class? It may also be important to determine the pattern of phonological strength and weakness; some children may be uniformly weak at all phonological subskills, whereas others may be strong at one sort of phonological ability but weak at others. The level and pattern of phonological skill then enables the teacher to know where and at what level to begin phonological training. Do all phonological skills need to be trained or just subskills within the phonological domain? Does the child need to commence with simple rhyming and syllable-level training or does he or she have rudimentary rhyming and syllable awareness that may enable the teacher to commence training at the level of onset-rime or even the phoneme? Lastly, screening measures such as the PAT may be used as a measure of progress during the course of phonological training by the repetition of the subtests at suitable regular intervals and the charting of rates of change in test scores over time.

Use of the PAT diagnostically and prescriptively

The following single case study illustrates how the PAT might be used diagnostically and as a prescription tool for teaching.

Andrew, aged 7 years and 11 months, had a Wechsler Intelligence Scale for Children III (WISC III) Verbal IQ of 101 (Wechsler, 1992) and could thus be regarded as being of average ability. He scored at barely the 6-year level on a standardized test of single-word reading (Wechsler Objective Reading Dimensions (WORD); Rust, Golombok and Trickey, 1993) and was unable to read any non-words from the Graded Nonword Reading Test (Snowling, Stothard and MacLean 1996). On the PAT, it is possible to make reference not only to the norms (given in centiles) but also to the graphically represented PAT profile (Figure 8.2). Andrew's scores on the rhyme detection, rhyme production, beginning and end phoneme deletion, and letter knowledge subtests were all at or under the 10th centile, that is, well below average. He had no difficulty with word completion, syllables or phonemes (50th centile) or with speech rate (75th centile).

Andrew clearly had no problems in respect of speech rate, and his simple or implicit segmentation abilities were well established. He was, nonetheless, experiencing great difficulty in many other aspects of phonological skill and in acquiring letter knowledge. He was unable to detect or produce rhyme, which suggested that his awareness of onset-rime boundaries was underdeveloped. Although he clearly had implicit phonological segmentation skills, he was not as yet explicitly manipulating phonemes within words, hence his inability to delete beginning or end phonemes from words. Andrew's pattern of difficulty, taken with his marked reading underachievement and his total lack of decoding ability, was clearly indicative of his having a specific literacy difficulty that had the hallmarks of a dyslexic problem. He needed to embark on a systematic literacy training programme that emphasized phonological awareness and related skills. Of the phonological abilities in which Andrew was deficient, rhyming is the ability that appears earliest in the developmental progression of phonological skills. It was therefore recommended that this be trained first. Later on, Andrew would need to work on his phonological manipulation skills through exercises that teach him to add, delete, substitute

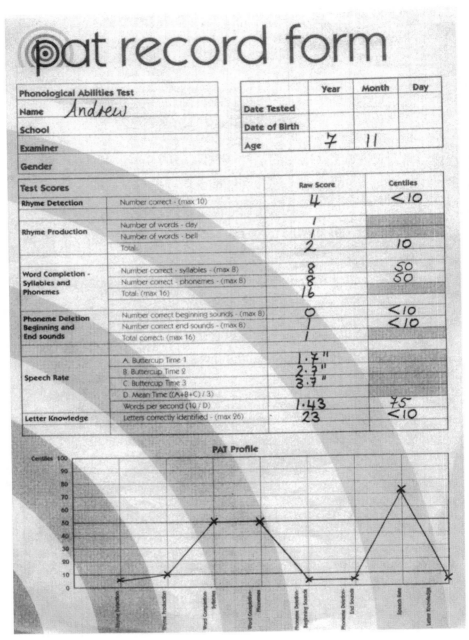

Figure 8.2 PAT profile for Andrew, a 7-year-old with phonological difficulties.

or transpose phonemes within words. Andrew would also need to be trained in his letter knowledge, with a teaching approach that emphasized multisensory learning (feeling, writing, naming) of both letter names and sounds, and where there was the opportunity for a lot of practice and reinforcement.

When Andrew was more phonologically aware, and when he knew all his letters, he should be exposed to 'linkage' exercises that help him make important connections between his improving speech sound sensitivity and his experience of print. After Andrew had worked through a programme such as this, he would be ready to embark on a structured phonic-based programme that would teach him about grapheme-to-phoneme consistencies and about sequential decoding skill. These teaching methods will be discussed more comprehensively later in the next chapter and again in Chapter 11.

Screening — the way ahead

Although screening instruments are increasingly being used to identify young at-risk poor readers, there are still a number of outstanding concerns about their use. First, the age at which children should be screened for reading difficulties is an important pedagogical concern. Phonological skills are less stable in young children, a factor that can impair their predictive relationship to later reading skill. Consequently, it may be inadvisable to attempt large-scale screening of pre-school children, but instead to concentrate screening and early identification around the first year of formal schooling — say from $4^1/_2$ to 5 years upwards. Second, there is the need to adopt increasingly refined measures of phonological abilities that are sensitive to the core deficit in reading disorder. Part of this refinement process will stem from the determinance of the relative importance of some phonological skills above others (for instance, rhyming versus segmentation) in predicting early literacy success. Third, we need to include measures that reflect the interaction of phonological awareness skills with other reading-related abilities, in particular letter knowledge acquisition. Indeed, we might want to develop a measure that reflects 'phonological linkage', the term adopted by Hatcher, Hulme and Ellis (1994) to describe the magnitude of the connection between phonological skill and experience of print. One way to do this might be to include the active learning of a specific word or word set as part of the assessment; for instance, seeing if a child could use his or her available phonological skills to 'sound out', learn and retain a presented word.

An effective early screening instrument aims primarily to identify children at risk of reading failure, but it may be possible for it to do more than this. Through studying the pattern of the child's relative strengths and weaknesses in reading-related skills, we may provide both a prescription for the amelioration of the deficits whilst highlighting specific compensatory resources on which he or she may be able to draw. It will therefore be important to include other language-related tasks, such as verbal memory and semantic/syntactic tasks. An important reason for bringing in syntactic and semantic measures is because these types of linguistic knowledge may be predictive of the child's capacity to compensate for a core phonological weakness. Also, in some children, deficiencies in broader language skills may affect subsequent reading development, particularly when children read prose material in context and when they need to understand and recall what they have read.

Lastly, we may want to develop screening instruments that draw on teacher observations more and which ultimately involve classroom teachers to a greater degree so as to ensure their continued commitment to monitoring and helping at-risk children. This brings us back to where we started at the outset of this chapter, when we looked at how teachers might use their knowledge and expertise to identify the early slow reader. Flynn (2000) explored this possibility by developing a teacher rating scale that was designed to mirror the skills covered in an established kindergarten screening test (the Literacy Screening Battery; LSB). This test comprised measures of vocabulary, syntax, alphabetic sounds, phoneme segmentation, form copying and visual discrimination. These same tests were adapted into a series of scales on which teachers rated individual children's performance from one to 10.

Flynn (2000) compared this skill-based teacher-rating instrument with simply asking teachers to predict whether a given child was likely to become a poor reader, in a sample of 2000 kindergarten children. Use of the rating instrument increased the accuracy of predicting later reading skill by 34 per cent. Thus, it may be efficacious to involve teachers in at-risk screening, providing they are given access to validated and objective instruments on which to base their decisions. Also, there is no reason why teachers should not use a standardized screening test, such as the PAT, in conjunction with rating scales, to assess and to target at-risk children. For instance, it may be appropriate for the school's learning support teacher to administer the standardized screening test whilst the class teacher completes a rating scale on a whole-class or selected subsample basis. This spreads the testing and rating load across school personnel and, because two teachers are involved in evaluating each child, the reliability of the screening procedure is likely to be increased accordingly.

Summary

- The goal of early screening is to identify children at risk of reading failure before they have proceeded too far along the reading route, ideally, on entry to elementary school, or even before.

- Early screening instruments typically adopted only one measure of phonological skill to predict reading outcome. However, error rates for these instruments proved unacceptably high, with the result that more recent screening instruments have made use of multiple measures in order to improve the reliability of prediction.
- Research has shown that the administration of two phonological awareness tests, with a test of letter knowledge, to 5-year-olds can accurately predict later reading skill in up to 90 per cent of cases.
- Early screening instruments may also be used diagnostically and prescriptively, that is, to develop a profile of phonological strength and weakness that can aid diagnosis and suggest strategies for teaching.

CHAPTER 9

Preventing reading failure

Once a young child has been identified as at risk of reading failure, and assuming that he or she has been found to have weaknesses in phonological processing, the next step is to provide a systematic intervention programme that will improve the child's phonological skills and so ameliorate the impending reading problem. There are now several curricula aimed at developing phonological awareness in young children and which have been empirically validated in training studies.

Arguably, the first study aimed at systematically training phonological awareness was that conducted by Bradley and Bryant (1983). Sixty-five 6-year-olds were selected for the study, all of whom had recorded low sound categorization scores when they were aged 4 and 5 years. The children received two years of intervention. They were divided into four groups, two experimental and two control groups. The first experimental group received instruction in sound categorization, essentially phonological awareness training, throughout the two years, whereas the second group received phonological awareness training for the first year followed by teaching in sound-to-letter correspondences during the second. The children in the first control group received instruction using the same material that had been employed with the experimental group, but they were trained to categorize it semantically (that is, by 'meaning') as opposed to phonologically. The second control group was an 'unseen' group that received no specific training.

At the end of the intervention, Bradley and Bryant (1983) found that the children in the 'sound categorization only' group had made disappointing progress in their reading. Indeed, they did not differ from the children in the semantic training group. However, the children who had received both sound categorization and sound–letter training had made significantly greater progress in reading than the children in the semantic training group; the reading scores of the children receiving the combined phonological–letter knowledge training were some eight to 10 months ahead of those in the semantic training group. This early study suggested that in order to enhance the efficacy of phonological awareness training, it may need to be combined with letter knowledge training. We shall return to this issue a little later on after we have looked at some other early phonological training studies.

Another early training study was conducted by Lundberg, Frost and Petersen (1988) with Scandinavian children. These authors developed a programme that consisted of daily phonological games that were given to 235 pre-school children in a group context over a period of one year. Since the programme involved no letters, text or print, it was postulated that a link between this early phonological training and subsequent reading success would provide powerful evidence of a causal relationship between phono-logical awareness and reading. When the children were assessed at the end of that year, just at the point of school entry, the trained children outperformed untreated control children on tests of phonemic awareness. More import-antly, the children who had received phonological awareness training obtained significantly higher reading scores than those in the control group when they were tested at seven-monthly intervals right through to grade 3.

Lundberg (1994) evaluated the predictive power of this pre-school inter-vention by randomly allocating 50 'at risk' children (that is, those performing poorly on phonological awareness tests) to either of two groups: a training group who participated in phonological awareness training activities during their pre-school year, and an untrained control group. The control group made slow progress in reading over the next three years at school; in contrast, the trained group performed at a similar level to a 'not at risk' control group, and by grade 3 were said to be achieving normal levels of attainment. The results of the Lundberg studies have had far-reaching effects on educational policy within Scandinavia, to such an extent that group-based phonological awareness activities conducted for 15–20 minutes per day are now routinely included in kindergarten classrooms throughout that country.

The Lundberg programme was first translated into English by Adams and Huggins (1993). There was a further English adaptation by Fielker (1997) that was used as the basis for a training study by Brennan and Ireson (1997). These authors carried out a training programme with 5-year-old English-speaking children attending an American school in the UK. The programme consisted of a series of games that followed the sequence of phonological activities used in the studies by Lundberg and colleagues. The first set of games were listening and sound games, many of which used environmental sounds, such as ticking clocks, as opposed to speech sounds. A period of rhyming games followed, using nursery rhymes, stories containing rhymes and games for rhyme production. At the next stage, syllables were introduced in the form of hand-clapping activities, first involving the children's own names and then moving on to other multisyllabic words; later on, the children used plastic markers as concrete representations of the syllables. Lastly, phonemes were introduced, first in the initial position and later on embedded in medial positions within words. Note that the sequence of activities followed the order of developmental progression of phonological skills described earlier in Chapter 2.

Brennan and Ireson found that that the original Danish phono-logical activities translated effectively into English. Additionally, these authors noted that most of the games could be readily conducted with children in groups as large as 12 or even 15; having said that, they acknowledged that it became necessary to divide the children into smaller groups of five or six children for the phoneme awareness activities. At the end of the year, the children in the trained group showed significantly greater gains in reading and spelling than children in a control group who had followed a normal kindergarten programme. The children in the trained group also did better on a wide range of phonological awareness tasks, with the trained children showing significantly greater gains on these tests than the control group.

Recall that in the Bradley and Bryant (1983) training study, there was some evidence that the benefits of phonological awareness training for beginner readers could be enhanced if the phonological training was combined with the learning of letter names/sounds. A number of other studies have supported the view that phonological awareness training should be explicitly linked either to the learning of letter names or sounds (Ball and Blachman, 1988; Schneider, Roth and Ennemoser, 2000) or to direct reading experience (Cunningham, 1990).

Ball and Blachman (1988) looked at the effects of phonological training on 151 5-year-olds over a seven-week period. The children were allocated to one of three groups. A phoneme awareness group received instruction in word segmentation, letter names and sounds, and in sound categorization. The language activities group was given general language enhancement exercises, together with the learning of letter names and sounds. A control group received conventional classroom instruction. The children were tested before and after training on a range of educational measures and on a test of phoneme segmentation. At post-training testing, the phoneme awareness group performed at a significantly higher level than the other two groups on the test of phoneme segmentation. These children also achieved significantly higher reading scores than those in the other two groups. Ball and Blachman (1988, p. 64) concluded that 'the most pedagogically sound method of phoneme awareness training is one that eventually makes explicit the complete letter-to-sound mappings in segmented words'.

Schneider, Roth and Ennemoser (2000) compared the efficacy of three early intervention programmes that were adopted with 138 at-risk German-speaking kindergarten children who had obtained low scores on phonological screening measures. One group had 'letter sound only' training, a second group had 'phonological awareness only' training, and the final group had 'combined training in both phonological awareness and letter knowledge'. Schneider, Roth and Ennemoser (2000) found that the combined training yielded the strongest effects on both reading and spelling in grades 1 and 2. This study provides clear evidence that combining phonological awareness training with instruction in letter–sound knowledge during the early school years has more powerful effects on subsequent literacy development than either phonological awareness or letter–sound training alone.

Lastly, Cunningham (1990) looked at the benefits of phonological training within the context of learning to read text. Kindergarten and first-grade children were allocated either to a phonological 'skill and drill' group, a 'meta-level' group in which phoneme awareness training and reading were actively and explicitly linked, or a 'listening to stories' control group. Both experimental groups were better than the control group on phonemic awareness tests given after 10 weeks of training. They also scored higher on the test of reading given after the training. However, the improvements were significantly greater for those children who had meta-level instruction than for those experiencing skill and drill training.

Examples of phonological awareness training programmes

We have seen that in each of the four studies above, young children who received phonological awareness training combined with letter knowledge or reading instruction made greater gains in later reading than those children who had only 'pure' phonological training. A number of authors have drawn on this experimental work to develop teaching schemes that are designed to get kindergarten and first-grade children off to a good start in literacy so as to prevent reading failure. Three of these, one Australian, one American and one British will be described in some depth in order to give a flavour of the content that might be effectively used with young starter readers.

Byrne and Fielding-Barnsley (1991a) developed a phonological training programme in Australia called Sound Foundations. This is designed to train phoneme identity in 4-year-olds and uses colourful illustrations of words that either begin or end with the same sound. Nine phonemes receive particular attention and are trained in a play-oriented way using posters, card games, dominoes and audiotapes of stories and poems (Figure 9.1). To evaluate the programme, two groups of children were studied (Byrne and Fielding-Barnsley, 1991b). There were 64 children in the experimental group, with an average age at the outset of the study of 55 months. These children were taught six of the nine key phonemes (five consonants and one vowel) in

Figure 9.1 Outline drawings of two posters from Sound Foundations, depicting words beginning with /m/ (a), and words ending with /g/ (b). (Source: Byrne and Fielding-Barnsley, 1991a.)

small groups of four to six children. They received a half-hour session per week, concentrating on one phoneme in one position each week. In each lesson, the teacher used poems, stories and posters whilst drawing the children's attention to the sound and 'how it is made by the mouth'. Throughout the lessons, the relevant letter was displayed and the children were told that it 'said' the phoneme.

In all, there were 12 sessions, 10 for the five consonants in beginning and end positions, one for the vowel, and a final session that used card games and which functioned as a reinforcement and revision lesson. Thus, the children received approximately six hours' exposure to the concept of phoneme identity. There were also 62 children in a control group who were treated in the same way as the children in the experimental group, but with one important difference. These children were taught to classify objects in the posters and games not by common phoneme but by semantic category.

The children were matched at the outset of the study on a range of pre-test variables, including grasp of phoneme identity, rhyme recognition, receptive vocabulary, concepts of print and recognition of letter names and sounds. At post-training testing, the children were given phoneme identity tests that included both taught and untaught sounds (the three key phonemes not specifically taught). Additionally, a forced choice decoding test in which a word constructed from the trained sounds, such as *sat* was shown and the children were invited to choose between *sat* and *mat* as its pronunciation. The findings revealed that improvements in the ability to identify phonemes was much greater in the experimental than the control group and that the experimental group improved just as much on the untrained items as the trained ones. In fact, 61 of the 64 children in the experimental group were found to have achieved phoneme awareness during the four months between pre- and post-training testing. Additionally, it seemed that once pre-school children have grasped the notion of phoneme identity for some sounds, it generalizes unaided to other sounds. The experimental group also achieved far higher scores on the forced choice decoding task which was designed to determine if the children had discovered the alphabetic principle; the experimental group scored significantly above chance level, whereas the control group achieved only chance level.

Not only did the pre-schoolers trained on this phoneme identification programme show benefits in their reading immediately after the study but these were still evident even at three-year follow up (Byrne and Fielding-Barnsley, 1995). The experimental group achieved higher reading scores than the control group in grades 1 and 2 that were particularly evident for the decoding of non-words. There were no benefits for spelling. However, an important and telling result at grade 2 follow-up was that the experimental group scored above the control group on reading comprehension. This was an effect specific to the consequences of improved word-level reading skill, not of general language factors, since there was no difference between the groups in respect of listening comprehension. These results are actually very impressive, bearing in mind that the children had received only six to seven hours of phonological awareness training as pre-schoolers.

Byrne, Fielding-Barnsley and Ashley (2000) returned to this same sample of children in order to see whether the benefits of early phonological training could be sustained for as long as six years after the intervention took place. It turned out that the children who had received the early instruction were still showing some benefits in their average word identification levels. The children in the experimental group outperformed the control children on a list of irregularly constructed words, on non-word decoding and on a 'global print identification measure' based on the sum of regular and irregular words and non-words.

However, when Byrne, Fielding-Barnsley and Ashley looked at children's individual rates of progress, they found that a significant number of children who had responded well to early phonological training (and who had achieved high levels of phonemic awareness at the end of training), had nonetheless gone on to become poor readers. This raised the question of a failure to find a clear 'vaccination effect' of successful phonological training. The children who had responded to phonological training but who went on to become poor readers were found to be amongst the slowest to reach a secure understanding of phoneme identity during the training period. Byrne, Fielding-Barnsley and Ashley suggest that children who are slow to grasp reading-related ideas early in development, even though they do finally grasp them, are liable to remain slow to acquire other principles that contribute to accurate word identification. The practical implication of this finding is that such children need to be monitored closely as they confront the later demands of acquiring an English orthography; it is likely that they will need continuing support during their elementary school years.

The American programme developed by Blachman et al. (1994) uses a simple task, they refer to as 'say-it-and-move-it' to teach kindergarten-age children to move disks to represent the sounds in words. The children begin by learning to move one disk to represent one sound, for example /i/. Eventually, they learn to represent two-phoneme words, for example *up*, and then three-phoneme words, for example *fan*, by moving two or three discs to represent individual sounds as they say each word slowly. After segmenting an item into its constituent phonemes, the children repeat the original word as a whole unit. Once successful at this level of segmentation, children learn to connect the phonological segments to the letters that represent these segments.

Blachman et al. (1994) have demonstrated that children's phonological awareness can be heightened by use of this structured phoneme segmentation task. The kindergarten phonological awareness training programme is followed with a five-step programme in the first grade that continues to emphasize phonological awareness and understanding of the alphabetic code. The five steps are:

- A brief review of sound–symbol associations.
- Instruction in phoneme analysis and blending by manipulating individual letters on a small chart, for example changing *sat* to *sam*, *sam* to *ham*, *ham* to *him*.
- A brief review of regular words and high-frequency (commonplace) irregular words to develop fluency.
- Reading stories from phonetically controlled reading books.
- Written dictation of regular words and sentences.

A primary goal of this programme is to help children to develop accurate and fluent recognition of the basic syllable patterns in English, that is, closed syllables such as *sun*, open syllables such as *he*, vowel team syllables such as *train*, vowel plus *r* syllables such as *car*, and consonant *le* syllables such as *bubble*. At the end of their first grade, children who received this training programme significantly outperformed control children on measures of phoneme awareness, letter name and letter sound knowledge, regular word and non-word reading, and spelling.

Lastly, 'Jolly Phonics' (Lloyd, 1992, 1998) is a phonics programme from the UK that addresses reading readiness through teaching phoneme segmentation and blending skills, letter names and sounds, and reading and spelling within a play-oriented context. The children begin by learning the sounds and names for the letters: *s, a, t, i, p* and *n*. By use of blending and segmentation techniques, accompanied by actions that help children to remember both the sounds and the key words beginning with that sound, they eventually learn 42 phonemes and their corresponding letters or letter combinations. Jolly Phonics has been used successfully with older kindergarten children (5-year-olds). In a study by Sumbler and Willows (1996), children matched on pre-test letter name and letter–sound knowledge were allocated either to a Jolly Phonics or a 'whole language' classroom. When tested after the training, the children who received Jolly Phonics scored higher, not only on the letter knowledge tasks but also on standardized measures of reading and spelling (including non-word reading). Moreover, Jolly Phonics has been demonstrated to be a successful training programme for 4- to 5-year-old children from low-income homes (Morgan and Willows, 1996).

Stuart (1999) demonstrated that Jolly Phonics is a highly effective teaching instrument for inner city children who are second language learners. One hundred and twelve 5-year-olds, 96 of whom were learning English as a second language, were allocated to one of two groups. One group received Jolly Phonics, which emphasized phoneme awareness and phonics, whereas the other group received a more holistic 'book reading' approach that, nonetheless, contained some letter- and word-level instruction. The children were tested on measures of spoken and written language, phonological awareness and alphabet knowledge, before a 12-week intervention programme. The children were tested on all the measures immediately after the intervention, and again one year later.

At the end of the intervention programme, the children in the Jolly Phonics group were superior to those in the control group on the measures of phonological awareness, letter knowledge, reading and writing. These differences between the groups were sustained when the children were reassessed one year later. At follow-up, the children in the Jolly Phonics group had a mean advantage of 10 months in reading and 11 months in spelling over the children in the control group. Stuart (1999, p. 587) concludes 'early concentration on teaching phoneme awareness and phonics can radically improve reading and spelling standards in inner city second language learners'.

What are the necessary components of a successful phonological training programme?

We have looked in some depth at three examples of phonological training programmes that might be used with kindergarten or first-grade children. Although there are clear similarities between them, there are also some differences in methodology and emphasis. What are the necessary components of a successful programme? Spector (1995) suggested seven facets to effective pre-school programmes to teach phonological awareness:

- Engaging children in activities that direct their attention to the sounds in words. In particular, children need to appreciate that words share common sounds.
- Encouraging children to segment and blend words. Children need to learn about both isolating sounds within words and about joining sounds together to form words.
- Including training in letter–sound relationships. We have seen that successful training programmes integrate segmentation and blending activities with instruction in letter knowledge.
- Teaching segmentation and blending as complementary skills. In other words, having children switch back and forth between segmentation and blending so that they can come to appreciate that they are related complementary skills.
- Sequencing activities systematically. For instance, introducing words with simple consonants before consonants blends, for example *cat* before *clap*.
- Encouraging transfer to novel tasks. Children need to practise segmentation and blending with words that have different sound structures, and within a variety of contexts.
- Ensuring that teachers have a clear understanding of the rationale for a phonological awareness training programme. Teachers need to understand the goals and purposes of the training programme and, importantly, their relation to reading progress in order to be committed, flexible and innovative in implementing the programme.

The importance of teacher training and monitoring to the successful outcome of a phonological awareness training programme was clearly brought out in a study conducted by Schneider et al. (1997). Regular classroom teachers delivered a phonological training programme, based on that developed by the Lundberg group, to 205 kindergarten children in Germany. Whole-class sessions were conducted for 15–20 minutes per day for approximately six months. The children's reading and spelling skills were assessed in grades 1 and 2. The results were not as dramatic as had been hoped; however, it was noted that children in the classrooms where the programme was implemented consistently showed significantly better reading achievement at the end of grade 1 than in control classrooms or in classrooms where the children were trained inconsistently. Schneider et al. (1997) repeated their training study, paying more careful attention to teacher training, and with more stringent monitoring of the implementation of the programme in the classrooms. As a result, the children in the training group showed substantial gains in reading and spelling at the ends of grades 1 and 2.

Although most of the above facets of a successful training programme appear indisputable, there remains some controversy in relation to both the specific skills to be taught and the size of the unit to be emphasized. Let us consider each of these in turn. We have seen that Spector (1995) strongly emphasized blending and segmentation as the recommended methods of training phonological skills. However, Byrne and colleagues (Byrne and Fielding-Barnsley, 1991b, 1995; Byrne, Fielding-Barnsley and Ashley, 2000) have argued that training in phoneme identity is more strongly related to reading than training in segmentation ability. Murray (1998) attempted to resolve this conflict of opinion by examining the relative impact of phoneme identity training compared with phoneme segmentation training on the early development of reading. One group of children was given phoneme identity training (similar to that described by Byrne in his training studies), a second group was given training in phoneme manipulation, and a final (control) group was given general language experiences.

Murray found that children in the phoneme manipulation group performed significantly better on blending and segmentation tasks, whereas children in the phoneme identity group performed better on measures of early decoding ability. This finding suggests that training in phoneme identity may facilitate young children's insight into the alphabetic principle and, therefore, enhance their early reading skills. Murray (1998) proposed that his data indicate that phoneme identity knowledge and manipulation skills are two independent skills and that proficient decoding, and ultimately successful reading, require both. He recommends that children receive instruction first in phoneme identity followed by learning how to manipulate phonemes through blending and segmentation.

Although there is an increasing consensus that early training in phoneme identity and in segmentation and blending may enhance children's later reading progress, there is controversy as to whether training in rhyming and syllabification plays a role. We saw in the earlier chapters that children's awareness of syllabic and rime structure precedes that of phonemes. We also looked at some research studies that have suggested that phoneme awareness is a more powerful predictor of early progress in learning to read than is rime awareness. What do training studies suggest about the salience of training in rhyming technique and in awareness of rime units for early reading?

A study by Layton et al. (1998) examined the effectiveness of a pre-school programme aimed specifically at training rhyming skills to children with poor phonological ability. Forty-three children were randomly assigned to one of two groups, a rhyme training group and a control group. One group of children received instruction in learning and reciting new rhymes, generating rhymes, and identifying rhymes and non-rhymes. The control group children were given activities that required them to categorize non-linguistic materials. The children in the experimental group improved in their phonological skills relative to the control group by the end of the intervention period but, critically, there were no significant differences between the groups in reading and spelling when they were tested a year later. This does raise the issue that training programmes that are based on rhyme alone may not be sufficient to improve reading and spelling skills.

Duncan and Seymour (2000) also expressed concern that training rhyming skills may not be sufficient to promote good early reading development. These authors conducted a study of 4-year-old children in their final year at nursery school. After preliminary assessments of the children, the three parallel classrooms were allocated to two intervention and one control condition. One intervention class received instruction in nursery rhymes, action rhymes and rhyming songs in the framework of standard nursery school play activities. The other intervention class received instruction in alliteration and initial phonemes. Training was conducted over a five-month period in twice- or thrice-weekly sessions. The third class constituted an untreated control group. The children in the rhyme intervention group performed at a higher level than the other two groups on a rhyme production task given at the end of training. However, there was no difference between the groups when the children's reading skills were assessed at the end of grades 1 and 2. Duncan and Seymour concluded that an intervention that successfully improved pre-school rhyming skills had no substantial effect on later reading progress.

Although the benefits to be gained from rhyme-oriented training programmes appear to be very limited, it may not be appropriate to exclude rhyming activities completely. Indeed, Bowey (2000) argued a case for pre-school children to be trained in onset-rime awareness so that they learn to focus their attention on sound. Bearing in mind that awareness of onset-rime precedes that of phonemes in the developmental continuum of phonological skill, it may well be important for children with very limited phonological skills to work through activities that emphasize syllables and rimes before proceeding to the 'harder' phonemic units. However, Bowey cautions against assuming that onset-rime training will generalize to phoneme sensitivity tasks. She suggests that children who have become 'onset-rime aware' will still need explicit instruction in phoneme-level skills to ensure that the skills necessary to promote acquisition of the alphabetic principle are in place. We shall come back to the issue of the relevance of training in rhyming in Chapter 11 when we address teaching methods that help dyslexic children.

If rime awareness training reaps little direct benefit for early reading, can we expect training at the level of the syllable to be of benefit? The simple answer is, probably not. Gipstein, Brady and Fowler (2000) conducted a series of studies that have shown that awareness of syllable structure probably has little salience for children beginning to learn to read — at least in English orthography. There is, however, some evidence that syllable awareness plays a greater role in French speakers (Bruck and Genesee, 1995). The reason for this distinction stems from the differences in clarity of syllabic boundaries in English and French. It is very hard in English to know where one syllable ends and the next begins. For the word *butter*, is it /bu-ter/, /but-er/ or /but-ter/? It is proposed that this ambiguity in English detracts from the status of the syllable and thus reduces its salience for learners of written English. In contrast, French has far clearer syllable boundaries, thus affording learners of written French a consistent framework that promotes syllable-level organization within both speech and orthography.

Gipstein, Brady and Fowler (2000) demonstrated that English-speaking children are more naturally disposed to identify onset-rime units, which have considerable consistency in English, than they are to identify syllables. Consequently, syllable awareness training would be unlikely to form a critical component of a phonological awareness training programme for English speakers, other than perhaps briefly at the beginning to draw children's attention to the gross sound structure of words. This would not, however, exclude the possibility that awareness of the syllable at an explicit level may become more important later on as children move into reading multisyllabic words in second and third grades.

Do all pre-schoolers need phonological awareness training?

The evidence presented thus far may well give the reader the impression that explicit phonological awareness training is critical to the normal development of reading skills — and that children who do not receive this in their kindergarten or early school years are likely to be markedly disadvantaged. Although we have very clear evidence for phonological awareness being a powerful predictor of reading ability, and bearing in mind the findings of training studies, it is tempting to conclude that all children should be given phonological training as part of their classroom learning routine from an early age. However, we should not lose sight of the fact that phonological training can be quite time-consuming, demanding on teachers and, in theory, could take time away from other important classroom activities. If some children do not need phonological training in order to promote literacy development then clearly we need to know this, given the cost in terms of time and energy involved in delivering such programmes.

A very recent study conducted at the University of York has thrown light on this important issue. Hatcher, Hulme and Snowling (2001) completed a very large-scale study of children attending 25 schools in the north of England who were recruited at the age of 4 years for an evaluation of whole-class teaching of phonological training programmes. Cohort 1 consisted of 410 children who were randomly allocated to four matched groups:

- a structured phonic reading programme
- a phonic reading programme with additional rhyming activities
- a phonic reading programme with additional phoneme awareness activities
- a phonic reading programme with additional rhyming and phoneme awareness activities.

Cohort 2 consisted of 513 children who comprised an unseen control group. They were children from the same schools as those in Cohort 1 who were in the year ahead. The children were assessed on four separate occasions: Time 1 at the age of 4^1/$_2$ years (pre-test), Time 2 at 5 years 2 months, Time 3 at 6 years 2 months (post-test) and Time 4 at the age of 6 years 9 months (follow-up). The intervention for Cohort 1 took place between times 1 and 3. It is important to point out that the training was whole-class-based, not in small groups.

First, Hatcher, Hulme and Snowling found that training in rhyme awareness increased children's rhyming ability at post-test, whereas the training in phoneme awareness increased their phoneme sensitivity, relative to the performance of the phonic-reading-only children who did not receive additional phonological training. Interestingly, training in rhyme awareness also improved later phoneme awareness. The intervention cohort showed greater improvements in literacy skill development relative to the unseen control group, but these results achieved statistical significance only for spelling (not reading) at post-test. Also, there were no differences between the treatment groups; the additional phonological training did not bestow benefits above those achieved by the phonic-reading-only programme.

Given the disappointing findings that emerged when the results for the very large cohort and groups were analysed as a whole, Hatcher, Hulme and Snowling decided to look at their data again, but in a rather different way. They focused on those children who could be regarded as 'at risk' at Time 1 (pre-test). One hundred and thirty-seven children were selected who constituted the bottom third of Cohort 1 in terms of their scores on measures of rhyme and phoneme awareness, letter knowledge and listening vocabulary. The researchers then looked at the performance of the children in this subcohort according to the teaching group to which they had been allocated. The children who had the best reading outcome at times 3 and 4 were those who had received phonic reading together with phoneme awareness training; these children improved in their phoneme awareness (but not rhyme awareness) skills and in their reading. The children who received the rhyme training did far less well.

Lastly, Hatcher, Hulme and Snowling charted the progress over time of the reading skills in the children in the at-risk cohort. The children in the phonic-reading-only group tended to show a relative decline over time. However, this decline was effectively arrested in those children who had received the phonic reading and additional phonological training intervention. In this study, the gains in reading were quite small. It does, however, need to be borne in mind that the intervention was whole-class-based and was delivered by classroom, not specialist, teachers.

Hatcher and colleagues concluded from their findings that the optimal early phonological training strategy should begin by screening at-risk children at ages 4 to 5 years using standardized phonological awareness and letter knowledge tests. These children should then have access to individual or small group phonological training programmes that particularly emphasize phoneme awareness instruction that is linked to literacy instruction. It would seem unnecessary, and indeed wasteful of resources, to provide phonological training for all children. The majority of 4- and 5-year-olds have established, through normal language learning experiences, phonological awareness skills sufficient to support the early stages of literacy development. Screening and targeting selected at-risk pre-school children makes far better use of teacher time and resources, and enables children to be taught individually or in small groups, a procedure that appears to reap greater and faster benefits than whole-class teaching.

The next chapter looks at assessment issues and techniques for practitioners working with young children who are delayed in reading, many of whom are dyslexic, and who require a more detailed evaluation of their learning and educational profiles.

Summary

- Training programmes that promote phoneme awareness during the kindergarten and early elementary school years have been shown to have both short- and long-term benefits in improving children's reading skills.
- The benefits of phoneme awareness training can be substantially enhanced when the training is actively and explicitly linked either to the learning of letter names and sounds, or to direct reading experience.
- Early training in phoneme identity may facilitate children's insight into the alphabetic principle, whereas training in the complementary skills of phoneme segmentation and blending may be important for the development of effective decoding strategies.
- Early training at the level of syllables or onset-rime units has produced equivocal results in terms of improving children's reading skills; however, it may be important for children with limited phonological skills to work through activities that emphasize 'larger and easier' syllable and rime units before proceeding to 'harder' phoneme units.
- There is emerging evidence that explicit phonological awareness training may be unnecessary for many children who develop, through normal language learning experiences, phonological skills sufficient to support beginning literacy development.
- The most appropriate use of resources may be to select and to target at-risk children for individual and small group phonological training.

CHAPTER 10

A model for the assessment of reading impairment in young children

The previous chapters concentrated on screening for, and prevention of, reading failure in young children who have not yet formally begun to learn to read. The present chapter will focus on the comprehensive diagnostic and prescriptive assessment of the child referred with known reading problems, who will typically be aged 6 to 7 years. We begin by looking at a conceptual framework for assessing the child presenting with reading difficulties, before going on to consider in some detail how such an assessment might be conducted by a psychologist or teacher.

A conceptual framework for approaching the assessment of the child who is slow to read

The present book is very much focused on reading problems that arise from a specific cognitive deficit, that is, those children who have a phonological or related deficit and who will, therefore, be diagnosed as dyslexic. However, an assessor needs to appreciate that not all children presenting with reading delay will turn out to be dyslexic. Some children fail to learn to read at the appropriate age because they have generalized learning difficulties and are consequently experiencing problems with all types of learning. Others may be experiencing reading problems because they have learning difficulties that are not purely dyslexic in origin, for instance broader language difficulties or problems of attention control. Some children may have made a late start because of disruptions in their schooling experiences, for instance, many changes of school, high teacher turnover, inconsistent teaching methods. Occasionally, there are major family disruptions that can affect the child emotionally in such a way that he or she is both distracted and anxious within the classroom so that even good teaching fails to make an impact.

The psychologist or teacher confronted by the child with delayed reading should not, therefore, launch into an assessment that presumes that he or she is dyslexic as this could result in important information, which may have a critical bearing on the child's presenting reading problem, being overlooked. Rather, it is helpful, indeed necessary, to gather broad-based background information that may be achieved through face-to-face discussion with parents and teachers or with the aid of standardized questionnaires. Relevant background information that needs to be sought before assessing the child includes:

- Consistency and type of schooling experiences, including number of schools the child has attended.
- Developmental history, concentrating especially on early speech skills (including the age at which the child began to talk, age when first short sentences emerged, and clarity of speech in the pre-school years).
- Medical history, particularly focusing on major illnesses, and sensory problems (especially hearing impairment).
- Family factors that might have disrupted the child's life or caused undue stress or anxiety, for instance divorce, illness or bereavement, many moves of home address.
- Personality and behavioural features of the child, including temperament and attentional skills (sometimes simple questionnaires such as The Strengths and Difficulties Questionnaire (Goodman, 1997) can be helpful in eliciting this kind of information).
- Family history of learning and educational difficulties.

Once background information has been gathered, and non-learning factors excluded (or at any rate taken into account) it is then appropriate to embark on an assessment protocol to evaluate the child's learning and educational skills. A thorough assessment should include the following:

- Cognitive (typically IQ) testing to establish a 'baseline' of the child's general learning ability against which his or her other skills may be compared.
- Standardized tests of reading, spelling and mathematics to ascertain the child's level of knowledge related to age-appropriate norms.
- Diagnostically oriented literacy measures that might include non-word reading tasks, or reading and spelling error analyses.
- Tasks that evaluate underlying deficits that might be expected to contribute to literacy delay, in particular those that tap into phonological processing abilities.
- Specific tests that permit a differential diagnosis when dyslexia may not be the critical or the only cause of the child's educational difficulties — such tests might include measures of spatial and fine motor ability, attention control or oral language development.

- Additional tests of related skills and abilities that might function as compensators for poor phonologically-based reading skills, for example tests of visual memory or semantic skill.

A figurative model that represents these domains is given in Figure 10.1.

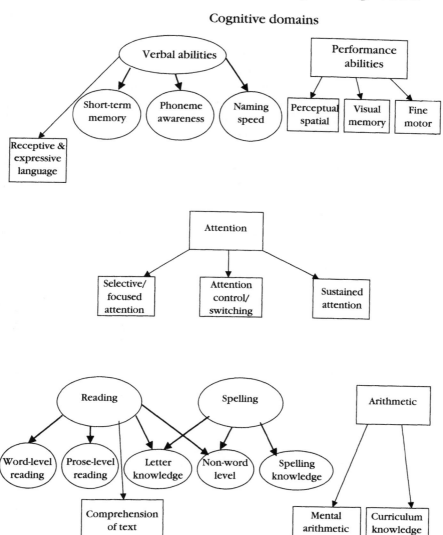

Figure 10.1 A proposed model for assessing the young impaired reader.

In the model (Figure 10.1), the cognitive/educational domains and tasks represented in the oval shapes signify the core areas of difficulty in dyslexia. These skills need to be assessed thoroughly when the difficulties and educational needs of the dyslexic child are being evaluated. The remaining domains, represented within the rectangles, are not core deficits, but are important to assess as part of a differential diagnosis. A deficiency in any of these non-core areas might be suggestive of a co-morbid problem, whereas, in contrast, a strength on a given task could point to a possible compensatory resource.

We shall look at each of these assessment domains in some detail. But, before doing so, a brief digression is necessary to discuss the psychometric properties of tests that are important to ensure that the assessment will accurately reflect the child's abilities and difficulties. The three major factors to be taken into account when evaluating an assessment instrument are as follows.

Standardization

It is important to know whether the child's performance on a test is comparable with that of other children of the same age. To do this, the test needs to be standardized on a large sample of children who are representative of the population for which the test has been developed. The larger the normative sample, the more confident we can be about interpreting whether the child's attainment is 'age-appropriate'.

Reliability

The child's performance on a test can sometimes be affected by extraneous factors, such as his or her motivation, distractibility and tiredness, and even by guessing. A reliable test is one whose susceptibility to these extraneous sources of variation is minimized, that is, where most of the variance in scores between one child and the next is associated with the stable characteristic we are trying to measure. There are two main ways of assessing reliability. One is to administer the test to the same group of children on two separate occasions, separated by a few weeks or months. The correlation between the scores obtained on the two occasions gives a measure of test–retest reliability. Another way of assessing reliability is to measure the test's internal consistency, that is, the extent to which the different items in the test are correlated with the overall score.

Validity

A valid test is one that measures what it claims to measure. One way of quantifying validity is to consider to what extent the test correlates with an already tried-and-tested measure of the construct being assessed ('construct validity'). For instance, we might demonstrate that a new test of language comprehension correlates highly with an established similar test that has been widely adopted clinically or that has been extensively researched. Another way of assessing validity is to measure how a given test correlates with a later specified outcome measure; this is predictive validity. So, a test of phonological awareness given to 5-year-olds would have good predictive validity if it correlated highly with the children's reading scores one year later.

The role of ability testing

Psychologists usually begin an assessment with a comprehensive measure of general cognition, typically an intelligence test. It is important to recognize that although a specific difficulty such as dyslexia can occur across the full ability range, it may not be meaningful to conceptualize the child's educational problems in these terms if he or she is of particularly low ability. Thus, the child who registers an IQ of 60–70 will be very likely to be delayed in developing reading skills because he or she is delayed in all aspects of learning and education. That is not to say that there may not be a dyslexic component to such a child's problems, for instance if his or her phonological skills are particularly underdeveloped relative to other learning abilities. But it would not be especially helpful to conceptualize the child's problems and educational needs purely in terms of dyslexia as this would ignore other considerations relevant to school placement, type of learning support and so on.

There has been a lot of controversy over the use of IQ tests in respect of defining dyslexic problems. A common criterion used to allocate learning support resources to children with reading difficulties is that referred to as the 'discrepancy definition', that is, where there is a significant discrepancy or gap between the child's actual reading level and that which would be expected for a child of that age and ability level. Stanovich and Siegel (1994) argued against the use of IQ measures and the discrepancy definition on the grounds that, first, reading problems occur across the full ability range and second, that they are best conceptualized in terms of phonological difficulties. These authors propose that tests of phonological skill are more relevant to assessing the underlying difficulties and needs of the child presenting with reading delay than are IQ tests.

Although it is certainly true that phonological tests are far better predictors of reading ability than is IQ, and must be administered as part of any dyslexia-oriented diagnostic assessment, nonetheless, IQ measures are invaluable in any fine-grained assessment of the child presenting with reading problems, for the following reasons.

First, they are necessary to determine whether the child's reading delay is a specific difficulty or whether it is part of a more global learning problem. The child with an IQ of 100 or above but with below-average reading skills would be conceptualized as having a specific literacy difficulty. In contrast, the child with an IQ of 60 or 70, who is behind in reading, would be regarded as having global learning problems, that is, the reading difficulties are merely one aspect of a generalized learning problem that affects all the child's abilities and skills.

Second, the use of IQ tests can provide valuable information as to whether the child has any co-occurring difficulties. For example, the child may well have a phonological dyslexia but could also have additional spatial or fine motor problems that might affect other aspects of his or her educational performance, for instance handwriting, specific aspects of mathematics and written presentation/organization. The assessor would be able to detect these co-occurring deficits by use of a Performance (that is, non-verbal) IQ measure that makes use of visual- and puzzle-based materials in order to assess spatial, perceptual and fine motor skills (often under time-constrained conditions).

Third, Verbal IQ tests are invaluable as part of an evaluation of the child's speech and language skills which are important in forming the substrate on which written language abilities are built. A Verbal IQ test, which is most usually orally administered, evaluates language-related skills such as abstract concepts, verbal factual knowledge, vocabulary and verbal reasoning and inference. The findings from a Verbal IQ test, alongside qualitative observations of the child's language structures (for example, grammar) and speech quality, may help to determine whether there are global language problems (say, beyond those of phonological awareness) which would warrant referral to a speech and language therapist for more comprehensive evaluation.

Fourth, IQ tests are helpful in providing parents and teachers with objective information on which they might base their expectations of the child's likely rate of progress and eventual academic attainments. Children of lower ability may not respond quite as rapidly to learning support and may not achieve the very high academic standards of children of superior ability. It is important to know this so that less able children are not unfairly and unrealistically pressurized, whereas the considerable capabilities of the child with superior intelligence are not underestimated.

Lastly, intelligence tests may be helpful in isolating specific cognitive strengths that might be used by the child as compensating strategies in helping to resolve the reading problem. For instance, determining that the child has a high Verbal IQ might direct the teacher to promote the use of contextual facilitation processes in reading, so helping to compensate for phonological or phonic deficiencies the child might have.

Detailed descriptions of specific IQ tests are not relevant to the focus of this book, and are much more comprehensively described elsewhere (see Turner, 1997). Suffice to say that there is a fairly wide range of IQ tests which psychologists may use to address the above issues. These include: the Wechsler Pre-school and Primary Scale of Intelligence — Revised (WPPSI-R) (Wechsler, 1990), the Wechsler Intelligence Scale for Children III UK (WISC

III UK) (Wechsler, 1992), the British Ability Scales (BAS) (Elliott, Murray and Pearson, 1983) and the Differential Ability Scales (DAS) (Elliott, 1990). These IQ tests are referred to 'closed tests'. They are available only for administration by chartered psychologists. Because most of them address a wide range of cognitive subskills, and may take as long as a full hour to administer, they provide a very comprehensive and well-validated description of the child's cognitive levels and pattern of strengths and weaknesses. To give the reader a flavour of the content of a commonly used IQ test, brief descriptions of the core subtests from the WISC III UK are given in Table 10.1.

Table 10.1: WISC III UK Intelligence scale*

Verbal scale

- *Information*: a test of general knowledge, for example. '*What is the day that comes after Tuesday?*'
- *Similarities*: a test of verbal concepts in which the child must state how two words are alike, for example. '*How are 'rose' and 'daisy' alike?*' (credited responses could include '*They are both flowers*', '*They grow*', '*They have petals*').
- *Arithmetic*: a test of mental mathematical computation, for example. '*How many are three pencils and four pencils all together?*'
- *Vocabulary*: a test in which the child is asked to define words, for example. '*What is a sheep?*' (credited responses could include '*It's an animal*', '*It makes wool*', '*It has four legs and lives on a farm*').
- *Comprehension*: a test of verbal reasoning in the context of social problem-solving, for example. '*Why do we put petrol in a car?*' (credited responses could include '*It's fuel for the engine*', '*To make the car go*').

Performance scale

- *Picture completion*: a test of visual perception in which the child must identify a missing part from a picture, for example. identifying a missing 'nose' from the picture of a man's head.
- *Picture arrangement*: a test of sequencing ability in which the child rearranges a set of three to six pictures, putting them in the correct order to tell a story, for example. 'telling' a story about buying a present for a friend.
- *Block design*: a test of spatial ability in which the child assembles either four or nine blocks to copy a specific design, for example putting four red and white blocks together in order to make a v shape.
- *Object assembly*: a further test of spatial ability in which the child makes a composite figure from presented elements, for example putting six pieces together to make a house.
- *Coding*: a strictly timed pencil and paper copying task in which the child copies symbols according to a specified code or 'key', for example. A is associated with[†], B is associated with <, C is associated with #.

*Note that the examples given are similar, but not identical, to those in the WISC III UK scale.

Of course, teachers are more restricted in terms of what they are able to use to evaluate their pupils' ability levels. Those wanting to give a cognitive screen, as opposed to the detailed evaluation provided by the psychologist, should consider administering a test of non-verbal reasoning and a test of vocabulary. An example of a test of non-verbal reasoning is that which employs a matrices task. The Ravens Progressive Matrices (Ravens, Court and Ravens, 1978) has been used for many years, but given its out-of-date standardization sample, it may be more appropriate to consider instead the Naglieri Nonverbal Ability Test (NNAT) (Naglieri, 1996) which is very similar in structure but has a more recent standardization sample. A good test of vocabulary is the Peabody Picture Vocabulary Test (PPVT) (Dunn and Dunn, 1981) which has American norms, or its British equivalent, the recently revised, British Picture Vocabulary Scale – Revised (BPVS–R) (Dunn et al., 1997). Measures of receptive vocabulary such as these have been demonstrated to correlate highly with Verbal IQ. An item from the BPVS–R is shown in Figure 10.2.

Figure 10.2 An item from the British Picture Vocabulary Scale — Revised (the child must point to the picture that shows 'panda', (in this case picture 4). (Source: Dunn et al., 1997.) Reproduced by permission of nfer-Nelson Publishing Co.

Assessing educational skills

It is important to obtain normatively based standardized measures of literacy achievement. Again, some of these are 'closed' tests, in particular those linked to the Wechsler scales or the BAS, but tests available to teachers include several published by the National Foundation for Education Research (NFER-Nelson). Giving a standardized test of single-word reading, for example the Wechsler Objective Reading Dimensions (WORD) (Rust, Golombok and Trickey, 1993), to assess word recognition skill is a crucial starting point. The skilled examiner may want to use the information from such a test not only in quantitative terms to obtain a standard score or reading age but also to derive additional qualitative information. For instance, the examiner may choose to look at the child's reading errors and determine whether these are phonetic or non-phonetic in type. Phonetic errors (sometimes called 'regularization errors') take note of the sound-to-letter consistencies within the word, but the word is, nonetheless, pronounced incorrectly. These errors are indicative of the child having developed at least some decoding strategies. Non-phonetic reading errors, commonly produced by young dyslexic children, fail to take note of the sound–letter relationships within the word, and are, therefore, suggestive of the use of global 'visual' word attack strategies or even of 'guesswork'.

Examples of phonetic (regularization) and non-phonetic (visual) reading errors, taken from the reading attempts of 5- to 7-year-old dyslexic children, are given in Table 10.2. For a fuller description of reading errors and their interpretation in dyslexic children, see the chapter by Goulandris in *Dyslexia, Speech and Language* (Snowling and Stackhouse, 1996).

Table 10.2: Phonetic and non-phonetic reading errors of 5- to 7-year-old dyslexic children*

Non-phonetic (visual) reading errors	Phonetic (regularization) reading errors
First (*fruit*)	dŏzing (*dozing*)
Anger (*ajar*)	anny (*any*)
Away (*animal*)	jell-os (*jealous*)
Sat (*sight*)	pyre (*pier*)
And (*am*)	ch-ord (*chord*)
Change (*courage*)	uni-cue (*unique*)

*The words given in parentheses are those presented to the child in print.

It may also be valuable to give a prose reading test, for example the Neale Analysis of Reading Ability II (NARA II) (Neale, 1997). Since many verbally able children with reading problems are able to capitalize on context cues to assist their word recognition, they are often able to obtain higher scores on a test such as the NARA II than on a single-word reading test. Prose reading tests are also helpful in evaluating the child's reading speed (perhaps more relevant in assessing older rather than younger children) and in determining reading comprehension.

There has been much attention paid of late to diagnostically oriented reading measures. For very young children (aged 6 and under) it is important to give a test of letter knowledge (see the Phonological Abilities Test (PAT); Muter, Hulme and Snowling, 1997) which determines whether the child's ease of learning individual letter identities is an important issue in explaining his or her reading failure. Importantly, children should be given a test of decoding ability in the form of a non-word reading test (see the Graded Nonword Reading Test; Snowling, Stothard and Machean, 1996; or the non-word reading test from the Phonological Assessment Battery, PhAB; Frederickson, Frith and Reason, 1997). By the age of $5^{1}/_{2}$ to 6 years, most children have acquired the ability to decode simple three-letter consonant– vowel–consonant (C–V–C) words (the Graded Nonword Reading Test has five of these, for example 'mot' and 'kib'). Between the ages of 6 and 7 years, children should be reading single-syllable non-words with consonant clusters (examples from the Graded Nonword Reading Test include 'kisp' and 'twesk'). A failure to develop decoding ability is a defining feature of dyslexia. Indeed, in many dyslexic youngsters, their non-word reading score is below their word recognition and prose reading scores, a pattern that allows us to have especial confidence in making a diagnosis of dyslexia.

Although spelling is of less importance in the early years of literacy acquisition than is reading, assessors will want to have an idea of how the child's writing skills are developing. Administration of a standardized single-word spelling test (for instance, the spelling test from the WORD; Rust, Golombok and Trickey, 1993) allows the assessor to obtain the child's level of spelling knowledge in normative terms, and to assess qualitatively, through error analysis, the child's word attack strategies.

As with reading, it may be helpful to contrast the child's frequency of phonetic versus non-phonetic spelling errors. Phonetic errors occur when the child's attempted spelling contains all the speech sounds in the target word but is nonetheless spelled incorrectly. Non-phonetic spelling errors occur when the attempted spelling does not sound like the target word; indeed, the reader would be unable to identify such a spelling unless he or she knew which word the child was intending to spell. Dyslexic children make non-phonetic spelling errors far more frequently than normally developing spellers and for far longer during their school years. Examples of non-phonetic spelling errors made by 6- and 7-year-old dyslexic children are given in Table 10.3. The spelling efforts and errors made on the WORD test by a boy aged 6 years and 9 months, diagnosed with dyslexia, are given in Table 10.4. Again, for a fuller discussion of spelling errors and their interpretation in dyslexic children, see Goulandris (1996) in Snowling and Stackhouse (1996).

Table 10.3: Examples of phonetic and non-phonetic spelling errors made by 6- and 7-year-old dyslexic children

Phonetic spelling errors	Non-phonetic spelling errors
Picher (*picture*)	chiy (*climb*)
Rite (*right*)	bune(*done*)
Dun (*done*)	kineght (*knight*)
Celes (*careless*)	moust (*most*)
Luc (*look*)	peg (*pig*)
Sol (*sole*)	jup (*jump*)
Weke (*weak*)	nady (*hand*)
Wisel (*whistle*)	fsh (*fish*)
Ate (*eight*)	cur (*car*)
	jupn (*jump*)
	und (*under*)

Table 10.4: Words spelled correctly and spelling errors made by a dyslexic boy aged six years 9 months

Words spelled correctly	Spelling errors
Cat	Mosd (*most*)
No	Jup (*jump*)
Cat	Ud (*under*)
Car	Thes (*things*)
Look	Cati (*counting*)
Play	Rit (*right*)
Fish	Ety (*eight*)
To	Dun (*done*)

Of relevance to assessing the younger child is the finding by Bryant and Bradley (1980) that children just beginning to acquire literacy skills may show a dissociation in their reading and spelling knowledge. This is because many children read visually (or logographically) to begin with, that is, they adopt a 'global' approach and only adopt a more systematic decoding approach rather later on. In contrast, many children spell phonetically right from the beginning. This explains why some children can read words they cannot spell and even spell words they cannot read. Reading and spelling converge and become more integrated skills later on. It is not unusual in 6-year-olds to find that their spelling vocabulary is more advanced than their reading vocabulary, with the result that the reading age is substantially below the spelling age. This effect tends to disappear by the time the child is achieving literacy levels at the 7-year standard — and for older dyslexic children, it is usual to find that spelling age is well below reading age.

When assessing young children, it is important to consider whether a difficulty in literacy constitutes a specific educational problem or whether it is part of a more generalized educational deficit. Consequently, many assessors find it helpful to administer tests of number skill, alongside those of literacy attainment. For psychologists, the Wechsler Objective Numerical Dimensions (WOND) (Rust, 1996) is particularly helpful because it separates number operation knowledge from mathematical reasoning and conceptualization. There are many dyslexic children who have no difficulty with number and it is, therefore, possible to contrast a high mathematics age with far lower reading and spelling ages. This is an important finding because it adds further weight to the diagnosis of a specific literacy problem, whilst isolating an educational strength that parents and teachers might promote, and in so doing, help to build the child's confidence. Having said that, there are substantial numbers of dyslexic children, especially those occupying the more extreme end of the dyslexic continuum, who do have significant difficulty with number. This is an under-researched area in dyslexia but in many children may well be a consequence of their frequently diagnosed short-term verbal memory difficulties that compromise their abilities in mental maths.

Assessing phonological abilities

Obtaining a cognitive/attainment profile of the child is crucial to determining whether there is a substantial degree of underachievement whilst also throwing at least partial light on the nature and extent of the child's problems. A comprehensive profile, that is geared towards a management and teaching prescription, is incomplete without what might be termed 'diagnostic testing'. Diagnostic testing aims to delineate the nature of the child's underlying difficulties. In respect of dyslexic children, it is important to administer a range of phonological tests. A model of phonological deficit in dyslexia that has much relevance for clinical and educational practice is that developed by Wagner and colleagues (Wagner, Torgesen and Rashotte, 1994; Wagner et al., 1997). These workers view phonological processing ability as comprising three separate, though related, skills: phonological awareness tapped by tests of phonological blending and segmentation; phonological working memory assessed by tests of memory span or non-word repetition; and phonological access in long-term memory assessed by naming speed measures. It is important to evaluate each of these areas in the child presenting with reading problems.

In the younger age range, there are several tests that can be recommended for evaluating 'phonological awareness' (the best single predictor of early reading). First, the Phonological Abilities Test (PAT) (Muter, Hulme and Snowling, 1997) is a test that can be used not only as a screening instrument but also for assessing phonological awareness in children who are making a slow start in learning to read; it contains measures of implicit and explicit phonological segmentation skill as well as tasks of rhyming ability. The structure, methodology and rationale of PAT has already been described in Chapter 8.

Second, the Comprehensive Test of Phonological Processing (CTOPP) (Wagener, Torgesen and Rashotte, 1999) was developed in the USA. This test assesses phonological awareness, phonological memory and rapid naming. There are two versions of the test, one developed for children in the 5- to 6-year age range and the other developed for use with older individuals aged from 7 to 24 years. In the 5- to 6-year age range there are three core phonological awareness subtests: Elision (deletion of a specified phoneme in a single-syllable word); Blending Words (joining sounds together to form single-syllable and multisyllabic words); and Sound Matching (asking the child to choose from an array which word begins with the same sound as the target word). For the older age group, only Blending Words and Elision are the core phonological awareness subtests, but there is a wide range of supplementary tests that include segmenting real and non-words, and phoneme reversal. The CTOPP was normed on 1656 individuals across the USA according to a stratified sampling procedure that ensures that it represents the nation as a whole. The phonological awareness measures in the 5- to 7-year age range correlate highly with standardized reading tests administered one year later, with correlations ranging from 0.71 to 0.80.

A further UK-based phonological test battery is the Phonological Assessment Battery (PhAB) Frederickson, Frith and Reason, 1997). This test provides norms for children aged from 6 years to 14 years and 11 months, and consists of six subtests, of which three tap into phonological awareness skills: Alliteration, Rhyme Fluency and Spoonerisms. The PhAB is intended as a diagnostic and prescriptive instrument 'in particular ... for children whose literacy progress is causing concern, (Frederickson, Frith and Reason, 1997, p. 3). Criterion-related validation studies have confirmed that the PhAB tests show significant correlations with a standardized reading measure, the Neale Analysis of Reading Ability (NARA) (Neale, 1989). The clinical applicability of the PhAB was demonstrated by comparing the PhAB scores of children with significant reading underachievement with those in the standardization sample; the specific reading-disabled group obtained significantly lower scores on the PhAB phonological awareness subtests, with the notable exception of Rhyme Fluency.

'Phonological working memory' is probably most reliably assessed by use of a digit, letter or sentence span test. The CTOPP has a Memory for Digits task that involves repeating digits forward, whereas the WISC III UK has a Digit Span task that requires the child to repeat digits forwards and backwards. The WPPSI–R, which is the downward extension of the WISC, with norms in the 3- to 7-year age range, has a sentence span test. Examples of non-word repetition tasks that tap phonological working memory skills are the Children's Nonword Repetition Test (CNRep) (Gathercole and Baddeley, 1996) and the Non-Word Repetition test from the CTOPP. It should be noted that phonological memory tasks are not as strong predictors of later reading as are phonological awareness measures. The phonological memory measures from the CTOPP correlate with later reading in the 5- and 6-year age groups at a far lower level than do the phonological awareness measures: 0.4–0.5 for phonological memory, in contrast to 0.7–0.8 for phonological awareness.

Lastly, 'phonological access in long-term memory' may be tapped by naming-speed tasks or by measures of speech rate. On the CTOPP, the two core naming-speed tasks for 5- and 6-year-old children require the rapid naming of series of colours and of objects, whereas the older children name letter and numbers. The PhAB has both digit- and object-naming tasks, and the PAT includes a speech rate test. Rapid-naming tasks are more strongly correlated with reading skill in the early years of learning to read than are phonological memory measures, but again the rapid-naming tasks fail to achieve the high levels of correlation with reading evident in the phonological awareness tests. The CTOPP rapid-naming speed tasks given at 5 and 6 years of age correlate with reading a year later in the region 0.65–0.70.

Children with severe dyslexias are likely to experience problems on all three types of phonological tasks. However, there are some children who may have difficulty with one or two of the phonological tasks, but not all three. Phonological awareness tests are particularly strongly diagnostic of dyslexic difficulties, but it is not uncommon to assess children who are able to blend and segment phonemes within words, but who exhibit short-term verbal memory limitations or naming-speed problems, or both. Whether we are looking here at dyslexia of varying degrees of severity or complexity or whether there are qualitatively different subtypes of dyslexia is still an area of some debate. Recall that we looked at this issue in some depth in the earlier chapter on phonological deficits in dyslexic children. Some practitioners refer to children who have difficulties on all three types of phonological measures as having 'phonological dyslexia', whereas those who have short-term memory and/or naming speed deficits (in the absence of marked phonological or non-word reading problems) are referred to as having 'surface dyslexia'.

Testing for co-occurring difficulties and for strengths

It may be appropriate for the assessor to administer additional tests for two reasons. The first is to identify co-occurring weaknesses beyond the dyslexic problem that may be affecting educational progress and development. The second purpose of additional testing is to identify specific cognitive strengths that might be used by the dyslexic child as compensators for his or her phonological and decoding deficiencies.

It is a well-documented fact that the probability of two disorders co-occurring is greater than expected from the population incidence of either disorder alone (Caron and Rutter, 1991). This tendency for two separate disorders to occur together in the same individual is sometimes referred to as 'co-morbidity'. Consequently, the child who has a 'pure' dyslexia will exhibit a rather different behavioural manifestation than the child who has dyslexia and additional, that is, co-occurring problems. Probably the two most frequently observed and recorded additional difficulties that co-occur alongside dyslexia are attention problems and motor/perceptual difficulties.

Attention problems

Many parents and teachers complain that a common feature of children with reading difficulties is their apparently poor concentration. When the population of a large UK primary school was screened, Adams et al. (1999) found that 12.5 per cent of poor readers were rated by their teachers as having significant problems with attention, an incidence far above what would be expected in the general child popu. on. Of course, it is not always easy to determine whether the child with a reading difficulty is inattentive because he or she has a co-morbid difficulty or because the reading problem is causing frustration and stress sufficient to result in 'switching off' in class. Pennington, Grossier and Welsh studied the nature of attentional difficulties in dyslexic children by looking at three groups of children: 'pure' dyslexic children; children with attention deficit and hyperactivity disorder (ADHD); and children who had both dyslexia and ADHD (the co-morbid group). Pennington, Grossier and Welsh (1993) gave the children dyslexia-sensitive phonological tasks and a further set of tests that measured attention, organization and planning skills (what are sometimes called 'tests of executive function'). The pure dyslexic children performed poorly on the phonological tasks but quite normally on the executive tests. The children with ADHD had difficulty with the executive tests but performed normally on the phonological tasks. The children in the co-morbid group performed very similarly to the dyslexic group, in that they exhibited phonological but not executive function deficits. It seems very likely that the so-called co-morbid group in this study comprised dyslexic children who had developed attentional problems in response to their reading difficulties.

It is important to recognize that most children with persisting reading problems might well appear inattentive in the classroom because the frustration, anxiety and feelings of failure generated by their learning problem affects their motivation. However, there may be instances where long-standing concerns are being expressed by parents and teachers about a child either being overactive or of having attentional problems that seem both severe and pervasive. This might well raise the possibility of their having a co-morbid attention deficit. Having said that, it does need to be recognized that many young children aged 4, 5 or even 6 may show some attentional immaturities that do not warrant their being labelled as having a true attention deficit. In fact, there is evidence that many children who present as inattentive in the very early years of elementary school outgrow these problems by the time they are 7 or 8.

If a given child's early inattentiveness has not shown signs of resolving, or at least improving, by the age of 7 to 8 years, it may warrant more formal investigation. Questionnaires can be helpful in determining whether an attentional problem is of long standing (perhaps even pre-dating the reading problem), and is sufficiently marked to justify a description of 'co-morbid attention deficit'. The Connors Rating Scales — Revised (CRS–R) (Connors, 1996), which can be completed by parents or teachers, may be helpful in this respect.

Furthermore, it may be appropriate to attempt specific testing to determine whether there is a true difficulty in concentrating that is not accounted for by the child's phonologically-based reading problem. Recall that it was mentioned earlier that attentional difficulties in ADHD children may be tapped by giving them tests of executive function. A useful recent test is the Test of Everyday Attention for Children (TEA-Ch) (Manly et al., 1998) which contains a number of executive function tasks that have been shown to discriminate children with true attention deficits. The TEA-Ch is a multifaceted test that evaluates a range of attentional abilities. A recent validation study of the TEA-Ch demonstrated that children's performance on the 10 subtests that make up the test can be explained by three independent attention factors (Manly et al., 2001). The first of these, selective attention, describes the child's ability to focus on a specific activity while screening out distractor stimuli; this factor is best tapped by the Map Mission subtest, which requires the child to search (and to circle with a pen) specific target symbols on a map. The second factor, sustained attention, describes the child's ability to maintain an 'attention set' while carrying out a lengthy task that requires continued vigilance; sustained attention is best captured by the Score! subtest in which the child listens to an audiotape and counts the number of unevenly spaced 'tones' (up to 15 of them) presented over 10 trials. Attentional control, or switching, refers to the child's capacity to switch from one task or mental set to another whilst inhibiting a previously acquired set; the subtest that best encapsulates this skill is Opposite Worlds, in which the child must switch between naming the digits 1 and 2 in the conventional way (Sameworld condition), and saying the opposite for each digit in the Oppositeworld condition ('one' for 2 and 'two' for 1).

Clearly, if there are sufficient concerns about the child's attention that have been confirmed through behavioural observation, completion of questionnaires and standardized testing, then it becomes necessary to address these attentional problems in their own right. It is beyond the scope of this book to enter into a description of management techniques to assist children with attentional problems. Suffice to say that severely affected children may need to be referred to a psychiatrist with a view to considering medication, whereas lesser affected children may be significantly helped by structured educational programmes or behaviour management advice.

Perceptual, spatial and motor problems

The other main co-morbid difficulty in dyslexic children is that characterized by motor, perceptual and sometimes spatial difficulties. This is an under-researched area, and there is much confusion of terminology that limits both accurate assessment and appropriate management. Sometimes, children with these difficulties are referred to as having 'non-verbal learning difficulties', a term much favoured in the USA. In the UK, children with perceptual and motor problems are more likely to be diagnosed as 'dyspraxic'. A term that is coming into increasingly popular use is that of 'developmental co-ordination disorder' (DCD). Children with these difficulties will typically perform badly on at least some of the Performance subtests of IQ scales that tap into spatial, perceptual and motor skills. Although there is little evidence that having a developmental co-ordination disorder has a direct effect on reading and spelling, it is very likely to affect handwriting speed and quality, written presentation and organization (Lord and Hulme, 1987). Of course, as with the case of apparent attention problems in dyslexic children, it is important to recognize that some children may have handwriting problems that arise not from a motor deficit, but which follow as a consequence of their spelling difficulties. If, however, a dyslexic child does present with especially marked perceptual and motor difficulties, it may be appropriate to refer him or her to a paediatric occupational therapist or physiotherapist for a fuller investigation and, possibly, prescribed therapy.

Cognitive strengths

We saw in earlier chapters that verbally able dyslexic children may be able to draw on their good language skills in order to provide a 'verbal contextual facilitation effect', particularly when they are reading in context. It follows that it may be helpful to carry out broader language-based testing that might well determine whether a particular child will be in a strong position to take advantage of this compensatory mechanism. Thus, Verbal IQ tests, vocabulary measures and even specific tests of grammatical (including syntactic and semantic) knowledge could be used to ascertain the level of the child's language functioning. Children with strong language capabilities may be prescribed a teaching programme that includes drawing their attention to the information contained in surrounding context as an aide to precise word identification. Some dyslexic children may have other strengths they can draw on as effective compensators for their deficient phonological and decoding skills. For instance, JM (Hulme and Snowling, 1992) had very good visual memory skills which enabled him to learn to read by building up a visual memory store of words. Consequently, there may be a place for visual memory tests in an assessment protocol in order to decide whether 'visualization' learning techniques have a role in the prescribed teaching programme of a given dyslexic child.

Summary

- A model of assessment is proposed that places standardized cognitive and attainment testing within a framework that also draws on both qualitative observations of the child's skills and background factors, such as a family history of learning difficulties.
- Testing of cognitive ability has an important part to play in determining whether the child's reading delay is a specific difficulty or whether it is part of a more global learning problem.
- Standardized tests of reading and spelling enable the assessor to quantify the child's degree of literacy delay, whereas a qualitative analysis of the errors made provides additional information about the child's preferred word attack strategies.
- Phonological processing tasks (which include measures of phonological awareness, short-term verbal memory and naming speed) are essential in determining whether the child has a core phonological deficit that will undermine progress in reading.
- Tests of attention and visuo-motor skills help to determine whether there are co-occurring difficulties (additional to the reading problems) which may affect the child's educational progress and development.

- A complete cognitive profile of the child should not only specify his or her difficulties, but also highlight strengths (for example, high verbal abilities, a good visual memory) on which the child may be able draw in order to compensate for deficient phonological and decoding skills.

CHAPTER **11**

Teaching young dyslexic children

In the previous chapter, we looked at how we might assess the child with early reading delay and arrive at a formulation of his or her cognitive/educational profile that takes account of both strengths and weaknesses. This chapter describes an influential approach to teaching early delayed readers, namely 'reading recovery', that began in New Zealand and then went on to have a major effect on the methodology of early teaching intervention in many other countries. This is followed by detailed descriptions of two important and carefully designed studies that have addressed the efficacy of specific teaching methods for children with dyslexic difficulties. A discussion of some specific teaching programmes follows, including one that makes use of computer technology to teach the dyslexic child. Lastly, we touch briefly, and turn a critical eye on, 'alternative' therapies.

'Reading recovery' — a systematic approach to teaching young children with reading delay

'Reading recovery' is an enormously influential approach to the early intervention of young poor readers that was developed by Dame Marie Clay (Clay, 1985) in New Zealand. Since then, reading recovery has been implemented worldwide. Reading recovery provides a systematic methodology for identifying, selecting, teaching and evaluating the progress of children who make a slow start in beginning reading. The core principle of Clay's (1985) philosophy is that the effective remediation of young delayed readers depends upon the provision of a structured and individual reading programme that is delivered by a trained teacher. Each school is expected to train one or two teachers by sending them to attend a one-year training course.

Children are selected for inclusion in reading recovery only on achievement criteria, irrespective of cause. They are 'screened' in the second year at school, usually at around the age of 6 years, by use of achievement instruments that include measures of letter and word knowledge, concepts about print, spelling and writing skill. Each school decides at what level to set criteria for inclusion in its reading recovery programme, this being determined by the availability of teaching resources. Thus, a well-resourced school, with say two reading recovery teachers, might select the bottom 10 per cent of readers for inclusion in the programme, whereas a school with only one trained teacher might be in the position to select only the bottom 5 per cent. Each child's programme is tailored to his or her individual needs, and commences at 'where the child is' in terms of their literacy knowledge. The child receives half an hour per day of one-to-one tuition for a period of, typically, 12–20 weeks. The aim of reading recovery is to improve children's reading skills to the point where further assessment confirms that their reading attainment matches that of their peer group. The small percentage of children who fail to meet this discharge criterion after 20 weeks' tuition (usually less than 1 per cent) are then referred for more detailed evaluation and continued learning support. We might expect that contained in this 'failure' group are children with severe dyslexic difficulties for whom sustained remedial tuition is necessary. The daily individual tuition that is the core feature of reading recovery means that it is, of necessity, very costly.

What of the content of the reading recovery programme? So far, the phonological component of reading has been strongly emphasized as a critical variable in determining outcome and as an essential feature of a screening, prevention and assessment programme. However, reading recovery as conceptualized by Clay (1985) did not explicitly promote phonological training (though recent versions of reading recovery have incorporated more phonological/phonic content). The aim of the original reading recovery programme was to encourage children to use all the strategies they have available and to promote independence and fluency. A typical reading recovery lesson might include letter and individual word identification, text reading, concepts about print (for example sequencing of sentences within stories), developing a writing vocabulary and dictation. Clay and her colleagues claimed great success for the reading recovery programme. However, reading recovery is not without its critics. One point to bear in mind is that because the teaching programme contains so many different components, it is hard to work out which are the most critical to achieving a successful outcome. We shall see in the next section how important it is to isolate the important and indeed necessary components of a training programme, and that to do this requires stringent design methodology as part of the evaluation procedure.

Staying for the moment with the phonology component issue, the importance of a phonological training component within reading recovery was addressed in a study conducted by Iverson and Tunmer (1993). These authors selected three matched groups of 32 6-year-old poor readers on the basis of their low performance on a word recognition test and on a battery of tests and observation procedures that make up the Clay Diagnostic Survey (Clay, 1985). The first group of children received the 'classic' reading recovery programme delivered by a trained and experienced tutor. The second group received a modified reading recovery programme that contained an additional teaching component — namely, exercises that explicitly trained phonological skills and their connection to print. The third group received standard remedial tuition. Children in both reading recovery groups had individual lessons on a daily basis. The discharge criterion was that of matching their age peer group on reading skill.

At the end of the training programme, the children in both reading recovery groups had made better progress than the children in the standard remedial group. Importantly, it was the children in the modified reading recovery programme group, who received explicit phonological training, who made the most progress. It took the children in this latter group signifi-cantly fewer lessons to reach the discharge criterion than those in the classical reading recovery programme. Indeed, Iverson and Tunmer concluded that the phonology-based modified programme was 37 per cent more efficient than the traditional reading recovery programme. Clearly, the specific content of reading recovery is critical to the determination of its success, both in terms of reading outcome and cost effectiveness.

Another problem for reading recovery is whether its apparent short-term efficacy can be sustained to achieve long-term reading success. Sylva and Hurry (1995) conducted a British trial into the efficacy of reading recovery using 22 schools in which reading recovery was implemented and 18 schools in the same education authority in which it was not. The six poorest readers in their age group from each school were selected for the study; three or four children were assigned to the reading recovery programme while the others formed 'within school' control subjects. In the control school, all six children were allocated to a 'between groups' control group and received standard remedial tuition. There was a more explicit phonic component to reading recovery in this study than was advocated in the original approach by Clay (1985). The children used plastic letters to build and break up words, and they were encouraged during story writing to listen to and record the sounds of words. The children received up to 33 weeks of daily individual tuition.

On completion of the training, children in the reading recovery group were found to be well ahead in reading when compared with those in the within-school and between-school control groups. However, when the children were followed up a year later, the results were far less impressive. Although the children in the reading recovery group were still reading ahead of those in the between-schools control group, this was not the case when they were compared with those children in the within-schools control group. Compared with their age peers in their own school, the children who had received reading recovery were not significantly advanced in their reading skills. Clearly, for any programme that is intensive, individual and, therefore, costly, it is imperative to demonstrate that any gains made in reading can be sustained long-term and that the programme can reap benefits for the child's school performance at least through the important elementary school years.

Although the above is somewhat critical of the content of the reading recovery programme, it should be emphasized that as an overall methodology for early intervention in reading failure, reading recovery has a lot to commend it. First, it incorporates an objective and sensible criterion-referenced-based method for screening and selecting children who are failing to read at an early age. Second, it strongly emphasizes the importance of a daily individual and structured training programme delivered by experienced teachers. Third, reading recovery aims to work with a child's individual strengths and difficulties to achieve a goal of fluent reading. Lastly, there is a clear methodology for determining discharge from training, but with a 'safety net' for those children who fail to progress as they should and who do, therefore, need further detailed evaluation and support. What does need to be addressed more rigorously is the specific content, in particular the inclusion of explicit phonological training, and the means by which the efficacy of the training programme can be extended to ensure long-term success for reading-disabled children.

How do we evaluate the success of teaching programmes?

New reading teaching programmes are coming on to the market and being made available to teachers at an astonishing rate. Structured phonological-based training programmes for dyslexic children are advocated here for two reasons. First, they are derived from a well-defined, thoroughly researched, theoretical model of normal and abnormal reading development. Second, methodologically rigorous research has clearly demonstrated the efficacy of the phonological teaching scheme in terms of improving children's reading skills, as well as isolating the specific components that contribute to the success of the programme. There are now many 'alternative' therapies for addressing reading difficulties, which feature prominently in the media and which are widely embraced by desperate parents. Although not wanting to sound overly sceptical about these new training programmes or therapies, it is important to recognize that any new treatment does need to be subjected to rigorous examination. To give the reader a feel for how research into the efficacy of teaching procedures should be conducted, two excellent

training studies with young poor readers that stand as models of good clinically relevant experimental research, one British and one American, are now
described.

The seminal study by Hatcher, Hulme and Ellis (1994) demonstrated
empirically the efficacy of a phonological training programme conducted
within the context of learning to read. These authors carried out a training
study with 128 poor readers, aged 7 years, who had reading quotients of less
than 86 on a standardized word recognition task (constituting the poorest 18
per cent of readers). The children were randomly allocated to one of four
groups. The authors ensured that the groups were carefully matched for age,
IQ and reading age. The 'reading + phonology' group received phonological
awareness training, reading experience and activities that linked the two
components. The 'phonology alone' programme experienced the same
phonological training given to the 'reading + phonology' group, but had no
explicit reading instruction or phonology linkage exercises. The 'reading
alone' group read books, had multisensory training and learned letter names,
but had no phonological training. A control group received conventional
classroom instruction.

Before training, the children were tested on a wide range of cognitive,
phonological awareness and educational measures. Those in the three experimental groups received 40 30-minute sessions of individual instruction over a
20-week period. Twenty-three teachers, trained specifically to implement the
teaching programmes, worked with children in all three experimental conditions; that is, each teacher taught the same number of children from each of
the experimental conditions. At the conclusion of the teaching phase, the
children were re-tested. At post-training testing, the 'reading + phonology'
group scored significantly higher than the other groups on measures of
reading that included word recognition, text reading and non-word reading.
To determine whether the effects of the intervention were long lasting,
measures of reading were taken again nine months after the teaching
programme was completed. The improvements in reading shown by the
'reading + phonology' group were sustained at follow-up. It is important to
note that the tests given at the pre-training testing, post-training testing and
follow-up phases were administered by an experimenter who had not taught
any of the children and who was 'blind' as to the group to which each child
belonged.

Hatcher, Hulme and Ellis wanted to make two important points from the
results of their study. First, they had demonstrated that a structured phonologically based reading programme can significantly improve the reading
standards of delayed 7-year-olds. Indeed, the 'reading + phonology' group
made over a year's progress in text reading accuracy and reading comprehension over a seven-month period, although the teaching lasted for just 20

sessions. This amounts to gains of approximately 1.7 months for each month of elapsed time. In contrast, the control group made gains in reading of just 0.9 months per month elapsed.

The second point that Hatcher, Hulme and Ellis wanted to reinforce was that phonological training is most effective in enhancing progress in literacy when it is combined with the teaching of reading and writing. The 'reading + phonology' group made far more dramatic progress in reading than either the 'phonology alone' or 'reading alone' groups. Also, the beneficial effects of the 'reading + phonology' intervention were not purely mediated by changes in phonological skill. Larger improvements in phonological skills at post-test were obtained for the 'phonology alone' group without an equal improvement in literacy skill. Thus, phonological training is at its most effective when it encourages the formation of explicit connections or links between children's underlying phonological skills and their experiences in learning to read. As we shall see later, the materials used in this study eventually formed the basis for a phonological awareness training programme, Sound Linkage (Hatcher, 1994), now in its second edition (Hatcher, 2000).

The second study described in some depth is one of a series conducted in the USA by Torgesen and colleagues. In this particular study, Torgesen et al. (1999) wanted to contrast two phonologically based teaching programmes that were delivered to young at-risk poor readers. The researchers selected 180 kindergarten children of normal verbal ability who had obtained low scores on both a letter naming task and a phoneme deletion task. The children were then randomly assigned to one of four groups: a no-treatment control condition (NTC); a regular classroom support condition (RCS); the embedded phonics condition (EP) and the phonological awareness + synthetic phonics (PASP) condition.

At pre-training testing, the children were given an extensive battery of tests that included measures of phonological processing (including phonological awareness, short-term verbal memory and rapid-naming ability), receptive and expressive language, verbal and non-verbal ability, word recognition and non-word reading, and letter–sound knowledge. The children in the two treatment conditions were then provided with four 20-minute sessions of one-to-one instruction per week for two-and-a-half years. In the PASP teaching condition, the emphasis was largely on word-level learning; this strongly emphasized phonological awareness training, teaching sound–letter correspondences and decoding of single words. Indeed, teachers in the PASP condition spent 80 per cent of the teaching time on word-level instruction and only 20 per cent on text-level activities. In contrast, the children in the EP condition spent 43 per cent of their training time on word-level activities and 57 per cent on text-level activities (the latter involved reading or writing connected text).

When the children were reassessed on completion of training, Torgesen et al. found that the children in the PASP condition had significantly stronger phonological awareness, phonemic decoding and word-level reading skills than those in the EP condition. Indeed, the word-level skills of the children in the PASP condition were in the middle of the average range. In contrast, the children in the EP and RCS conditions did not demonstrate a significant improvement in word-level skill when compared to the no-treatment control group.

The findings of Torgesen et al. echo those of Hatcher, Hulme and Ellis (1994) by highlighting the importance of phonological and decoding training in effecting significant improvements in reading in young 'at risk' poor readers. Although this is a very positive result, the study by Torgesen et al. raises two salutary issues. First, although the children in the PASP group improved in their word-level skills, this improvement did not extend to the important reading component of reading comprehension. Second, there were enormous individual differences, with some children benefiting very little from the teaching programme even though it had been conducted on a four times per week basis over two-and-a-half years. In the PASP condition, which produced the best overall group results, 24 per cent of these children remained significantly impaired in their phonemic (non-word) reading skills and 21 per cent remained impaired in their real-word reading ability.

Torgesen et al. suggested that the characteristics of 'difficult to teach' children extend beyond the domain of phonological weakness. They found that two of the most reliable predictors of response to intervention were the child's home environment (as measured by parental occupation and education) and the rated level of behaviour problems (especially attention and activity level) within the classroom.

The above studies provide us with models of how the evaluation of teaching programmes needs to be conducted. Consequently, when confronted by a new teaching regime or therapeutic method we need to ask whether its efficacy has been rigorously tested. Describing anecdotes of how individual children were helped by a specific method or therapy is not enough; although anecdotes may be used for the purposes of illustration, they do not constitute unequivocal proof that a teaching or therapeutic method actually works. We need to be reassured that the new approach has been subjected to a properly designed treatment trial of the type used by Hatcher, Hulme and Ellis (1994) and Torgesen et al. (1999). If we look closely at each of these studies, we can see that these authors have employed very similar methodologies to ensure that the findings obtained and the conclusions drawn are both clear and unequivocal.

What are these common features? To begin with, large numbers of children, matched on ability, reading level and phonological skill, were randomly allocated to treatment groups. Importantly, control groups were included. In both studies, the treatment or teaching conditions were both specific and well-defined. Extensive testing, by use of reliable and well-researched instruments, had been conducted at the outset (pre-test), at the conclusion of treatment or training (post-test) and, in the case of the study by Hatcher, Hulme and Ellis (1994), at longer-term follow-up as well. The experimenters conducting the testing did not know to which group each child belonged, and did not deliver the training or treatment. The children in the experimental groups received the same amount of intervention from teachers or therapists who had equivalent skills and experience and who worked with children from all the groups. Lastly, the test scores were subjected to appropriate statistical analysis to ensure that the purported differences between the training or treatment conditions were both statistically significant and educationally meaningful.

Methodologically sound training and treatment studies such as those described above are usually submitted to scientific journals that subject them to rigorous scrutiny through peer review. The study by Hatcher, Hulme and Ellis (1994) was reported in *Child Development* and the paper by Torgesen et al. (1999) in the *Journal of Educational Psychology*. One final point is that training or treatment studies require replication by other, preferably independent, researchers. There have been instances in which a treatment method has apparently been validated scientifically and then reported in a reputable journal, but thereafter other researchers have been unable to replicate the results. It is, therefore, important not to be overly enthusiastic about a one-off treatment study that describes dramatic results from a new treatment or training method. All new methods await the confidence that can come only through replication studies from independent researchers.

Teaching programmes to use with young dyslexic children

We now have compelling evidence that phonologically based reading programmes can facilitate improved reading progress in young at-risk 5-year-old children (Torgesen et al., 1999) and in slightly older children who have fallen behind in their reading development (Hatcher, Hulme and Ellis, 1994). The teaching methods used in these studies have been described in fairly minimal detail, sufficient to highlight the differences between the treatment and control conditions of each study. However, the programmes adopted by Hatcher, Hulme and Ellis (1994) and Torgesen et al. (1999) are now available commercially for use by specifically trained learning support teachers in their work with reading-delayed children. It is, therefore, appropriate to look at how these programmes might be implemented in the real world setting.

The study by Hatcher, Hulme and Ellis (1994) produced such encouraging results that Hatcher decided to develop and publish the materials that had been adopted in the form of a phonological training package called Sound Linkage (Hatcher, 1994, 2000). The programme begins with a series of short phonological tests that enable the teacher to determine what specific phono-logical skills the child has at his or her disposal, and his or her overall level of phonological ability. The phonological activities that make up the training component in Sound Linkage are divided into nine sections and are graded in order of difficulty, which then determines the sequence in which they are taught. The ordered activities are:

1 Identification of words as units within sentences.
2 Identification and manipulation of syllables.
3 Phoneme blending.
4 Identification and supply of rhyming words.
5 Identification and discrimination of phonemes.
6 Phoneme segmentation.
7 Phoneme deletion.
8 Phoneme substitution.
9 Phoneme transposition.

Some of the activities are accompanied by illustrations; two examples of these are given in Figure 11.1.

Many of the above activities will already be familiar to readers since they were described in the earlier discussion of phonological awareness in Chapter 2. However, some of the specific activities are now described in a little more detail. One of the earliest Sound Linkage activities (word-level units — first in the above list) requires children to push plastic counters into a line of squares marked on a card whilst simultaneously saying each word in a sentence. For instance, the child might be supplied with six counters and then told the sentence 'The girl is going to school'. The child is then expected to push the counters on to the squares whilst simultaneously saying each of the six words. At the level of the syllable, children might be asked to clap in time with the spoken syllables within a word or to delete a syllable from a two-syllable word, for example *farmhouse* without the *farm* says *house*.

Children move on to phoneme-based activities by working initially on phoneme blending, for example *p–i–g* joins together to make the word *pig*, and then move through rhyme production and detection activities to the identification of phonemes (for example, which of these words begin with

(a)

(b)

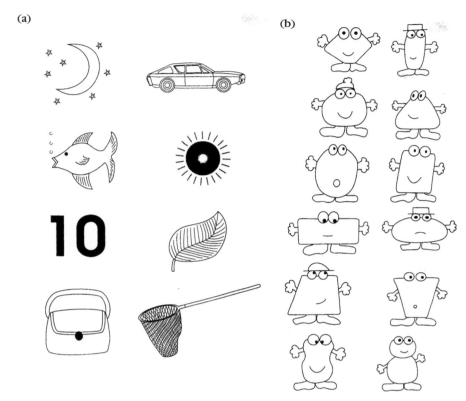

Figure 11.1 Illustrations from Sound Linkage: (a) First sound in a word: the child must point to the picture that goes with an initial sound uttered by the teacher (for example /fff/ for *fish*); (b) 'Same end' sound: the child determines whether the Mr Men pictures with the funny names have the same end sound (for example *Mr Kop* and *Mr Mip*; *Mr Eez* and *Mr Ooz*).

the same sound? *doll–table–tap*). At a more advanced level of phoneme awareness, children segment words into sounds by, for instance, indicating the beginning, medial or end sound of a given word (for example, in the word *dog*, the child must specify what sound it begins with, what is the middle sound and what is the end sound).

The ability to delete or substitute sounds in words is an advanced skill not achieved by many children until they have already begun to read. In these exercises, children are asked to delete a specified sound from a word, for example *bold* without the [b] says *old*, or at a more difficult level *stick* without the [t] says *sick*. Another example of these more advanced phonemic skills would be the substitution of a medial vowel sound for another, for example replacing the [i] in *sick* with an [o] to make *sock*.

These phonological training exercises would be expected to form a signifi-cant component of a teaching programme for the young dyslexic child. Sound Linkage may be inserted into any of a number of existing structured reading support programmes. In his own work, Hatcher has incorporated Sound Linkage into the Clay (1985) reading recovery framework described in some depth earlier in this chapter. Each 40-minute teaching session is broken into three sections. In the first section that begins the teaching session, children read a book that can be read with at least 95 per cent accuracy. This provides them with the opportunity to rehearse known words and also to build up their reading speed and fluency. They then read a slightly harder book that was introduced during the third part of the previous session while the teacher maintains a running record that codes the children's reading responses. The running record not only helps determine the book's reading difficulty level but also provides data about the child's reading behaviour that can help inform teaching strategy. It is in Section 2 that Sound Linkage plays an important role. If necessary, children revise the names and sounds of the letters. This is done using a multisensory teaching approach which requires the child to feel, write, and name the letters, and through the construction of individual alphabet books containing pictures and words associated with each letter. Children then carry out phonological training exercises from the Sound Linkage package appropriate to their level of phonological ability.

Another component of Section 2 is the acquisition of a sight vocabulary, again through a multisensory approach. Children write commonplace words in as many different settings as possible, such as using sand, chalk or plastic letters. The words are written both in isolation and in a short story. Once the children have acquired a reasonable level of phonological awareness and a modest sight vocabulary, they carry out phonological linkage activities. These typically combine phonological segmentation activities with the spelling out of words using plastic letters. The final section of each lesson requires children to read a new book that is geared towards the instructional level of 90–94 per cent accuracy. For a fuller description of how Sound Linkage is incorporated within a reading recovery framework, see Hatcher's chapter in Snowling and Stackhouse (1996).

A field study of the above method revealed encouraging results (Hatcher, 1996). Teachers recruited for this programme received 14 weeks' training involving three days of in-service work, five half-day tutorials and the teaching of two reading-delayed children. For the study, 78 7-year-old children, who were about 18 months delayed in their reading at the start of the intervention, were selected. The children made average gains of eight months in word reading and 11 months in spelling over the three months of intervention. For each month of intervention, this represents gains of 2.67 months for reading and 3.67 months for spelling. Thus, incorporating phonological training within an existing well-tried structured reading programme shows not inconsiderable promise for tackling the reading deficits shown by dyslexic or reading-delayed children.

A popular phonological awareness training scheme used extensively in the USA is the Auditory Discrimination in Depth programme developed by Lindamood and Lindamood (1984). Indeed, it was the Lindamood programme that formed the core of the PASP teaching condition in the study by Torgesen et al. (1999). This programme begins with instruction designed to make children aware of the specific mouth movements required to produce each phoneme. As part of this instruction, children also learn labels for each phoneme that are descriptive of these mouth movements and positions. Thus, for example, the label 'lip popper' is used for the phonemes /b/ and /p/, the label 'tip tapper' is assigned to the phonemes /t/ and /d/, whereas the phonemes /k/ and /g/ are labelled 'scrapers'.

Once the children attain a high level of knowledge in oral awareness, they engage in an extensive series of exercises in which they represent sequences of phonemes with either mouth-form pictures or coloured blocks. This training aims to enable them to acquire sensitivity to the sequences of sounds in syllables, and it also enables them to learn to represent these sequences with concrete visual objects. As the children learn to label each phoneme with a descriptive name, they are also taught to associate specific letters with each phoneme. Once they become facile at representing sequences of letters with concrete objects, it is a natural transition to begin to represent them with letters.

Like Sound Linkage, the Lindamood programme aims to improve children's sensitivity to the sound structure of words whilst forging connections between their knowledge of phonemes and other concrete representations of these, be they visual objects or, ultimately, letters. What makes the Lindamood programme different to other phonological training packages is the emphasis on articulatory gestures. To what extent these enhance the efficacy of the programme overall and whether they make more of a difference for the child with particularly severe phonological problems are questions for further research.

The Lindamood-Bell Company has developed a computer-based programme that helps reinforce and extend the teaching principles inherent in their auditory training. Because computer-teaching programmes involve the interaction of child with machine, as opposed to tutor, it is possible for a single tutor to work with many more children. Thus, limited human learning support resources are spread more widely and used more efficiently. These computer programs are being adopted within the computer training model of Olson and Wise and colleagues at the University of Colorado. These researchers have developed a talking computer system to provide speech support for children who have decoding difficulties — 'reading with orthographic and segmented speech feedback', (ROSS) (Olson, Foltz and Wise, 1986). ROSS provides high-quality synthetic speech that pronounces words when children target them with a mouse while reading stories on a computer screen.

Olson, Wise and colleagues used the computer support approach for children as young as 7 years old. The children usually receive four half-hour sessions per week. The typical procedure is to pre-test poor readers in the study, to train them in the use of ROSS over a one-to-two-week period before then allowing them to read stories on the computer independently for three of the four weekly sessions. The difficulty level of the stories is adjusted for each subject, so that each child should not require computer feedback for more than 5 per cent of the words on the screen. The computer is programmed to present occasional multiple choice comprehension questions and to present some of the targeted words in a review test. The tutor monitors each child's oral reading and encourages targeting of unknown words during one session per week. Total training time on the computer is approximately 14 hours over a 12-week period.

Olson and Wise (1992) posed the following question. Could reading stories on the computer with speech support improve gains in phonological decoding and word recognition more than gains in similar control subjects who remained in their remedial reading or language arts classes? The answer to their question emerged a clear 'Yes'. The trained children averaged about four times the gains in phonological decoding (non-word reading) and about twice the gains in word recognition than did those children in the control group. In general, ROSS was demonstrated to be a successful adjunct to direct teacher–child methods in the promotion of segmentation and decoding skills in reading-disabled children. However, these authors noted that the children who had the lowest initial levels of phoneme awareness at the outset tended to gain significantly less from reading with speech feedback than those with more advanced phonological skills.

In a training study conducted by Wise and Olson (1995), children with low levels of phonemic awareness were first taught to become aware of the distinctive articulatory movements associated with different speech sounds, by use of the Lindamood and Lindamood (1984) auditory discrimination training programme (and reinforcer computer materials). The children were then switched to the ROSS programme. The results following training showed dramatically improved performance (relative to a comprehension-training group and the findings of previous ROSS studies) in phoneme awareness and, importantly, in decoding skill. The children in the Lindamood and

ROSS programme made three times the gains in phoneme awareness and twice the gains in phonological decoding than the comprehension training group. However, these dramatic improvements were not sustained at a long-term follow-up conducted nine months later.

Wise and Olson commented that it is likely that longer phonologic-al and computer training programs, conducted over at least a year, are likely to be necessary to ensure sustained and generalized improvements in children's reading skills. Longer training periods provide more time for children to automatize and integrate their phonological processes with reading of stories with speech support in the ROSS programme. It is important also to appreciate that computer-based reading packages function as a supplement or adjunct to one-to-one child–tutor programmes. They are not intended to act as a replacement for the interactive teacher–learner relationship that is critical to enable delayed young readers to crack the alphabetic code. What computers can do is to provide additional feedback and print exposure that is needed to improve fluent and flexible word recognition in the individual child, whilst releasing the tutor so that he or she can directly train another child in phonological and decoding skills.

Most phonological/phonic programmes have taught at the level of the smallest unit, that is, the phoneme. However, there has been an upsurge of interest in larger sublexical units, specifically at the level of onset and rime (what teachers have usually termed 'word family' learning; for instance, learning related groups of words such as *light, might, fight,* etc.). Goswami and colleagues (see Goswami, 1994, for a review) argued that children aged as young as 5 years can benefit significantly from instruction in onset-rime awareness and specific instruction in orthographic analogies. There are two main arguments as to why this approach may be particularly helpful for the dyslexic child. First, decoding using larger chunks at the level of the rime rather than the phoneme acts to reduce the load on memory when phonological segments need to be synthesized to form pronunciations. We have seen that many dyslexic children do show limitations in their short-term verbal memory. Second, larger sublexical units show greater consistency and regularity than do smaller unit graphemes within English orthography. Consequently, it should be easier to learn and to apply generalizations about these larger units without being confused and confounded by the many exceptions that occur at the level of smaller units, such as phonemes. However, on a cautionary note (as we saw in Chapter 2), some experimental studies have shown that rime training may not reap such long-term benefits as teaching smaller phoneme–grapheme correspondences (Bruck and Treiman, 1992). Additionally, it may be necessary for children to have some decoding skill before they can make sense of an analogical approach to reading (Ehri and Robbins, 1992). Furthermore, although Goswami demonstrated powerful analogy effects in experimental studies, there is recent evidence that children may not use analogies spontaneously, at any rate not until they have had the opportunity to develop a sight vocabulary on which to base their analogical inferences (Muter, Snowling and Taylor, 1994; Savage, 1997). Despite these criticisms, there has been a series of training studies with reading-disabled readers conducted by Greany, Tunmer and Chapman (1997) that have demonstrated that children with reading ages as low as 6 to 7 years are able to profit from instruction in rime analogies when compared to reading-age matched control subjects. These authors studied 57 reading-disabled children aged 8 years who had reading ages of between 6 and 7 years. These children were then compared with 57 younger normal readers in a reading-age-matched study design. Although the reading-disabled children performed at a higher level than the younger control subjects on a receptive vocabulary test, they performed far less well on measures of phonological segmentation and non-word reading. The 57 reading-disabled children were then allocated to one of three groups, all of whom received three- or four-times weekly individual instruction over a 12-week period. One group received standard remedial reading instruction. A second group received systematic instruction in the use of rime-based spelling units, for example *seat–beat–neat*. The third group focused on word-specific learning and sentence-level reading strategies.

At post-training testing, the children taught rime analogies not only significantly improved on experimental measures of rime awareness, word recognition and non-word reading, but they also significantly outperformed the other two groups. Even more importantly, the children in the rime analogy group also showed an average six-month gain in their reading age on a standardized test, suggesting that the word identification strategies acquired by these children generalized to reading unfamiliar words. It seems plausible, therefore, to add an analogical training component to a phonological-based training programme, perhaps not at the outset, but rather later, when children have acquired the alphabetic principle and a sight word vocabulary that is at or near to the 7-year level.

Visual training and alternative therapies — do they have anything to offer?

The structured phonological teaching approach advocated here for dyslexic children is one that is firmly grounded in a well-validated theory of reading development. Additionally its efficacy is now well established through empirical training studies. Of late, there has been a plethora of alternative therapies that are claimed to 'cure' dyslexia, and very often other learning difficulties as well. It would take many pages to discuss all of these in turn;

instead, we now focus on just five of them in order to give the reader a flavour of what is on offer, whilst casting a critical eye on what these alternative therapies claim to do.

Monocular occlusion

A popularly held view in the UK, much endorsed by learning support teachers who work with dyslexic students, is that such children lack ocular motor dominance (see Stein, 1989, for a review). Dyslexic children are purported to have difficulty in integrating information between the two eyes, which then impairs visual localization of letters, with children apparently complaining that letters 'jump about' or 'seem blurred'. Stein (1989) has proposed that this phenomenon is due to a defect in the visual magnocellular system that results in a difficulty in detecting visual motion (see Chapter 6 and Stein (2001) for a fuller discussion). This results in failure to establish a reference eye that may be tested by use of an orthoptic measure described by Dunlop (1972). The problem may be resolved by the child wearing occluded spectacles so that one eye is effectively patched.

Stein and Fowler (1985) attempted to validate this technique in a study of dyslexic children, half of whom wore occluded glasses while those in the control group wore plain glasses. Those who had developed a fixed reference eye advanced in reading by almost a year, whereas those who had failed to develop a fixed reference eye advanced by less than six months. This study was subjected to scrutiny by Bishop (1989), who made the following three criticisms that called into question the validity of the findings of Stein and Fowler. First, there was a failure to randomly allocate the dyslexic children to the treatment versus control groups. Second, there was no control over the children's receiving of learning support tuition during the time they were wearing the spectacles. Lastly, there was no check on whether, and for how long, individual children wore their prescribed spectacles. To complicate matters further, when Bishop carried out further statistical analyses of the data from Stein and Fowler the differences in reading skill between the occluded eye group and the control group were no longer present. Similarly, Goulandris et al. (1998) found that orthoptic difficulties were no more prevalent in a group of dyslexic children than in control subjects.

In a recent study by Stein, Richardson and Fowler (2000), 143 children who were significantly underachieving in reading and who were also found to have binocular instability (on the Dunlop test), were randomly allocated to one of two groups. In both groups, the children were required to wear yellow spectacles for all reading and writing activities, but one group had the left lens occluded while the other group did not. At a follow-up assessment three months later, the children were found to be significantly more likely to have gained binocular stability if they had been wearing occluded glasses. Furthermore, gaining stable binocular control appeared to be associated with improved reading. The children who gained binocular control through occlusion improved their reading by 9.4 months during this three-month period, compared with an improvement of only 3.9 months in those who were not patched and who did not gain stable fixation.

Although this appears to be a very impressive finding, there are two caveats of which we should be aware. First, the original cohort from which the subject sample was selected comprised over 700 children, all of whom had been referred with reading problems and eye strain or visual confusions when reading. The authors then excluded those children who were not actually significantly underachieving in reading, together with those who demonstrated stable binocular fixation (indeed, 45 per cent of the cohort passed the Dunlop test). Thus, fewer than 20 per cent of the original cohort was deemed suitable for the study. It thus seems that binocular occlusion as a treatment method may have relevance for only a small proportion of children presenting with reading difficulties. This has not, however, discouraged Stein (2001, p. 23) from making statements such as 'this progress (in response to occlusion) is far greater than most remediation techniques achieve with dyslexics', thus tending to give the impression that the technique has relevance for all dyslexic students. Furthermore, in the study by Stein, Richardson and Fowler, there was no clear indication of what reading methods of instruction or other intervention strategies were being employed during the three months the children were wearing the spectacles. It could be the case that the reading improvements noted in the occlusion group were not related to the achievement of binocular stability but were, in fact, a response to teaching input.

Despite these concerns over methodological issues, and with the failures to confirm and to replicate the link between oculomotor dominance and reading progress, the use of the Dunlop test and of occluded glasses remains a common feature of the management of dyslexic children in the UK.

Coloured or tinted lenses

A very popular alternative therapy in the field of dyslexia is that of prescribing the poor reader tinted lenses or coloured overlays to use when reading. This therapy was first advocated by Irlen, who claimed that some poor readers suffered from 'scotopic sensitivity' which amounted to an uncomfortable glare and distortion effect when confronted by black print on a white page. The Irlen Institute in the USA and the UK was established to assess individual children's and adults' level of scotopic sensitivity, and to prescribe and supply coloured lenses. Great claims have been made in the popular press for the instant curative effect of coloured lenses for even long-term poor readers. However, the evidence quoted in newspapers has almost invariably been anecdotal in nature and, as we have seen, this constitutes very flimsy evidence indeed. Research studies carried out by Irlen and associates have resulted in accusations of bias, with criticisms of the methodology that was used.

However, that is not to say that there is not something about the use of coloured lenses or overlays that might help, if not cure, some dyslexic individuals. A study carried out at Cambridge University (Wilkins et al., 1994) suggested that coloured lenses might have a role to play alongside systematic teaching in the management of the dyslexic child. Wilkins et al. carried out a study of 51 9- to-14-year-old children who were prescribed lenses by use of an assessment instrument called a 'colorimeter'. The colorimeter permits the child to select a colour filter that gives maximum reduction of distortion of print under controlled conditions. Each child was then prescribed two different sets of lenses, which to the naked eye differed very little in actual colour. One lens, the experimental one, significantly reduced the level of print distortion for the child. The other lens, the control, did not significantly reduce distortion. The children in the study were 'blind' as to which lens was which. The children were then randomly allocated to two groups — the first group wore the control lens for four weeks followed by the experimental lens for a further four weeks, whereas the second group wore the lenses in reverse order, that is, experimental lens followed by control lens.

The children and their parents kept a diary documenting the wearing of the lenses and the level of discomfort and/or distortion they experienced while reading. They were tested on the Neale Analysis of Reading Ability, NARA (Neale, 1989) prior to commencement of the study and at the end of each month's trial. Of the 51 children who participated in the study, 48 claimed that the experimental lens, but not the control lens, reduced their perception of distortion and of discomfort. But the critical test of the efficacy of tinted lenses is whether the wearing of the experimental lens resulted in greater gains in the children's NARA reading scores than the wearing of the control lens. In fact, the gains in reading were greater for the period during which the children wore the experimental lens than for the period when the children wore the control lens — but the difference between the two sets of gains in reading did not quite achieve statistical significance.

Wilkins et al. went on to conclude that the wearing of tinted lenses is unlikely to have a direct effect on the child's level of reading skill. Rather, these authors proposed that wearing the lens reduces eye discomfort and print distortion, and that this makes reading an easier and more comfortable experience for the child. As a consequence, he or she is likely to engage in reading for longer periods at a time, thus increasing print exposure, which then exerts a direct influence on the levels of reading skill. Many opticians and optometrists are now making use of colorimeter instruments in their practice so that access to prescribed tinted lenses is made relatively easy and fairly inexpensive. However, it is important to appreciate that scotopic sensitivity is unlikely to be a contributory factor to the reading difficulties of other than a relatively small number of children, and that it is a supplementary management strategy that should not be regarded as a substitute for systematic reading instruction.

Primitive reflex therapy

This approach to the treatment of dyslexia (and also of other learning difficulties) draws on a neurological theory that seems to have little direct bearing on the acquisition of reading and related language skills; specifically, that learning-disabled children have failed to replace their early primitive reflexes with more mature postural reflexes. Nonetheless, this treatment method has attracted the attention of many parents who have been prepared to embark on what amounts to a time-consuming and expensive procedure.

Blythe, from the Institute of Neurophysiological Psychology, Chester, a private treatment centre which provides reflex therapy in the UK, recently described a study conducted there which purported to establish a clear link between the persistence of primitive reflexes and the presence of learning difficulties in children (Blythe, 2001). Blythe and colleagues looked at the reflex profile of 54 diagnosed dyslexic individuals. This involved rating (on a five-point scale) the relative presence or absence of primitive reflexes such as the Moro reflex, the palmar reflex and the asymmetric neck reflex. Ninety two per cent of the dyslexic subjects in their study were reported to show significant presence of these primitive reflexes, which usually disappear in infancy. However, it should be noted that this study suffers from the absence of a control, or indeed another clinical comparison, group. It follows that there could not be a 'blind' assessment procedure to reduce bias.

Nonetheless, on the basis of studies such as this, treatment packages are prescribed that involve the carrying out of specific movement sequences aimed at resolving these primitive reflexes. Advocates of this treatment method claim that, as the primitive reflexes disappear, so the child's reading improves.

It is tempting to dismiss a theory and treatment method that makes claims for a connection between palmar hand reflexes and reading! However, it is important to recognize that all theories and treatment methods are capable of being subjected to empirical investigation and indeed, in the case of primitive reflex therapy, one such trial has now been carried out.

McPhillips, Hepper and Mulhern (2000) selected 66 children who met a double criteria of being 24 months behind age level on the NARA and who showed evidence of having an unresolved asymmetric tonic neck reflex. The children were then randomly allocated to three groups, matched on age, verbal IQ, gender and tonic neck reflex level. The children in the experimental group were requested to engage in a specific movement sequence (aimed at replicating and ultimately resolving their neck reflex) for 10 minutes per day for a period of 12 months. Children in the placebo group performed non-specific movement sequences that were not based on the replication of primitive reflexes. The third group was a 'no treatment' control group.

Both the assessors and the participants in the study were 'blind' as to group allocation, that is, this was a 'double-blind' trial. On completion of the trial, the children in the experimental group showed a significant decrease in the level of their neck reflex while the children in the placebo and control groups showed no change. More importantly, although all the children in the study showed improvements in their reading over the course of the study, the increase in reading score was substantially greater for those children in the experimental group.

Although this study seems impressive in terms of its design methodology and its findings, it is not without its problems. It is hard to determine from the authors' description what reading instruction the children received during the course of the treatment trial, and whether this varied between the groups. Nor is it clear whether the children were expected to conduct the exercises themselves or whether these were meant to be supervised by a parent or teacher. Indeed, it could not be validated whether the children carried out the exercises on the prescribed basis since the assessors were not present during the exercise sessions. Finally, it may be that some of the statistical analyses were inappropriate; the children's neck reflexes were assessed by use of a rating scale which cannot be subjected to the same (parametric) statistical procedures as for analysing children's test scores. Yet the authors used the same method of analysis for all their data.

It is important that, for any treatment method to be regarded as efficacious, there must be more than one study trial conducted. In other words, it is necessary to replicate the above study with a different group of children. However, even allowing for that, it is still a concern that there has been a failure on the part of advocates of primitive reflex therapy to establish any convincing connection between infant motor reflexes and the complex process of learning to read. It is possible that the failure to resolve primitive reflexes may constitute a biological marker of an immature neurological system in the learning-disabled child, but that this marker is in itself unrelated to cognitive level of functioning and, therefore, to reading. Parents and teachers should be cautious about embarking on a costly and time-committing therapy that may have no direct bearing on the child's reading and related cognitive skills.

Dyslexia, dyspraxia, attention treatment (DDAT)

DDAT is a much-publicized and heavily marketed therapy that assumes that dyslexia, and indeed many other learning difficulties, arise from a malfunction in the cerebellum (in spite of evidence for such a malfunction being scanty at best). Testing techniques, that include measuring postural control (balance) and eye tracking, are used to determine which areas of the cerebellum need stimulation. A series of motor exercises is then prescribed that are claimed to improve cerebellar function; this is then alleged to be followed by dramatic gains in reading, writing, attention control and so on.

There are two completed studies of the DDAT method which are reported on the organization's website, but which have not as yet been published in peer-reviewed journals. The first of these, described as the 'Phase One Study', studied a sample of 40 children who had attended a DDAT centre; only 20 of the children completed the programme which is a rather alarming dropout date. The main results are presented as 'improved percentage ratings' on the balance and tracking tasks. Additional data on academic performance and concentration skills took the form of parental ratings. The children who completed the DDAT programme were said to have improved on all these ratings, but no comparison group was studied and no statistical analyses conducted.

A second study, termed 'Retrospective Study Two', followed 50 children over a six-month period while they carried out the DDAT programme. The children were given the Dyslexia Early Screening Test (DEST) (Nicolson and Fawcett, 1996) prior to commencing the training programme, and again at its conclusion. There was no control group, but the children's scores on the DEST were compared to what was referred to as the 'national average'. However, it does need to be recognized that the DEST does not have full published normative data, so this comparison does not have the status it would have, had the children been tested on a fully standardized measure. Furthermore, the children's rates of improvements were expressed as percentages, but in a rather misleading way. For instance, children who had scored at the twentieth centile on the DEST before treatment, and who had then scored at the thirtieth centile after treatment, were described as having improved by 50 per cent. In addition to making the progress seem more dramatic than it really is, the use of this method of expressing progress means that gains from a lower starting point will result in greater percentage increases.

It is not hard to see that the quality of the research into the efficacy of the DDAT treatment falls far short of the requirements of a methodologically sound training study, such as that conducted by Hatcher, Hulme and Ellis (1994) or Torgesen et al. (1999) described earlier in this chapter. Until far more rigorous research has been carried out to show that DDAT is an effective treatment for reading difficulties, it is to be hoped that parents and teachers will approach it with justifiable caution.

Essential fatty acid supplements

This treatment approach is based on the hypothesis that dyslexic children show an impairment in their metabolism of essential fatty acids derived from their diet. It follows that supplementing the diet of dyslexic children with increased levels of highly unsaturated fatty acids, contained in tuna fish oil for instance, might help improve their reading. Again, the theoretical basis for a connection between fish oils and ability to read seems a very tenuous one.

The main research into this treatment method has been carried out by Richardson at Imperial College, University of London. Two of these studies (Richardson et al., 2000; Richardson et al., 2001) are now briefly described. In the first of these, 41 children with diagnosed dyslexia and accompanying attention deficit disorder were randomly allocated to one of two groups in a double-blind trial. The children in the experimental group received fatty acid supplements in the form of tuna fish oil capsules while the children in the placebo control group consumed similar looking capsules but without a fatty acid content. After three months' treatment, the children in the experimental group showed a greater reduction in their ratings on an attention deficit assessment scale than did those in the placebo group.

A second, similar randomized double-blind trial was carried out to look at the effect of fatty acid dietary supplements on progress in reading in dyslexic children. This study employed a larger subject sample (35 in the experimental group, 43 in the placebo control group), all of whom were two-and-a-half years behind in reading. After six months' treatment, reading progress was said to be much greater in the experimental than in the control group. Putting the findings of these two studies together, it may be possible to argue a case for fatty acid supplements improving the attention control of dyslexic children, which might then improve reading indirectly via the print exposure factor, that is, children with improved concentration sit still for longer to read books!

Much more research is needed to establish a plausible link between fatty acid deficiency, attention and learning to read, and to determine whether this oral ingestion method of treatment might have a role to play in the management of some dyslexic children, perhaps the subgroup with accompanying attention problems. One point for parents to bear in mind is that Richardson and colleagues (Richardson et al., 2000; Richardson et al., 2001) have found that their studies have a high participant attrition rate, that is, many parents and children drop out of the study during the course of treatment. One possible reason for this is the high dosage of fatty acids required, which means the children have to consume copious quantities of large capsules; not surprisingly, many parents find it difficult to persuade their children to continue with the treatment after a relatively short time.

The message I want to convey from this discussion of just five of the many alternative therapies is, first, to be cautious and realistic (if not sceptical) about what they might have to offer, and second, to not see any of them as a substitute for well-substantiated and systematic phonological approaches to the teaching of reading.

Summary

- Reading recovery is a systematic and integrated approach to screening, identification and intervention in the early stages of reading failure; the poorest readers in a class (usually of 6-year-olds) are given daily, individual reading instruction until their reading level matches that of their peer group.
- Teaching programmes that explicitly train up phonological skills, within the context of learning to read, have been demonstrated to substantially benefit children who are slow to acquire literacy skills.
- Recommended teaching programmes that are now becoming widely employed by teachers include Sound Linkage (Hatcher, 2000) and the Lindamood Phoneme Sequencing Program (LIPS) that has been developed from the Auditory Discrimination in Depth programme (Lindamood and Lindamood, 1984).
- There are now increasing numbers of visually based and alternative therapies available; however, these treatments for reading delay need to be regarded with some caution as most have yet to be subjected to rigorous scientific evaluation.

CHAPTER 12

Assessing and teaching the young poor reader — four case studies

The two previous chapters described a model for assessing young children with reading difficulties before going on to discuss teaching methods and materials that might be used to ameliorate their literacy problems. A series of short case studies of young children follows, illustrating the implementation of these assessment and teaching techniques. Each child's assessment procedure is described and a formulation of his or her difficulties (and, where relevant, strengths) is given. Lastly, the reader is offered an exploration of how this formulation may be used to derive a prescription for management and teaching. The first two children present with a developmental dyslexic profile. The two remaining children have reading difficulties (and other problems) that are a consequence of neurological impairment. The intention is for the four case studies to illustrate a number of important issues described in this book, both theoretical and practical.

Case Study 1 — Daisy

Daisy was a bright 7-year-old girl with developmental dyslexia. She was referred for an assessment of her slow reading development that was affecting not only her ability to cope within the classroom but also her self-confidence. She had been attending quite a high-expectation school, but her parents were thinking of moving her to another school with a well-established learning support unit. There were no concerns about Daisy's early developmental milestones; she was a healthy child, popular with her peers and able to concentrate well. Her older sister had already been assessed as having dyslexia, and her father reported that he also had had reading and spelling problems.

At the assessment, Daisy had a great deal of difficulty initially separating from her mother, to whom she had become increasingly 'clingy' of late. However, with firm but gentle management, she was eventually able to separate; she settled quickly thereafter and went on to work co-operatively, and with good concentration for over an hour and a half.

First of all, Daisy was given the Wechsler Intelligence Scale for Children III UK (WISC III UK), on which she achieved a Verbal IQ of 124 ('superior' range), but a relatively lower Performance IQ of 105 ('average' range). Her verbal scores were very high, especially for vocabulary and verbal reasoning, although she scored at only a low-average level on the Digit Span subtest. On the Performance Scale, she had considerable difficulty with the Object Assembly subtest, a jigsaw puzzle test that assesses visuo-spatial ability, and with Coding, a timed pencil and paper copying task (additionally, her attempts at copy drawing of geometric shapes were noted to be very immature). The results of the IQ tests had confirmed, first, that Daisy did not have generalized learning difficulties that could account for her slow progress with reading; second, that she was verbally bright; and lastly, that there were specific spatial and fine motor difficulties.

A range of educational tests was then conducted. Daisy's high Verbal IQ would lead us to expect her to perform at an above-average level on standardized attainment tests. The first finding of relevance was that Daisy had few problems in mathematics. She scored at an above-average level on a mental arithmetic subtest of the WISC, and she achieved at a level commensurate with her chronological age on a mathematics test Wechsler Objective Numerical Dimensions (WOND Mathematics Reasoning) Rust (1996). Although her standards in mathematics were reasonable, there were some localized gaps. For instance, she could not tell the time on an analogue clock, she could not identify the fifth in a series of objects and she could not interpret a simple graph.

Daisy was underachieving relative to both age- and Verbal IQ-expectation on tests of reading and spelling. Her reading and spelling ages on the Wechsler Objective Reading Dimensions WORD (Rust, Golombock and Trickey, 1993) tests were 6 years and 3 months, and 6 years and 9 months, respectively. Daisy was unable to read very simple commonplace words, such as *again* and *slow*, but could spell a word as difficult as *thing*. Recall that it was said earlier that in early development, reading and spelling vocabularies may be somewhat disconnected from one another — this appeared to be the case with Daisy. Daisy proved a poor decoder; she could read only three out of 20 of the non-words on the Graded Nonword Reading Test (Snowling, Stothard and MacLean, 1996) which placed her at barely the 6-year level. Analysis of her spelling errors revealed a propensity to make non-phonetic errors. Daisy's spelling weaknesses, her preponderance of non-phonetic errors, and her struggles with her handwriting are clearly evident from the spelling sample shown in Figure 12.1.

Was Daisy dyslexic? The evidence to date suggests that she was certainly making slow progress in her literacy development. Her educational difficulties were specific to reading, writing and spelling. With her high Verbal IQ, Daisy would be expected to contribute well to oral classroom discussions and to have

cat
ho
pig
con
Lock (*look*)
play
fish
to
most
lump
und (*under*)
thing
Svmn (*sum*)
rite (*right*)
ats (*eight*)
bun (*done*)

Figure 12.1: Sample of Daisy's handwriting and spelling.

no difficulty in following what is being taught within the classroom. Also, she appeared to be doing relatively well in mathematics. Adding in the positive family history of dyslexia, it did look as though Daisy's difficulties were likely to be dyslexic in nature. However, to be really confident that she did have a dyslexic problem, and to uncover more information about the nature of her literacy difficulties, it was necessary to carry out further specific tests.

In keeping with the three-element phonological processing model formulated by Wagner and colleagues, specific tasks were conducted that tapped short-term verbal memory, phonological awareness and naming speed. The first of these has already been commented upon; Daisy scored at around the $6^{1}/_{2}$ year mark on WISC III Digit Span, far below the level to be expected for a seven-year-old girl with a Verbal IQ of 124. Both the Beginning and End Phoneme Deletion subtests from the Phonological Abilities Test (PAT) (Muter, Hulme and Snowling, 1997) were then administered to assess her phonological awareness, specifically segmentation ability. Daisy scored two out of eight and six out of eight, respectively, that is at between the 5- and 6-year levels. Lastly, she was given the Digit Naming Speed subtest from the Phonological Assessment Battery (PhAB) (Frederickson, Frith and Reason, 1997) on which she scored at only the second centile. Thus, Daisy, was experiencing significant difficulty with all three components of phonological processing ability.

How do we formulate Daisy's difficulties? First, it was evident that she had a significant phonological dyslexia. Daisy experienced problems with all three components of phonological processing skill, and she was very weak at decoding. It was her phonological problems that accounted for her slow progress in reading and spelling and her high proportion of non-phonetic spelling errors. Additionally, Daisy had spatial and fine motor difficulties that were affecting not only her handwriting but also, very likely, localized visual aspects of mathematics. Finally, she was a sensitive little girl so, not surprisingly, anxiety and feelings of failure arising from her failure to progress in reading were beginning to affect her motivation and her self-confidence. Were there any specific strengths that Daisy might be able to capitalize upon to help her compensate for her literacy difficulties? Most obviously, she was a verbally bright little girl so it was appropriate to expect her to draw on her good language skills to help compensate for her phonological and decoding deficiencies. She may well also be able to take advantage of her strong visual memory — she scored at the 85th centile on a picture memory test that appears on the British Abilities Scale (BAS) (Elliott, Murray and Pearson, 1983).

The assessment procedure produced a formulation of Daisy's core and co-occurring difficulties, whilst also considering the effect these had on her educational development and on her emotional and behavioural adjustment. The formulation may now be used to generate a series of 'management recommendations' aimed at addressing her difficulties.

The first recommendation was to suggest that the appropriateness of Daisy's present school placement be reviewed. Fortunately, her mother had recognized that Daisy was not thriving either educationally or emotionally within her present school and had herself already begun to explore alternative settings that were not so academically fast-paced, where there was clear recognition of the needs of the dyslexic child, and where Daisy would be able to have access to regular, individual and specialist learning support.

Second, it was clear that Daisy would require at least twice-weekly one-to-one teaching following a structured programme that addressed her phono-logically-based literacy difficulties. It was suggested that a teaching scheme that emphasized phonological awareness training, phonological linkage exercises and, later on, the development of systematic decoding strategies, should meet her needs nicely. This programme is most appropriately conducted within a structured multisensory framework; this is one that aims to develop and to make use of all the child's sensory input channels for learning. The child's auditory channel is 'exercised' through the hearing and saying of words and their component sounds, the visual channel through looking at print, and the kinaesthetic channel through writing and the perception of mouth movements (the latter in the sense advocated in the Lindamood programmes). A multisensory approach like this would help

Daisy build up her relatively weaker auditory/phonological skills whilst capitalizing on her stronger visual memory.

Later on, Daisy might profit from segmentation-based teaching methods that emphasize larger sublexical units within words, that is, units above the level of the phoneme. A teaching method such as analogy training, which splits words at the level of onset and rime, would place a lesser load on Daisy's limited short-term verbal memory because the units of sound within a word are larger so there are fewer of them to segment and remember. Brooks and Weeks (1998) suggested that severely dyslexic children, who have difficulty in segmenting and memorizing phonemic units, might be helped by having their attention drawn to smaller words or subwords that are contained within many longer multisyllabic words. For instance, the word *carpet* is composed of two constituent words *car* and *pet*, both of which are likely already to be contained within the reading and spelling lexicons of the 6- to 7-year-old child. Similarly, the word *encounter* has embedded in it the smaller, more commonplace word *count*. Encouraging the child to look for embedded words or subwords may require some preliminary training in syllable identification and segmentation, together with work on identifying syllable boundaries.

Lastly, given that Daisy was a verbally able little girl, it would be appropriate, even at this early stage, to encourage her towards developing verbal contextual facilitation skills. We have seen that drawing the child's attention to the semantic and grammatical cues contained in the surrounding context of prose reading material may function as a powerful compensator for her less-than-adequate decoding skills. Consequently, Daisy should be encouraged to decode an unfamiliar word as far as she can, and then to use the surrounding context to 'plug the decoding gap', so arriving at the correct reading of the word through partial phonics supplemented by word knowledge and context cues.

Daisy's arithmetical skills appeared to be developing quite nicely, though she did have difficulty with what might be termed 'visual concepts within mathematics'; this is to be expected, given her co-occurring visuo-spatial difficulties. Visual concepts within an early elementary school curriculum would include fractions, setting out of arithmetic problems in column format, place values (hundreds, tens and units), distinguishing geometric shapes, telling the time on an analogue clock, reading a chart or graph, understanding left-to-right sequences and measurement. Daisy would need extra teaching time and attention paid to these visual aspects of her mathematics curriculum.

It would be appropriate to set in place classroom accommodations that would help Daisy to fulfil her potential, lessen her frustration and improve her self-confidence. These might include not marking her down for spelling errors in her written work, and providing her with extra time to complete written tests and examinations within the classroom. Another important accommodation would be to provide Daisy with an alternative means of expressing herself in written form, that is, through the use of computer technology. She was a poor speller and she had handwriting difficulties; using a word processor would enable Daisy to develop 'spellcheck' strategies, while the use of computer 'printouts' would improve her written presentation.

It was also suggested that Daisy's progress be monitored closely, with a formal review at age 9. This would provide an opportunity to update the picture in relation to the current status of Daisy's learning difficulty. It would also facilitate an evaluation of how much educational progress she had made during the interim period, using the present test results as a baseline against which to compare future levels of performance. Lastly, it would be appropriate at a review assessment to look ahead to Daisy's impending senior school needs and the continuing management issues arising from her learning difficulties.

Daisy's assessment findings, formulation and management recommendations are summarized in Table 12.1.

Case study 2 — Rupert

Rupert was a 5-year-old boy of average ability, but with early evidence of dyslexia. It is unusual to accept a child as young as 5 years for a formal assessment of early reading problems. However, there are circumstances in which this is justified, and Rupert proved to be one of those rare instances. He was referred by his parents because of concerns about his slow progress in establishing beginning reading skills and his tendency to be 'off task' and disruptive within the classroom of his previous school. Rupert had found it very hard to learn the names of colours and he was proving very slow to acquire alphabet knowledge. He was about to start at a new school, and with a mid-August birthday, his mother was querying whether he might benefit from being held back with a younger group of children. She wanted to make the decision before he started at his new school. There were concerns that if he were not appropriately placed and managed at his new school, he might well repeat the patterns of behaviour that had earned him a negative reputation at his previous school. Rupert's early developmental milestones were normal and he was a healthy child. Both his mother and older brother had experienced reading and spelling problems.

Assessing children as young as 5 years old, especially those whose teachers have complained about their behaviour, can challenge even an experienced psychologist or teacher. However, it soon became evident that Rupert had no difficulties in co-operating and concentrating in a structured

Table 12.1: Case Study 1 (Daisy) - Summary of assessment, formulation and management

Assessment		
Test	**IQ or centiles**	**Age level**
Ability tests		
WISC–III Verbal 10	IQ = 124 (superior)	
WISC–III Performance IQ	IQ = 105 (average)	
Attainment tests		
WORD Reading	12th centile	6y3m
WORD Spelling	25th centile	6y9m
Graded Nonword Reading	10th centile	6y
Handwriting		Below-average
WOND Mathematics	50th centile	7y+
Diagnostic tests		
WISC–III Digit Span (verbal short-term memory)	40th centile	6y6m
PAT Phoneme Deletion (phoneme segmentation)	10th – 25th centile	5–6y
PhAB Digit Naming Speed	2nd centile	
Complementary tests		
BAS visual memory	85th centile	Above-average

Formulation

Significant phonological dyslexia, with co-occurring spatial and fine motor deficits; compensatory resources include good verbal skills and visual memory

Management

- Relocation to a more supportive school with learning support resources
- Twice weekly learning support programme adopting phonologically based teaching techniques
- Support in acquiring visual-based mathematical concepts
- Classroom accommodations, to include use of a word processor and time allowances in school examinations
- Later review assessment to monitor progress and to address future educational needs.

one-to-one setting. Indeed, he coped admirably with a lengthy one-and-a-half-hour test session, punctuated by only two short rest breaks. He sat at the test table throughout without getting out of his seat and he was not unduly restless or distractible. It seemed highly improbable that Rupert had any fundamental concentration difficulties, although it was clear from earlier school reports that he did find it hard to stay on task within the larger classroom setting.

Because Rupert was only five at the time of referral, it was not possible to administer the WISC III intelligence scale. Instead, its downward extension, the Wechsler Pre-School and Primary Scale of Intelligence–Revised (WPPSI–R) (Wechsler, 1990) was given. This is constructed similarly to the WISC, but with more pictorially presented material appropriate to its younger standardization sample in the three- to seven-year age range. Rupert achieved a Verbal IQ of 106, a Performance IQ of 108 and a Full Scale IQ of 107 — well within the average range of ability.

Educational testing revealed that Rupert was making a slow start educationally, with reading being more affected than number skill. On the WPPSI–R Arithmetic test, he scored at the 4 years and 9 months level — only a little below his chronological age. However, his progress in reading was much poorer. Most standardized reading tests are normed from the 6-year level upwards and are consequently unsuitable for use with children as young as Rupert. Such tests also rarely have sufficient easy words to enable them to discriminate good versus poor readers at ages 5 and 6. Hatcher surmounted this problem by developing an Early Word Reading Test (Hatcher, Hulme and Ellis, 1994) that contains 42 of the most commonplace and simple words that children are likely to encounter in their reading experiences during their first two years at school. The test has been 'informally' standardized on several hundred children in Cumbria and London. Rupert was able to read only six out of 42 of these easy words, which placed him at barely the 5-year level. The words he read correctly were *stop, it, in, is, a, look*. He could not read other very simple words, such as *was, no, me, the*. What was even more striking was that Rupert had very limited letter knowledge. He was given the Letter Knowledge subtest from the PAT on which he scored 19/26, which was effectively at under the 4-year level. Thus, Rupert had made very little progress in establishing early reading skills, even though he had been in a formal school system for almost two years.

To explore why Rupert was making such a slow start in reading, he was given phonological tests that explored the range of processing skills advocated in the model of Wagner, Torgesen and colleagues. He was first of all given a memory for sentences test from the WPPSI–R on which he encountered little difficulty, scoring at the 5 years and 9 months level. His phonological awareness was evaluated by use of a range of tests that tapped implicit and explicit phonological segmentation skills and sound blending abilities. Rupert achieved a perfect score of eight out of eight on the Phoneme Completion subtest of the PAT, indicating that his simple or implicit phonological segmentation abilities were well established. He had yet, however, to achieve explicit segmentation skills that would enable him to manipulate phonemes within words. He failed to score at all on the Beginning Phoneme Deletion subtest, also from the PAT (none out of eight), which placed him at under the 4-year level. Rupert did not have any significant difficulty with phoneme blending; he scored at the 50th centile, that is, average range on Word Blending from the Comprehensive Test of Phonological Processing (CTOPP) (Wagner, Torgesen and Rashotte, 1999). Lastly, Rupert was given a naming speed task. Bearing in mind his difficulties in recognizing the letters of the alphabet, it was thought more appropriate to administer a naming speed task that did not require established knowledge of letters or numbers. He was, therefore, given the Rapid Colour Naming subtest from the CTOPP, on which he encountered enormous difficulty. He scored at only the first centile!

There are usually great reservations about applying a diagnostic label like dyslexia to a child as young as Rupert. However, it was clear from his learning profile that Rupert was markedly at risk of dyslexia. He was a child of normal ability who was making slow progress in establishing not only a basic sight vocabulary but also letter knowledge, in spite of having extensive exposure to print over almost the past two years. Rupert had a phonologically based learning difficulty that was characterized by underdeveloped phonological segmentation skills and especially poor naming speed (though he had been spared the short-term verbal memory difficulties that afflict sizeable numbers of dyslexic children). Although Rupert could blend sounds and segment words at an implicit level, he had yet to develop the crucial explicit segmentation skills that would permit him to acquire early decoding strategies. In addition, he had marked naming speed difficulties that suggested that he found it hard to access the phonological representations of words in his long-term memory store — hence his problems in learning colour names as a preschool child. Manis, Seidenberg and Doi (1999) suggested that children who exhibit naming speed problems find it very difficult to establish and memorize arbitrary associations between symbols. The first set of symbol associations that children encounter on entering elementary school are those of learning the connections between sounds and letters. It was thus not surprising that Rupert's alphabet knowledge acquisition had been so slow.

One of the first issues that needed to be addressed in the management of Rupert's learning difficulties was whether he should, on entering his new school, be placed with his own age group or whether he should be held back a year (the latter could be made all the easier by his having a late summer birthday). To some extent, this decision is not in the province of the assessor, but may be dictated by the policy statement of the school or the education authority, or even by the practicalities of place availability. Having said that, the advantages of holding Rupert back with a slightly younger group of children were not difficult to enumerate. First, Rupert would be afforded the time and opportunity to build up his basic literacy and numeracy skills before he faced the increased demands and pressures of the next class. Second, the work in the 'younger' class would be more in keeping with his present educational standards and would thus be more relevant and meaningful to him. Lastly, a change of school at the same time as being retained would not give him the experience of being left behind whilst his classmates moved on. It was important to recognize, though, that Rupert's repeating a school year did not constitute the solution to his difficulties. It merely reduced the academic demands and pressures on him while allowing him to profit from a recommended individual and specialist learning support programme.

Although Rupert was only 5 years old, the results of his assessment provided convincing evidence of his being dyslexic. Consequently, he required a special teaching programme that catered for his specific difficulties and his individual needs. It was recommended that Rupert be permitted a settling-in period at his new school, which would provide an opportunity for his teachers to get to know him and to see for themselves the difficulties he was experiencing and how they might be accommodated. It would then be necessary to set up a twice- or thrice-weekly one-to-one learning support programme that initially devoted a lot of time to training the three prerequisite skills that need to be in place before the child can acquire the alphabetic principle.

Rupert was clearly a logographic reader who was far from making the important transition to the alphabetic stage that is characterized by a child's acquisition of the alphabetic principle. How could his teacher help him to effect this necessary transition? First, he required explicit phonological awareness training. Encouragingly, when assessed, Rupert already had implicit segmentation ability, though not the explicit ability to manipulate sounds in words that would be necessary to promote the development of decoding skills. At least 10 minutes of each individual teaching session needed to be devoted to phonological training that particularly emphasized the emergence of explicit segmentation skill; so, for instance, phonological manipulation tasks such as adding, deleting, transposing and substituting phonemes in words. Alongside Rupert's phonological training, he needed a lot of practice and reinforcement of basic alphabetic sound-to-letter relations. The assessment established that Rupert could recognize by name or sound only 19 of the 26 letters of the alphabet, which placed him at under the 4-year level. A systematic letter training programme such as Letterland (Wendon, 1997) would be appropriate to his needs, to be backed up by frequent repetition, especially of the letters that he was finding particularly difficult. As a minimum, Rupert needed to know the names and sounds of all the vowels, together with the sounds of the consonants.

The final prerequisite needed before Rupert could acquire the alphabetic principle was that he established firm connections between his improving speech sound sensitivity and his experience of print — what Hatcher, Hulme and Ellis (1994) termed 'phonological linkage'. Carrying out phonological segmentation and manipulation exercises whilst representing their graphemic structure using plastic letters is an example of a suitable linkage exercise. Once Rupert had established the alphabetic principle, he should be able to respond to a structured phonic programme that begins by teaching him left-to-right decoding strategies with simple two-, three- and four-letter words. His knowledge of graphemes then needed to be extended beyond that of simple alphabetic letters to more complex units, such as consonant clusters, digraphs and diphthongs.

Because Rupert's dyslexia had been diagnosed at an unusually early age, it meant that he should reap the many educational and behavioural benefits of early intervention. However, one reservation about him having been diagnosed at so young an age was that we could not be as confident as we would like about the precision of the assessment levels. It was also necessary to be guarded about the exact status and severity of the dyslexic difficulty, as this can influence prognosis and long-term outcome. Consequently, it would be appropriate in Rupert's case to re-evaluate his general cognitive skills, his educational status and his specific phonological skills after approximately two years, that is, when he would be around 7 years of age. At this stage, it should be possible to make more precise statements about the severity of Rupert's difficulties and to be more confident in predicting the future course of his educational development and how it is likely to be affected by his dyslexia.

Rupert had not only experienced a worrying delay in his literacy development, but his parents and teachers also expressed concern about his behaviour within the classroom. He was frequently off-task and at times disruptive. It may have been that Rupert's behaviour reflected his increasing awareness of, and frustration over, his reading difficulties that, in turn, resulted in avoidance behaviour. It might be expected that, as he responded to an individual learning support programme of the type described above, Rupert's frustrations over his failure to progress would be reduced. This, in addition to his feeling more supported by parents and teachers, might well result in less avoidance behaviour and a decreased amount of disruptive classroom behaviour. To be fair, in Rupert's case, the situation was complicated even further by his having experienced a number of dramatic changes in his life over a comparatively short space of time; specifically, he had moved country, culture, home and school. It was recommended that Rupert be given a reasonable settling-in and adjustment period while his behaviour was monitored jointly by his parents and teachers. If, after a term or so, there were still concerns about his behaviour then clearly it would be necessary for Rupert and his parents to consult a clinical psychologist who advises on children's behavioural and emotional difficulties and needs.

Rupert's assessment, formulation and management recommendations are summarized in Table 12.2.

Table 12.2: Case Study 2 (Rupert) — Summary of assessment, formulation and management

Assessment		
Test	**IQ or centile**	**Age level**
Ability tests		
WPPSI–R Verbal IQ	IQ = 106 (average)	
WPPSI–R Performance IQ	IQ = 108 (average)	
Attainment tests		
Hatcher Early Word Reading test	N/A	Barely 5y
PAT Letter Knowledge	10th centile	< 4y
Graded Nonword Reading Test		N/A
Handwriting		Not assessed
WPPSI–R Arithmetic	40th centile	4y9m
Diagnostic tests		
WPPSI–R sentence memory	60th centile	5y9m
(Verbal short-term memory)		
PAT Phoneme Completion	75th centile	6y+
(implicit segmentation)		
PAT Phoneme Deletion	10th centile	5–6y
(explicit segmentation)		
CTOPP Word Blending	50th centile	5y6m
CTOPP Rapid Colour Naming	1st centile	< 4y
Complementary tests		
BAS Visual Memory	50th centile	5–6y

Formulation

Significantly 'at risk' of phonological dyslexia of developmental origin. Failure to establish explicit phonological segmentation skills has impaired the acquisition of decoding strategies. Poor naming speed suggests difficulties in accessing phonological representations in long-term memory, thus affecting letter knowledge acquisition.

Management

- Consideration of 'retention' with younger children, to reduce academic demands while allowing him to profit from a specific learning support programme
- Twice- to thrice- weekly learning support programme, emphasizing phonological awareness training, consolidation of letter knowledge skills and 'linkage' activities
- Review assessment at age 7, to confirm diagnosis and to determine severity and likely outcome
- Monitoring of behaviour, with later behaviour management intervention if problems persist.

Case study 3 — Patrick

Patrick was a 7-year-old epileptic boy with reading difficulties. He was referred by his consultant neurologist owing to concerns that his epilepsy might be affecting his educational development and progress. Patrick had had epilepsy since early infancy; his seizures were initially very difficult to control, but there had been a recent improvement in both frequency and severity of his fits. He was being gradually weaned off anti-epileptic medication. MRI scans had shown a right-sided epileptic focus.

Patrick's early speech was delayed. He had received intermittent speech therapy between the ages of 18 months and 5 years. Additionally, there were motor problems, for which Patrick attended both physiotherapy and occupational therapy. His parents and teachers also expressed concern about his poor attention, his difficulty in memorizing new information and his slow progress in reading. Patrick's special needs were recognized at his school, where he received two individual lessons per week in literacy and numeracy. There was a family history of dyslexia on father's side.

On the WISC III intelligence scale, Patrick achieved a Verbal IQ of 86, a Performance IQ of 77 and a Full-Scale IQ of 80. He was, therefore, a child of slightly lower than average ability, although his IQ was not actually outside the normal range. Patrick's verbal subtest scores clustered evenly around the low-average level, though he did show greater variability in his performance scores (having especial difficulty with the visual perception and spatial subtests). Given that Patrick's general abilities were on the weak side, it would be reasonable to expect his attainments in literacy and numeracy to fall short of age-expectation.

Patrick's reading, spelling and mathematical skills (WORD and WOND tests) fell consistently at the $6^1/_2$ year level; this was more than a year below his chronological age, although only marginally below the level to be expected given his abilities. He showed an understanding of only very concrete number concepts, he had yet to establish basic number bonds and he was dependent on counting on his fingers. Patrick's reading vocabulary was very limited and he could identify only 22 of the 26 letters of the alphabet. His ability to decode was restricted to simple three-letter consonant–vowel–consonant words; on the Graded Nonword Reading Test, he scored at under the 6-year-level. He made many non-phonetic spelling errors. Patrick's handwriting showed immature letter formation. A sample of his handwriting and spelling is shown in Figure 12.2.

Further diagnostic testing revealed that Patrick had memory difficulties, but not of the sort one expects to see in the dyslexic child. He scored at the 7-year level on the WISC III Digit Span subtest, only marginally below his chronological age and in keeping with his verbal abilities. Patrick did, however, have marked visual memory problems. He was given the Dot Locations subtest from The Children's Memory Scales (CMS) (Cohen, 1997) which requires the child

Figure 12.2: Sample of Patrick's handwriting and spelling.

to remember and to replicate a dot pattern on a grid by use of circular disks; he scored at only the third centile, which is well below average.

Patrick did, however, exhibit the phonological processing and decoding difficulties that we expect to see in the dyslexic child. He scored at the 5¹/₂ year level on both the Beginning and End Phoneme Deletion subtests from the PAT. As we have already seen, he was finding it very hard to read even very simple non-words.

Lastly, Patrick was given two subtests from the Test of Everyday Attention for Children (TEA-Ch). The first of these, Map Mission, assesses selective or focused attention; he scored at only the second centile. The second subtest, Score!, evaluates sustained attention. Again, Patrick obtained a very low centile score of three. These well-below-average scores on standardized tests of attention were in line with the behavioural observations made of Patrick; his attention span was very short, he was restless and distractible, and he tired quickly.

The formulation of Patrick's difficulties recognized that his cognitive presentation was complex, and reflected a number of deficits that have different causal origins. First, it was important to appreciate that Patrick exhibited mild generalized learning limitations that were reflected in his low-average IQ. Second, he had a phonological dyslexia which may well have been of developmental origin, bearing in mind the positive family history; he had poor phonological awareness, he found it hard to acquire alphabet knowledge and his decoding skills were very limited. Patrick exhibited two further difficulties that were likely to be of neurological origin, given his epileptic status. He had visual perceptual, spatial and visual memory deficits that were consistent with his right-sided epileptic focus. Also, he had attentional difficulties that are quite commonly observed in children who have an identified neurological problem.

Because Patrick had a number of difficulties that would be expected to impair his educational development, his management required a multifaceted approach that drew on both education and health resources.

Patrick was of low-average ability, but his IQ nonetheless fell within the normal range. Consequently, he would not be regarded as a child in need of special schooling. His needs should be met appropriately within a mainstream school. His teachers should be alerted to his slower-than-average rate of learning so that expectations of progress can be realistic and appropriate to his abilities. He would need to have new concepts introduced at a slower rate than that of his peers and he would require more repetition and reinforcement of new skills. Many children who exhibit slower rates of learning, in particular those like Patrick who have accompanying attentional problems, may profit from 'learning support assistance'. A learning support assistant is not a teacher but is an adult (with a relevant background and some training) who is allocated to work with a child for a specified number of hours in the week. The role of the assistant is to support the child by helping him or her to 'stay on task', reinforcing newly acquired skills and concepts, and generally facilitating access to the curriculum. Patrick was a child who would benefit from learning support assistance, especially during core lessons such as literacy and numeracy.

Patrick had literacy problems that were consistent with a dyslexic diagnosis. Consequently, he required a teaching programme that was similar in content to that recommended for Rupert. Patrick was a less able child so, clearly, new letter combinations and phonological/phonic strategies would need to be introduced at a slower pace, with more time allocated to reinforcement and practice.

Patrick had non-verbal learning difficulties that would continue to profit from physical therapies such as physiotherapy and occupational therapy. It was important to work on his handwriting skills, and to complement this by encouraging him to develop keyboarding and computing skills.

The effect of Patrick's attentional problems on his learning within the classroom would be lessened by the provision of learning support assistance. Additionally, it was important to put in place a programme that aimed to improve his attentional skills by setting targets for Patrick's achieving increased 'time on task'. This may be supported by his assistant, who was in a position to provide 'prompts' to help him maintain an attention set for a given activity, and who can provide appropriate rewards for task completion. Rewards might take the form of praise, or if something more concrete is needed, a star or sticker chart with 'back-up' treats.

Patrick's assessment, formulation and management recommendations are summarized in Table 12.3.

Table 12.3: Case Study 3 (Patrick) — Summary of assessment, formulation and management

Assessment		
Test	**IQ or centile**	**Age level**
Ability Tests		
WISC–III Verbal IQ	IQ = 86 (low–average)	
WISC–III Performance IQ	IQ = 77 (below average)	
Attainment tests		
WORD Reading test	16th centile	6y6m
PAT Letter Knowledge	< 10th centile	5y0m–5y6m
Graded Nonword Reading Test	< 10th centile	< 6y
WORD Spelling Test	18th centile	6y6m
Handwriting		Poor letter formation
WOND Mathematics	16th centile	6y m
Diagnostic tests		
WISC–III Digit Span (verbal short-term memory)	40th centile	7y0m
PAT Phoneme Deletion:		
Beginning sound	10th centile	5y6m
End sound	10th centile	5y6m
Complementary tests		
CMS visual memory	3rd centile	
TEA–Ch Map Mission	2nd centile	
TEA–Ch Score!	3rd centile	

Formulation

Patrick's low-average ability has implications for rate of learning. His phonological dyslexia, which is of probable developmental origin, is associated with phonological segmentation and decoding deficits. There are additional co-occurring attentional, visuospatial and visual memory difficulties of probable neurological origin.

Management

- Provision of learning support assistance to help Patrick access the curriculum and to support his attention control
- Twice- to thrice-weekly learning support programme, emphasizing phonological awareness training, consolidation of letter knowledge skills and 'linkage' activities
- Emphasis on slower introduction of new concepts and skills, accompanied by repetition and reinforcement
- Continuance of physical therapies to address visuospatial and related difficulties
- Setting in place an attention programme aimed at increasing attention span

Case study 4 — Amanda

Amanda was a 6-year-old girl with right-sided hemiplegia, who participated in a longitudinal research study of children suffering from congenital hemiplegia (see Neville and Goodman, 2000, for a comprehensive description of this neurological condition). Briefly, congenital hemiplegia arises as a result of a cerebrovascular accident (effectively, a stroke) which occurs during the second or third trimester of pregnancy. The damage may be to either the left or the right hemisphere of the brain and results in contralateral hemiparesis; MRI scans had shown that Amanda had a left-hemisphere injury with consequent right-sided hemiparesis that affected her gait and her hand control. She was a left-hander. Hemiplegic children have an elevated risk of epilepsy, and Amanda suffered from seizures, although these occurred infrequently (around twice per year) and were well controlled on anti-epileptic medication. Readers wishing to know more about the learning difficulties associated with childhood congenital hemiplegia are directed to a review article by Muter and Vargha-Khadem (2000).

Amanda attended a mainstream school. It was recognized that she had exceptional special needs. She received 15 hours per week of learning assistant support, and three individual teaching sessions with the school's special needs co-ordinator. Amanda attended a local hospital for physiotherapy. There was no family history of learning difficulties.

Amanda was assessed over a three-year period, initially at age 4, then again a year later at age 5 and, lastly, at age 6. The last assessment, conducted when Amanda was 6 years and 10 months old, is described below.

On the WISC III IQ scale, Amanda obtained a Verbal IQ of 90 and a Performance IQ of 72. Children who have congenital hemiplegia generally score within the normal range on IQ tests, provided their presentation is not complicated by the presence of seizures. We saw that Amanda suffered from seizures so it was no surprise to find that her IQ was lower than for the hemiplegic children in the study who were seizure free.

When a left-hemisphere brain injury is acquired in adulthood, it typically results in impairment of language skills, reflected in a selectively lowered Verbal IQ. However, this is not the case when neurological injury is incurred very early in life. A congenital injury takes place when the brain is still functionally plastic; that is, the localization of specific functions has not yet taken place. The early damaged brain is a remarkably adaptive organ; if a unilateral injury occurs before or at around the time of birth, the brain is still sufficiently plastic to enable a process of functional reorganization to take place. The brain reorganizes itself in such a way as to preserve important language functions, irrespective of the specific locus of injury. Thus, language functions may be a little depressed in congenital hemiplegia, but not significantly so.

If the language centre in the left hemisphere is damaged, other parts of the same hemisphere may take over language function. However, it is even more likely that homologous regions of the right hemisphere will come to subserve language functions — but at a price. If the right hemisphere is reassigned to take over at least some language functions then the skills usually subserved by this hemisphere will be sacrificed; that is, visuo-spatial abilities will become degraded. Consequently, hemiplegic children tend to exhibit Performance IQs that are significantly lower than their Verbal IQs. Amanda displayed the characteristic pattern of a congenital left-hemisphere-damaged hemiplegic child with seizures. Specifically, she had a slightly lower than average IQ, relatively well-preserved language skills but poor visuo-spatial ability.

Amanda's educational attainments were weakly developed. She could read only one word correctly from the BAS reading test (that is, *on*), which placed her at below the 6-year level. She could identify just 13 of the 26 letters of the alphabet (under the 4-year level on the PAT norms). Amanda was not given a formal spelling test. She was struggling with her handwriting. Her attempts at writing letters are shown in Figure 12.3. Amanda's mathematical skills were noted to be very poor; she scored at under the 6-year level on WOND Mathematics Reasoning.

Amanda's verbal memory appeared to be developing normally. She scored at the 45th centile ('average' range) on the WISC III Digit Span subtest. She also did well, scoring at the 50th centile, on the Memory for Stories subtest from The Children's Memory Scales (CMS); this suggested that Amanda had no difficulty in retaining and recalling context-based verbal information. She did, however, have difficulty with the visual memory test from the CMS (Dot Locations), on which she scored at only the 15th centile.

Figure 12.3 Amanda's letter writing.

Amanda's phonological awareness was very limited indeed. She scored at under the 5-year level on the Rhyme Detection test from the PAT. She could not score at all on the Rhyme Production test (also from the PAT), placing her at below the 4-year level. Amanda showed evidence of beginning to develop implicit phonological segmentation skills (5- to 5½ year level on the PAT Phoneme Completion test). She failed to score at all on the Phoneme Deletion test (placing her at under the 5-year level for explicit phonological segmentation skill).

Amanda's attention span was noticeably short when aged 4 to 5 years. However, by the time she was assessed at age 6, she was concentrating far better, and coped very well with a lengthy and demanding test session.

Amanda had learning difficulties that arose from neurological impairment. Her general cognitive abilities were mildly depressed, a probable consequence of her seizure condition. Like most children with congenital hemiplegia, Amanda's verbal abilities were relatively well preserved (despite her having a left-hemisphere injury). However, this sparing of her verbal skills, made possible by functional reorganization, seemed to have been achieved at the expense of Amanda's visuo-spatial abilities, which were poorly developed. Weaknesses in visual learning skills may affect mathematical development and handwriting. It was possible that Amanda's handwriting was further compromised by her being an enforced left-hander; no other family members were left-handed which led to a suspicion that had it not been for her hemiplegia Amanda would very likely have been a natural right-hander.

Amanda's literacy development was proving to be very slow. She was finding it hard to learn the alphabet and she had very weakly developed phonological awareness; these are core learning deficits that are expected in the developmentally dyslexic child. There was, however, no family history of reading difficulties, which raised the possibility that Amanda's literacy problems were of neurological origin. It might be hypothesized that it had been possible for Amanda's right hemisphere to take over most basic language functions (including verbal memory), but perhaps the right hemisphere was not able to assume higher-level phonological functions for which the left hemisphere may be uniquely specialized. So, in Amanda's case, the apparent dyslexia was not due to an inherited predisposition but rather to a neurological injury that had impaired that part of the brain which processes phonological information necessary to enable the child to develop reading skills.

The recommendations for the management of Amanda's learning difficulties shared common features with those given for Patrick. Amanda required learning assistant support, partly to help her to access the curriculum and to provide her with reinforcement experiences, but also to assist with the physical difficulties caused by her right-sided hemiplegia.

Amanda's individual literacy programme needed to emphasize a great deal of phonological awareness training that began at a very basic level. She was able to segment words at the level of the syllable but her poor rhyming ability suggested that Amanda had yet to develop onset-rime awareness. She had the beginnings of implicit phonological segmentation skill, but had not yet progressed to the level where she was able to manipulate phonemes within words. Consequently, Amanda's phonological awareness training programme needed to commence at the stage where she was working through very simple exercises that concentrated on sublexical units that are larger than the phoneme and that focus on the most easily identified sound positions (for instance, beginning sounds). Amanda also needed to engage in daily exercises that would help her to learn the alphabetic sound-to-letter relationships. Her programme should build in lots of opportunity for practice and reinforcement, necessitated by her slightly slower-than-average rate of learning and her poor visual memory.

Amanda required help, not only with her literacy skill development but also with her number work, which was very poor. Visual concepts within mathematics were likely to prove especially difficult for her to access and, consequently, she would need a lot of support in this area. The use of verbal explanations to convey visual concepts would be appropriate, given that Amanda's language skills were superior to her visual learning capabilities.

Because Amanda had poor visuomotor skills (and was an 'unnatural' enforced left-hander), she would need a lot of support from an occupational therapist and from her teacher in order to improve her hand control and to help her develop pencil skills. Like most hemiplegic children, she was dependent on technological aids to help her develop written expression capabilities.

Amanda's educational needs should be monitored closely and reviewed regularly. It might be that her intact right hemisphere would not have either sufficient capacity or degree of neuronal specialism to subserve higher-order language skills that characterize the cognitive profile of the older child. If Amanda encountered increasing difficulty in accessing the curriculum later in her elementary schooling, it might be appropriate to consider a special school setting for her. Amanda's assessment, formulation and management recommendations are summarized in Table 12.4.

Concluding remarks

It is important for any effective evaluation programme for the delayed reader to consider not only the teaching input that will be necessary to enable him or her to develop effective literacy skills but also other presenting factors within the individual child and family. Each reading-disabled child is different;

Table 12.4: Case Study 4 (Amanda) — Summary of assessment, formulation and management

Assessment		
Test	**IQ or centile**	**Age level**
Ability tests		
WISC–III Verbal IQ	IQ = 90 (average)	
WISC–III Performance IQ	IQ = 72 (below average)	
Attainment tests		
BAS Reading test	10th centile	< 6y
PAT Letter Knowledge	< 10th centile	< 4y
Handwriting		Poor letter formation
WOND Mathematics	7th centile	< 6y
Diagnostic tests		
WISC–III Digit Span (verbal short-term memory)	45th centile	6y6m
CMS Memory for Stories	50th centile	
PAT Rhyme Detection	10th centile	< 5y
PAT Rhyme Production	< 10th centile	< 4y
PAT Phoneme Completion	25th centile	5y0m–5y6m
PAT Phoneme Deletion	< 10th centile	< 4y
Complementary tests		
CMS visual memory	15th centile	

Formulation

Amanda's lower than average ability has implications for rate of learning. Her phonological dyslexia, which is of probable neurological origin, reflects the likelihood that her right hemisphere is unable to subserve higher-order phonological skills. There are additional co-occurring visuospatial and visual memory difficulties, the 'price' that is paid for sparing of verbal abilities following functional reorganization.

Management

- Provision of learning support assistance to help Amanda access the curriculum and to assist with her physical difficulties
- Regular literacy support programme, beginning with basic-level phonological awareness training and the establishment of letter knowledge skills
- Learning support in mathematics, to include verbalization methods to address visual concepts
- Strong emphasis on repetition and reinforcement of new concepts and skills
- Continuance of physical therapies to address visuospatial and motor difficulties
- Support to develop good computer skills
- Ongoing monitoring and review to address changing needs

although there may be some commonalities in terms of assessment and overall management, we also need to recognize that each child's diagnostic formulation and management plan must address his or her particular profile of strength and weakness. Enormous progress has been made over the past 10–15 years in our understanding of how children learn to read and of the specific difficulties experienced by reading-disabled children. This knowledge has informed assessment and teaching practices. However, there is still some way to go and much to be done before we are able to help all poor readers to achieve their full potential. The final chapter considers in brief some of the outstanding issues that future research needs to address.

CHAPTER 13

Questions we still have to answer

Throughout this book, the important contribution of phonological abilities to reading development in both normal and reading-disabled young readers has been highlighted. The implications for early reading practices within the classroom, and in particular for children whose phonological deficits are preventing them from becoming good readers, are not inconsiderable. However, there are still many unanswered questions, some of which are considered in this final chapter.

When do we screen and intervene?

The age at which children should be screened for phonological difficulties, and the stage at which intervention should begin, are important pedagogical issues. Phonological skills are less stable in young children, a factor that can impair their predictive relationship to later reading skill. Consequently, it may be inadvisable to attempt large-scale screening of pre-school children, and rather to concentrate screening and early identification around the first year of formal schooling. We have some evidence from studies that phonological tasks given to 5-year-olds are significant predictors of reading ability one to two years later. This is not necessarily the case for phonological measures administered to 4-year-olds; the predictive validity to later reading in this younger age group is much reduced.

There is also the question of children's developmental readiness to profit from a systematic phonological training programme and whether such programmes meet the needs of all late readers. It might be hypothesized that very able 5-year-olds with good oral language skills, but poor phonological capabilities, might respond rapidly to a phonological training programme. Other children of similar age with more generalized developmental language immaturities should perhaps be given more time to mature in their linguistic capabilities (if necessary, facilitated by speech and language therapy) before embarking on a structured phonological programme.

Which phonological skills should we assess and teach?

We have come a long way in our understanding of phonological awareness, but there remains controversy as to which skills (for instance, rhyming versus segmentation, phonological awareness versus naming speed) best predict reading development. This is an important issue because it has a bearing on which tasks are to be selected for screening and assessment procedures, and which skills are to be prioritized in training programmes. In general, the research to date suggests that phoneme segmentation tasks are better predictors of early reading than are rhyming tasks, and that phonological awareness tests have higher correlations with concurrent and later reading than do naming speed tasks. However, there are some detractors who would argue a strong case for the primacy of rhyming (Bryant) and for naming speed measures (Wolf) in predicting reading success and failure. Of course, prioritizing one particular task or skill does not preclude the use of another. We have seen that it is usual when assessing a dyslexic child to administer measures of naming speed and short-term verbal memory as well as tests of phonological awareness and non-word reading, even though the latter tests tend to be more strongly correlated with reading skill. The former measures may, nonetheless, provide additional information about a child's phonological profile that could help to determine prognosis and to influence management.

Do all children need phonological instruction?

Throughout this book I have adopted a perspective on reading development that strongly emphasizes the importance of early identification and intervention, with a strong advocacy for phonologically-based assessment and teaching methods. However, it is the case that screening every 5-year-old on phonological tasks and providing phonological training for all beginning readers may be both expensive and unnecessary. There is an emerging view, supported by recent work conducted by Hatcher and colleagues (Hatcher, Hulme and Snowling, 2001), that a large proportion of children do not require explicit phonological training, and that supplying this is merely attempting to teach them a capability they already have. It may be more economic, in terms of teaching time and resources, to screen all 5-year-olds on phonological (and letter knowledge) tasks, but to select for phonological training only those who fall below acceptable levels in terms of their phonological abilities. Further research is needed to determine what is the most time- and cost-effective way of delivering a phonological screening and training programme for children at the school entry stage.

How long and intensive should phonological training programmes be?

This is a very important question for us to consider, not just from the crucial economic point of view but also because this issue is likely to have a considerable bearing on the long-term efficacy and generalizability of phonological training programmes. Short phonological training courses may give the child a boost sufficient to propel him or her into the use of alphabetic reading strategies, but how sustained is the child's progress likely to be and will there be generalization to other literacy skills, in particular spelling? In fact, there is some evidence that even relatively short but focused phonological training schemes can result in long-term benefits.

Byrne and Fielding-Barnsley (1995) found that pre-school children who had been trained for just six to seven hours in phoneme identity and letter recognition continued to demonstrate a significant advantage over control children in decoding and reading comprehension when they were followed up three years later. However, in contrast, Torgesen et al. (1999) found that over 20 per cent of the reading at-risk children in their study, who had received frequent individual phonological-based instruction over a two-and-a-half-year period, still had significant reading problems at ages 7 to 8 years.

How do we explain these apparently contradictory results? A critical difference between these two studies is that in the research by Byrne and Fielding-Barnsley (1995) the children were normal unselected pre-school children. In the study by Torgesen et al. (1999) the children had been identified as at-risk poor readers on the basis of their performance on a phonological awareness and a letter knowledge test. The issue of resistance to treatment in selected subgroups of poor readers, such as those in the study by Torgesen et al. (1999), is discussed in more detail later in this chapter.

How advanced do children's phonological processing skills need to be before they obtain the maximum advantage out of these insights about the phonological structure of words? Is it enough that they are able to delete initial and final sounds or do they require a more advanced level of phonological manipulation that would enable them to delete a medial phoneme (for example, the /p/ from *split* to make *slit*)? These are questions that can be answered through empirical research. It is important, though, to remember that phonological skills develop in interaction with, and partly as a consequence of, exposure to print. Although purely auditory-based exercises form the beginning of most phonological training programmes, it is essential to introduce the graphemic forms of the sounds we wish to teach (whether as print or plastic letters). This ensures the forging of sound-to-letter connections, which is essentially what early reading is all about.

How do we train phonological abilities beyond those of phonological awareness?

Phonologically-based reading packages typically follow a developmental progression that teaches children phonological awareness skills, beginning with syllable and rime awareness and segmentation, before working through to the more advanced skills of phoneme segmentation and manipulation. They do not usually address other phonological abilities, such as verbal working memory or phonological processing speed.

It may be that little can be done to train children's memory capabilities or processing speed, and that even in the future we shall need to accept that the only trainable aspect of phonological skill is the awareness component. However, before we can be sure that this is the case, we need to know more about how phonological awareness relates to other phonological processing, and reading-related, skills, such as naming speed and phonological working memory. It may become increasingly relevant not only to measure these related abilities during assessment, as we do now routinely, but also to find ways of programming them into intervention packages. Is increased phonological processing speed merely a byproduct of more secure phonological awareness? If so training children's phonological segmentation capabilities to the point where they become automatized might also be expected to improve naming speed. If phonological awareness training results in changes in underlying phonological representations, one might expect changes in other aspects of the phonological system that are tapped by naming speed tasks. Alternatively, are naming speed tasks and phonological awareness tests measuring qualitatively different components of phonological skill that need to be addressed through different training strategies? Some researchers are now beginning to attempt to address these difficult questions, but there is still some way to go before we have any clear-cut answers.

Who are the treatment resisters?

Lastly, we need to address the crucial issue of individual responsivity to phonological awareness training programmes. We need to know which children are resistant to such training programmes and what factors predict responsivity. Do resistant children merely require more intensive, lengthier programmes or is it a question of looking at different types of teaching techniques? Some researchers have now begun to explore these issues.

Byrne (1998) suggested that children's verbal capabilities may affect the ease with which they acquire the alphabetic principle because Verbal IQ is a predictor of letter knowledge acquisition and phoneme awareness development. However, these effects are comparatively small, and it seems more probable that the primary influence of verbal ability is on higher-level processes, such as reading comprehension. Other studies have failed to find a connection between IQ level and response to treatment. In the intervention study by Hatcher, Hulme and Ellis (1994), neither Verbal nor Non-Verbal IQ predicted the children's response to intervention. The only predictors of training outcome in this study were the children's performance on a phoneme manipulation task and the type of instruction they received (a phonological training programme that made explicit links to print produced the best results).

Vellutino et al. (1996) studied 118 children who were split into two groups according to their responsivity to a tutorial reading programme. The children who made slow progress were significantly poorer than those who made fast progress (who had effectively 'caught up') on measures of letter knowledge at kindergarten and on measures of phoneme awareness and short-term verbal memory in grade 1. This suggests that children with pervasive and severe phonological and letter acquisition difficulties are likely to require more long-term specialist teaching intervention. Children who are delayed in reading but who have less marked phonological difficulties may need little more than a 'phonic boost' allied to increased print exposure to resolve their difficulties.

In the study by Torgesen et al. (1999), two of the most reliable predictors of responsivity to intervention were unrelated to cognitive or educational factors. Indeed, it was a social factor (parental educational level) and a behavioural factor (the child's attention control and activity level) that together best predicted responsivity to the training programme. Byrne (1998) suggested that intensity of instruction can influence the progress young children make in acquiring phoneme awareness and in improving their reading skills. In the study he conducted with Fielding-Barnsley (Byrne and Fielding-Barnsley, 1995), it was found that children who had received more frequent phonological training in groups of four to six children made faster progress than children taught according to the same programme but on a less frequent basis within a whole-class framework.

The issue of individual differences also draws attention to children's capacity for developing compensatory strategies. Is it possible in intervention programmes to promote children's syntactic, visual or other strengths in order to enable them to find alternative routes to word recognition beyond those of relying on their depleted phonological abilities? This is a very exciting area for intervention research; there are individual case reports that indicate that 'teaching to strengths' may be valuable for dyslexic children, but there are as yet no group-based studies that compare the relative efficacy of teaching to strengths as opposed to remediating the deficit.

Phonological awareness training and alphabetic coding skills are now becoming a feature of classroom teaching and of learning support programmes in many countries where children are learning an alphabetic orthography. To ensure that we optimize the benefits to beginner readers and children with reading difficulties, it will be necessary to further refine and develop phonologically-based assessment and intervention procedures. These, in turn, need to be grounded in empirical research and sound theory, a challenge that will be met as we move into the twenty-first century, with the goal of making long-term reading disability a rarity.

References

Achenbach TM (1991) Child Behavior Checklist. Burlington, Vt: University of Vermont, Department of Psychiatry.

Adams JW, Snowling MJ, Hennessy SM, Kind P (1999) Problems of behaviour, reading and arithmetic: assessments of co-morbidity using the Strengths and Difficulties Questionnaire. British Journal of Educational Psychology 69: 571–85.

Adams M (1990) Beginning to Read: Thinking and Learning about Print. Cambridge Mass: MIT Press.

Adams MJ, Huggins A (1993) Lundberg, Frost and Petersens' Program for Stimulating Phonological Awareness among Kindergarten, First-grade and Special Education students. Cambridge, Mass: BBN Labs, unpublished manuscript.

Altman G. (1997) The Ascent of Babel. Oxford: OUP.

Baddeley A, Hitch G (1974) Working memory. In: Bower GH (Ed.) The Psychology of Learning and Motivation, Volume 8. New York, NY: Academic Press; 47–90.

Baddeley A, Thomson N, Buchanan M (1975) Word length and the structure of short-term memory. Journal of Verbal Learning and Verbal Behaviour 14: 575–89.

Badian N (1994) Pre-school prediction: orthographic and phonological skills, and reading. Annals of Dyslexia 44: 3–25.

Badian, N (2000) Do pre-school orthographic skills contribute to prediction in reading? In: Badian N (Ed.) Prediction and Prevention of Reading Failure. Baltimore, Md: York Press; 31–56.

Ball EW, Blachman BA (1988). Phoneme segmentation training: effect on reading readiness. Annals of Dyslexia 38: 208–25.

Baron J (1979) Orthographic and word-specific mechanisms in children's reading of words. Child Development 50: 60–72.

Barron R (1991) Protoliteracy, literacy and the acquisition of phonological awareness. Learning and Individual Differences 3: 243–55.

Bishop DVM (1989) Unstable vergence control and dyslexia — a critique. British Journal of Ophthalmology 73: 223–35.

Bishop DVM, Adams C (1990) A prospective study of the relationship between specific language impairment, phonological disorders and reading retardation. Journal of Child Psychology and Psychiatry 31: 1027–50.

Blachman BA, Ball EW, Black RS, Tangel DM (1994) Kindergarten teachers develop phoneme awareness in low-income, inner city classrooms. Does it make a difference? Reading and Writing: An Interdisciplinary Journal 6: 1–18.

213

Blythe SG (2001) Neurological dysfunction as a significant factor in children diagnosed with dyslexia. Paper presented at the British Dyslexia Association International Conference, York, UK.

Boder E (1971) Developmental dyslexia: prevailing concepts. In: Mykelbust HR (Ed.) Progress in Learning Disabilities and a New Diagnostic Approach. New York, NY: Grune & Stratton; 293-321.

Boder E (1973) Developmental dyslexia: a diagnostic approach based on three atypical reading–spelling patterns. Developmental Medicine and Child Neurology 15: 663-87.

Bond GL, Dykstra R (1967). The co-operative research program on first grade reading instruction. Reading Research Quarterly 2: 5-142.

Bowey J (1986) Syntactic awareness in relation to reading skill and ongoing comprehension monitoring. Journal of Experimental Child Psychology 41: 282-99.

Bowey J (1995) Socio-economic status differences in pre-school phonological sensitivity and first-grade reading achievement. Journal of Educational Psychology 87: 476 -8.

Bowey J (2000) A case for early onset-rime sensitivity training in at-risk pre-school and kindergarten children. In: Badian N (Ed.) Prediction and Prevention of Early Reading Failure. Timonium, Md: York Press; 217-45.

Brady S, Shankweiler D, Mann V (1983) Speech perception and memory coding in relation to reading ability. Journal of Experimental Psychology 35: 345-67.

Bradley L, Bryant PE (1983) Categorising sounds and learning to read: a causal connection. Nature 301: 419-521.

Bradley L, Bryant PE (1985) Rhyme and Reason in Reading and Spelling. IARLD Monograph No. 1. Ann Arbor, Mich: University of Michigan Press.

Brennan F, Ireson J (1997) Training phonological awareness: a study to evaluate the effects of a program of metalinguistic games in kindergarten. Reading and Writing: An Interdisciplinary Journal 9: 241-63.

Brooks PL, Weeks SAJ (1998) A comparison of the responses of dyslexic, slow learning and control children to different strategies for teaching spelling. Dyslexia 4: 212-22.

Bruce LJ (1964) The analysis of word sounds by young children. British Journal of Educational Psychology 34: 158-74.

Bruck M, Genesee F (1995) Phonological awareness in young second language learners. Journal of Child Language 22: 307-24.

Bruck M, Treiman R (1992) Learning to pronounce words: the limitations of analogies. Reading Research Quarterly 27 375-8.

Brunswick N, McCrory E, Price CJ, Frith CD, Frith U (1999) Explicit and implicit processing of words and pseudowords by adult developmental dyslexics: a search for Wernicke's Wortschatz? Brain 1223: 1901-17.

Bryant PE (1998) Sensitivity to onset and rime does predict young children's reading: a comment on Muter, Hulme, Snowling and Taylor. Journal of Experimental Child Psychology 71: 29-37.

Bryant PE (2002). It doesn't matter whether onset and rime predicts reading better than phoneme awareness. Journal of Experimental Child Psychology 82: 2-28.

Bryant, PE, Bradley L (1980) Why children sometimes write words which they cannot read. In Frith U (Ed.) Cognitive Processes in Spelling. London: Academic Press; 335-70.

Bryant PE, MacLean M, Bradley L, Crossland J (1990) Rhyme, alliteration, phoneme detection and learning to read. Developmental Psychology 26: 429-38.

Burgess SR, Lonigan CJ (1998) Bi-directional relations of phonological sensitivity and pre-reading abilities: evidence from a pre-school sample. Journal of Experimental Child Psychology 70: 117–41.

Byrne B (1996) The learnability of the alphabetic principle: children's initial hypotheses about how print represents spoken language. Applied Psycholinguistics 17: 401–26.

Byrne B (1998) The Foundation of Literacy: The Child's Acquisition of the Alphabetic Principle. Hove: Psychology Press.

Byrne B, Fielding-Barnsley R (1989) Phonemic awareness and letter knowledge in the child's acquisition of the alphabetic principal. Journal of Educational Psychology 82: 805–12.

Byrne B, Fielding-Barnsley R (1991a) Sound Foundations. Sydney: Leydon Educational Publishers.

Byrne B, Fielding-Barnsley R (1991b) Evaluation of a program to teach phonemic awareness to young children. Journal of Educational Psychology 83: 451–5.

Byrne B, Fielding-Barnsley R (1993) Evaluation of a program to teach phonemic awareness to young children: A 1 year follow-up. Journal of Educational Psychology 85: 104–11.

Byrne B, Fielding-Barnsley R (1995) Evaluation of a program to teach phoneme awareness to young children: A 2- and 3-year follow-up and a new pre-school trial. Journal of Educational Psychology 87: 488–503.

Byrne B, Fielding-Barnsley R, Ashley L, Larsen K (1997) Assessing the child's and the environment's contribution to reading acquisition: what we know and what we don't know. In Blachman B (Ed.) Foundations of Dyslexia and Early Reading Acquisition. Hillsdale, NJ: Erlbaum and Associates; 265–85.

Byrne B, Fielding-Barnsley R, Ashley L (2000) Effects of phoneme identity training after 6 years: outcome level distinguished from rate of response. Journal of Educational Psychology 92: 659–67.

Caravolas M, Volin J (2001) Persistent phoneme awareness and word recognition deficits in Czech-speaking dyslexic children: Is the effect of transparent orthography overstated? Paper presented at the Society for the Scientific Study of Reading, SSSR. Boulder, Colorado.

Caron C, Rutter M (1991) Comorbidity in child psychopathology: concepts, issues and research strategies. Journal of Child Psychology and Psychiatry 32: 1063–80.

Casalis S, Louis-Alexandre M-F (2000) Morphological analysis, phonological analysis and learning to read French: a longitudinal study. Reading and Writing 12: 303–35.

Castles A, Coltheart M (1993) Varieties of developmental dyslexia. Cognition 47: 149–80.

Castles A, Datta H, Gayan J, Olson RK (1999) Varieties of developmental reading disorder: genetic and environmental influences. Journal of Experimental Child Psychology 72: 73–94.

Cataldo S, Ellis N (1988) Interactions in the development of spelling, reading and phonological skills. Journal of Research in Reading 11: 86–109.

Chall J (1967) Learning to Read: The Great Debate. New York, NY: McGraw-Hill.

Cipielewski J, Stanovich KE (1992) Predicting growth in reading ability from children's exposure to print. Journal of Experimental Child Psychology 54: 74–89.

Clarke P, Snowling M, Hulme C (2001) Rapid naming as a predictor of exception word reading. Poster presented at the Society for the Scientific Study of Reading, SSSR. Boulder, Colorado.

Clay M (1985) The Early Detection of Reading Difficulties (third edition). Oxford: Heinemann Educational.

Cohen MJ (1997) The Children's Memory Scales (CMS). San Antonio, Tex: Psychological Corporation, Harcourt Brace Publishers.

Connors CK (1996) Connors Rating Scales — Revised. London: Psychological Corporation.

Cossu G (1999) Biological constraints in literacy acquisition. Reading and Writing 11: 213-37.

Cossu G, Shankweiler D, Liberman I, Katz L, Tola G (1988) Awareness of phonological segments and reading ability in Italian children. Applied Psycholinguistics 9: 1-16.

Cunningham AE (1990) Explicit versus implicit instruction in phonemic awareness. Journal of Experimental Child Psychology 50: 429-44.

Cunningham AE, Stanovich KE (1997) Early reading acquisition and its relation to reading experience and ability 10 years later. Developmental Psychology 33: 934-5.

Cunningham AE, Stanovich KE (1998) The impact of print exposure on word recognition. In Metsala JE, Ehri LC (eds) Word Recognition in Beginning Literacy. Mahwah, NJ: Erlbaum; 235-62.

Denkla MB, Rudel RG (1976) Rapid automatised naming (RAN): dyslexia differentiated from other learning disabilities. Neuropsychologia 14: 471-9.

DeFries JC, Alarcon M, Olson RK (1997) Genetic etiologies of reading and spelling deficits: developmental differences. In Hulme C, Snowling M (eds) Dyslexia: Biology, Cognition and Intervention. London: Whurr Publishers; 20-37.

DeFries JC, Fulker DW, LaBuda MC (1987) Reading disability in twins: evidence for a genetic etiology. Nature 329: 537-9.

Doyle, J. (1996). Dyslexia: An Introductory Guide. London: Whurr Publishers.

Duncan LG, Seymour PHK, Hill S (1997) How important are rhyme and analogy in beginning reading? Cognition 63: 171-208.

Duncan LG, Seymour PHK (2000) Phonemes and rhyme in the development of reading and metaphonology: the Dundee longitudinal study. In Badian N (Ed.) Prediction and Prevention of Reading Failure. Timonium, Md: York Press Inc.; 275-97.

Dunlop P (1972) Dyslexia: the orthoptic approach. Australian Journal of Orthoptics 12: 16-20.

Dunn LN, Dunn LM (1981) Peabody Picture Vocabulary Test. Circle Pines, Minn: American Guidance Service.

Dunn LN, Dunn LM, Whetton C (1982) British Picture Vocabulary Scale. Windsor: NFER-Nelson.

Dunn LN, Dunn LM, Whetton C, Burley J (1997) British Picture Vocabulary Test — Revised. Windsor: NFER-Nelson.

Ehri LC (1992) Reconceptualising the development of sight word reading and its relationship to recoding. In: Gough PB, Ehri LC, Treiman R (eds) Reading Acquisition. Hillsdale, NJ: Erlbaum Associates; 107-43.

Ehri LC, Robbins C (1992) Beginners need some decoding skills to read words by analogy. Reading Research Quarterly 27: 13-25.

Ehri LC, Wilce LS (1985) Movement into reading: is the first stage of printed word learning visual or phonetic? Reading Research Quarterly 20: 163-79.

Elbro C, Borstrom I, Petersen D (1998) Predicting dyslexia from kindergarten: the importance of distinctness of phonological representations of lexical items. Reading Research Quarterly 33: 39-60.

Elliott CD (1990) Differential Ability Scales: Introductory and Technical Handbook. New York, NY: Harcourt Brace Jovanovich/Psychological Corporation.

Elliott CD, Murray DJ, Pearson LS (1983). British Abilities Scales. Windsor: NFER-Nelson.

Feagans L, Farran DC (1982) The Language of Children Reared in Poverty: Implications for Evaluation and Intervention. New York, NY: Academic Press.

Feitelson D, Goldstein Z (1986) Patterns of book ownership and reading to young children in Israeli school oriented and nonschool oriented families. The Reading Teacher 39: 924–30.

Fielker D (1997) Language Games for the Reinforcement of Language Awareness. Translation from the program developed by J Frost, A Lonnegaard (1995). Unpublished manuscript.

Fisher SE, Marlow AJ, Lamb J, Maestrini E, Williams DF, Richardson AJ et al. (1999). A quantitative trait locus on chromosome 6p influences different aspects of developmental dyslexia. American Journal of Human Genetics 64: 146–56.

Fisher SE, Francks C, Marlow AJ, MacPhie IL, Newbury DE, Cardon LR et al. (2002) Independent genome-wide scans identifying a chromosome 18 quantitative trait locus influencing dyslexia. Nature Genetics 30: 86.

Flynn JM (2000) From identification to intervention: improving kindergarten screening for risk of reading failure. In: Badian N (Ed.) Prediction and Prevention of Reading Failure. Timonium, Md: York Press Inc.; 133–52.

Flynn J, Rahbar M (1993) Effects of age of school entrance and sex on achievement: implications for paediatric counselling. Developmental and Behavioural Paediatrics 14: 304–7.

Fowler AE (1991) How early phonological development might set the stage for phoneme awareness. In: Brady S, Shankweiler D (eds) Phonological Processes in Literacy: A tribute to Isabelle Y. Liberman. Hillsdale NJ: Erlbaum Associates; 97–118.

Fox B, Routh DK (1975) Analysing spoken language into words, syllables and phonemes: a developmental study. Journal of Psycholinguistic Research 4: 331–42.

Frith U (1985) Beneath the surface of developmental dyslexia. In: Patterson K, Coltheart M, Marshall J (eds) Surface Dyslexia. London: Routledge & Kegan-Paul; 301–30.

Frith U (1997) Brain, mind and behaviour in dyslexia. In Hulme C, Snowling M (eds) Dyslexia: Biology, Cognition and Intervention. London: Whurr Publishers; 1–19.

Frith C, Frith U (1996) A biological marker for dyslexia. Nature 382: 19–20.

Frith U, Happe F (1998) Why specific developmental disorders are not specific: online and developmental effects of autism and dyslexia. Developmental Science 1: 267–72.

Frith U, Snowling M (1983) Reading for meaning and reading for sound in autistic and dyslexic children. British Journal of Developmental Psychology 1: 329–42.

Frith U, Wimmer H, Landerl K (1998) Differences in phonological recoding in German and English speaking children. Scientific Studies of Reading 2: 31–54.

Frederickson N, Frith U, Reason R (1997) Phonological Assessment Battery (PhAB). Windsor: NFER-Nelson.

Gallagher A, Frith U, Snowling MJ (2000) Precursors of literacy delay among children at genetic risk of dyslexia. Journal of Child Psychology and Psychiatry 41: 203–13.

Gathercole S, Baddeley A (1989) Development of vocabulary in children and short-term phonological memory. Journal of Memory and Language 28: 200–13.

Gathercole S, Baddeley A (1990) Phonological memory deficits in language disordered children: is there a causal connection? Journal of Memory and Language 29: 336–60.

Gathercole S, Baddeley A (1996) CNRep: Children's Nonword Repetition Test. London: Psychological Corporation, Harcourt.

Gathercole S, Baddeley A, Willis C (1991) Differentiating phonological memory and awareness of rhyme: reading and vocabulary development in children. British Journal of Psychology 82: 387–406.

Gayan J, Olson R (1999) Genetic and environmental influences on individual differences in IQ, phonological awareness, word recognition, phonemic and orthographic decoding. Poster presented at the meeting of the Society for the Scientific Study of Reading, Montreal, Canada.

Geschwind N, Levitsky W (1968) Human brain: left–right asymmetries in temporal speech region. Science 161: 186–7.

Gilger JW, Pennington BF, DeFries JC (1991) Risk for reading disability as a function of parental history in three family studies. Reading and Writing 3: 205–18.

Gillham WEC, Hesse KA (1976) The Basic Number Screening Test. Sevenoaks: Hodder & Stoughton.

Gipstein M, Brady SA, Fowler A (2000) Questioning the roles of syllables and rimes in early phonological awareness. In: Badian N (Ed.) Prediction and Prevention of Early Reading Failure. Timonium, Md: York Press Inc.; 179–215.

Glushko RJ (1979) The organisation and activation of orthographic knowledge in reading aloud. Journal of Experimental Psychology: Human Perception and Performance 5: 674–91.

Goodman R (1997) The Stengths and Difficulties Questionnaire. Journal of Child Psychology and Psychiatry 38: 581–6.

Goswami U (1986) Children's use of analogy in learning to read: a developmental study. Journal of Experimental Child Psychology 42: 73–83.

Goswami U (1990) A special link between rhyming skills and the use of orthographic analogies by beginning readers. Journal of Child Psychology and Psychiatry 31: 301–11.

Goswami U (1994) Reading by analogy: theoretical and practical perspectives. In: Hulme C, Snowling M (eds) Reading Development and Dyslexia. London: Whurr Publishers; 18–30.

Goswami U, Bryant PE (1990) Phonological Skills and Learning to Read. London: Erlbaum Associates.

Goulandris N (1989). Emergent Spelling: The Development of Spelling Strategies in Young Children. University of London: PhD Thesis.

Goulandris N (1996) Assessing reading and spelling skills. In: Snowling M, Stackhouse J (eds) Dyslexia, Speech and Language: A Practitioner's Handbook. London: Whurr Publishers; 77–107.

Goulandris N, McIntyre A, Snowling MJ, Bethel JM, Lee JP (1998) A comparison of dyslexic and normal readers using orthoptic assessment procedures. Dyslexia 4: 30–48.

Greany K, Tunmer WE, Chapman J (1997) The use of rime-based analogy training as an intervention strategy for reading-disabled children. In: Blachman B (Ed.) Foundations of Reading Acquisition and Dyslexia. Hillsdale, NJ: Erlbaum Associates; 327–45.

Grigorenko EL (2001) Developmental dyslexia: an update on genes, brains and environments. Journal of Child Psychology and Psychiatry 42: 91–125.

Grigorenko El, Wood FB, Meyer MS, Hart LA, Speed WC, Shuster A et al. (1997) Susceptibility loci for distinct components of developmental dyslexia on chromosomes 6 and 15. American Journal of Human Genetics 60: 27–39.

Hagtvet B (2000) Prevention and prediction of reading problems. In: Badian NA (Ed.) Prediction and Prevention of Reading Failure. Timonium, Md: York Press Inc.; 105–31.

Hansen J, Bowey JA (1994) Phonological analysis skills, verbal working memory and reading ability in second grade children. Child Development 65: 938-50.

Harm MW, Seidenberg MS (1999) Phonology, reading acquisition and dyslexia: insight from connectionist models. Psychological Review 106: 491-528.

Hatcher P (1994) Sound Linkage. London: Whurr Publishers.

Hatcher P (2000) Sound Linkage (second edition). London: Whurr Publishers.

Hatcher P (1996) Practising sound links in reading intervention with children. In: Snowling M, Stackhouse J (eds) Dyslexia, Speech and Language: A Practitioner's Handbook. London: Whurr Publishers;146-70.

Hatcher P, Hulme C, Ellis AW (1994) Ameliorating early reading failure by integrating the teaching of reading and phonological skills: the Phonological Linkage hypothesis. Child Development 65: 41-57.

Hatcher P, Hulme C, Snowling M (2001) Training rhyme and phoneme skills facilitates reading through phoneme awareness. Paper presented at Society for Scientific Study of Reading, SSSR, Boulder, Colorado.

Hecht SA, Burgess SR, Torgesen JK, Wagner RK, Rashotte CA (2000) Exploring social class differences in growth of reading skills from the beginning of kindergarten through fourth grade: the role of phonological awareness, rate of access and print knowledge. Reading and Writing: An Interdisciplinary Journal 12: 99-127.

Heath SM, Hogben JH, Clark CD (1999) Auditory temporal processing in disabled readers with and without oral language delay. Journal of Child Psychology and Psychiatry 40: 637-47.

Hoover W, Gough PB (1990) The simple view of reading. Reading and Writing: An Interdisciplinary Journal 2: 127-60.

Hulme C (1988) The implausibility of low-level visual deficits as a cause of children's reading difficulties. Cognitive Psychology 5: 369-74.

Hulme C, MacKenzie S (1992) Working Memory and Severe Learning Difficulties. Hove: Erlbaum Associates.

Hulme C, Roodenrys S (1995) Verbal working memory development and its disorders. Journal of Child Psychology and Psychiatry 36: 373-98.

Hulme C, Roodenrys S, Schweickert R, Brown GA, Martin S, Stuart G (1997) Word frequency effects on short-term memory tasks: evidence for a redintegration process in immediate serial recall. Journal of Experimental Psychology: Learning, Memory and Cognition 23: 1217-32.

Hulme C, Muter V, Snowling M (1998) Segmentation does predict early progress in learning to read better than rhyme: a reply to Bryant. Journal of Experimental Child Psychology 71: 39-44.

Hulme C, Hatcher PJ, Nation K, Brown A., Adams J, Stuart G (2002) Small but powerful: phoneme awareness is a better predictor of early reading skill than onset-rime awareness. Journal of Experimental Child Psychology 82: 2-28.

Hulme C, Snowling M (1992) Deficits in output phonology: an explanation of reading failure? Cognitive Neuropsychology 9: 47-72.

Hulme C, Snowling M, Quinlan P (1991) Connectionism and learning to read: steps towards a phonologically plausible model. Reading and Writing 3: 159-68.

Hynd GE, Hiemenz JR (1997) Dyslexia and gyral morphology variation. In: Hulme C, Snowling M (eds) Dyslexia: Biology, Cognition and Intervention. London: Whurr Publishers; 38-58.

Iverson S, Tunmer WE (1993). Phonological processing and the reading recovery program. Journal of Educational Psychology 85: 112-26.

Johnston R, Anderson M, Holligan C (1996) Knowledge of the alphabet and explicit awareness of phonemes in pre-readers: the nature of the relationship. Reading and Writing: An Interdisciplinary Journal 8: 217-34.

Katz RB, Shankweiler D, Lieberman IY (1981) Memory for item order and phonetic recoding in the beginning reader. Journal of Experimental Psychology 82: 474-84.

Katz RB, Healy AF, Shankweiler D (1983) Phonetic coding and order memory in relation to reading proficiency: a comparison of short-term memory for temporal and spatial order information. Applied Psycholinguistics 4: 229-50.

Kirk SA, McCarthy JJ, Kirk W (1968) Illinois Test of Psycholinguistic Abilities, ITPA — Revised. Chicago, Ill: University of Illinois.

Larsen JP, Hoien P, Lundberg I, Odegaard H (1990) MRI investigation of the size and symmetry of the planum temporale in adolescents with developmental dyslexia. Brain and Language 39: 289-301.

Layton L, Deeny K, Upton G, Tall, G (1998) A pre-school programme for children with poor phonological awareness: effects on reading and spelling. Journal of Research in Reading 21: 36-52.

Lefly DL, Pennington BF (1996) Longitudinal study of children at high family risk for dyslexia: the first two years. In: Rice M (Ed.) Toward a Genetics of Language. Mahwah, NJ: Lawrence Erlbaum Associates; 49-76.

Liberman IY, Shankweiler D, Fischer FW, Carter B (1974) Reading and the awareness of language segments. Journal of Experimental Child Psychology 18: 201-12.

Lindamood C, Lindamood P (1984) Auditory Discrimination in Depth. Allen, Tex: DLM/Teaching Resources.

Lloyd S (1992) The Phonics Handbook. Chigwell: Jolly Learning.

Lloyd S (1998) The Phonics Handbook (third edition). Chigwell: Jolly Learning.

Lonigan CJ, Burgess S, Anthony JL, Barker TA (1998) Development of phonological sensitivity in 2- to 5-year old children. Journal of Educational Psychology 90: 294-311.

Lonigan CJ, Anthony JL, Dyer S (1996) The influence of the home literacy environment on the development of literacy skills in children from diverse economic backgrounds. Paper presented at the Annual Convention of the American Educational Research Institution, New York.

Lord R, Hulme C (1987) Kinaesthetic sensitivity of normal and clumsy children. Developmental Medicine and Child Neurology 29: 72-5.

Lovegrove W, Martin F, Slaghuis W (1986) A theoretical and experimental case for a visual deficit in specific reading disability. Cognitive Neuropsychology 3: 225-67.

Lundberg I (1994) Reading difficulties can be predicted and prevented: a Scandinavian perspective on phonological awareness and reading. In: Hulme C, Snowling M (eds) Reading Development and Dyslexia. London: Whurr Publishers; 180-99.

Lundberg I, Frost J Petersen O-P (1988) Effects of an extensive program for stimulating phonological awareness in pre-school children. Reading Research Quarterly 23: 264-84.

Lundberg I, Olofsson A, Wall S (1980) Reading and spelling in the first school years predicted from phonemic awareness skills in kindergarten. Scandinavian Journal of Psychology 21: 159-73.

MacLean M, Bryant PE, Bradley PE (1987) Rhymes, nursery rhymes and reading in early childhood. Merrill-Palmer Quarterly 33: 255-81.

Manis FR, McBride-Chang C, Seidenberg MS, Keating P, Doi LM, Munson B et al. (1997) Are speech perception deficits associated with developmental dyslexia? Journal of Experimental Child Psychology 66: 211-35.

Manis FR, Seidenberg MS, Doi LM, McBride-Chang C, Petersen A (1996) On the bases of two subtypes of developmental dyslexia. Dyslexia 58: 157-95.

Manis F, Seidenberg M, Doi, L (1999) See Dick RAN: Rapid naming and the longitudinal prediction of reading subskills in first and second graders. Scientific Studies of Reading 3: 129-57.

Manly T, Robertson IH, Anderson V, Nimmo-Smith I (1998) The Test of Everyday Attention for Children (TEA-Ch). Bury St Edmunds: Thames Valley Test Co.

Manly T, Anderson V, Nimmo-Smith I, Turner A, Watson P, Robertson IH (2001) The differential assessment of children's attention: the Test of Everyday Attention for Children (TEA-Ch), normative sample and ADHD performance. Journal of Child Psychology and Psychiatry 42: 1065-81.

Mann VA (1986) Phonological awareness: the role of reading experience. Cognition 24: 65-92.

Mann VA, Liberman IY, Shankweiler D (1980). Children's memory for sentences and word strings in relation to reading ability. Memory and Cognition 8: 329-35.

Marshall C, Snowling M, Bailey PJ (2001) The Effect of a verbal learning strategy on rapid auditory processing: Evidence from normal and dyslexic readers. Poster presented at the Society for the Scientific Study of Reading (SSSR), Boulder, Colorado.

Maughan B (1994) Behavioural development and reading disabilities. In: Hulme C, Snowling M (eds) Reading Development and Dyslexia. London: Whurr Publishers; 128-43.

Maughan B (1995) Long-term outcomes of developmental reading problems. Journal of Child Psychology and Psychiatry 36: 357-71.

Maughan B (2000) Age At Onset: Variations in risk for conduct problems. Paper presented at Association for Child Psychology and Psychiatry 4th European Conference. London, January 2000.

Metsala J (1999) Young children's phonological awareness and non-word repetition as a function of vocabulary development. Journal of Educational Psychology 91: 3-19.

Mody M, Studdert-Kennedy M, Brady S (1997) Speech perception deficits in poor readers: auditory processing or phonological coding? Journal of Experimental Child Psychology 58: 112-23.

Morais J, Cary L, Alegria J, Bertolson P (1979) Does awareness of speech as a sequence of phones arise spontaneously? Cognition 7: 323-31.

Morgan J, Willows D (1996) Early phonological awareness training for at-risk children in junior kindergarten. Paper presented at the National Reading Conference, Charleston, SC, December.

Murray, BA (1998) Gaining alphabetic insight: Is phoneme manipulation skill or identity knowledge causal? Journal of Educational Psychology 90: 461-75.

Muter V, Snowling M (1998) Concurrent and longitudinal predictors of reading: the role of metalinguistic and short-term memory skills. Reading Research Quarterly 33: 320-37.

Muter V, Vargha-Khadem F (2000) Neuropsychology and educational management. In: Neville B, Goodman R (eds) Congenital Hemiplegia. London: MacKeith Press; 179-94.

Muter V, Diethelm K (2001) The contribution of phonological skills and letter knowledge to early reading in a multilingual population. Language Learning 51: 187-219.

Muter V, Snowling M, Taylor S (1994) Orthographic analogies and phonological awareness: their role and significance in early reading development. Journal of Child
Psychology and Psychiatry 35: 293–330.

Muter V, Hulme C, Snowling M (1997) The Phonological Abilities Test, PAT. London: The
Psychological Corporation.

Muter V, Hulme C, Snowling M, Taylor S (1998) Segmentation, not rhyming predicts early
progress in learning to read. Journal of Experimental Child Psychology 71: 3–27.

Muter V, Hulme C, Snowling M, Stevenson J (Submitted) Phonemes, rimes and language
skills as foundations of early reading development: evidence from a longitudinal latent
variable study.

McDougall S, Hulme C, Ellis AW, Monk A (1994) Learning to read: the role of short-term
memory and phonological skills. Journal of Experimental Child Psychology 58: 112–33.

McPhillips M, Hepper PG, Mulhern G (2000) Effects of replicating primary-reflex movements on specific reading difficulties in children: a randomised double-blind controlled trial. Lancet 355: 537–41.

Naglieri JA (1996) Naglieri Nonverbal Ability Test (NNAT). London: Psychological
Corporation.

Nation K, Snowling M (1998) Contextual facilitation of word recognition: evidence from
dyslexia and poor reading comprehension. Child Development 69: 996–1011.

Nation K, Allen R, Hulme C (2001) The limitations of orthographic analogy in early reading development: performance on the clue word task depends upon phonological
priming and elementary decoding skill, not the use of orthographic analogy. Journal of
Experimental Child Psychology 80: 75–94.

Neale M (1989) Neale Analysis of Reading Ability — Revised. Windsor: NFER-Nelson.

Neale M (1997) Neale Analysis of Reading Ability II (NARA II). Windsor: NFER-Nelson.

Neville B, Goodman R (2000) Congenital Hemiplegia. London: MacKeith Press.

Nicolson RI, Fawcett AJ (1996). The Dyslexia Early Screening Test. London: Psychological
Corporation.

Nikolopoulos DS (1999) Cognitive and Linguistic Predictors of Literacy Skills in the Greek
Language. The Manifestation of Reading and Spelling Difficulties in the Greek
Language. University College London: Unpublished PhD Thesis.

Olson R, Foltz G, Wise B (1986) Reading instruction and remediation with the aid of computer speech. Behavior Research Methods, Instruments and Computers 18: 93–9.

Olson R, Wise B (1992) Reading on the computer with orthographic and speech feedback: an overview of the Colorado Remedial Reading Project. Reading and Writing: An
Interdisciplinary Journal 4: 107–44.

Olson R, Wise B, Connors F, Rack J, Fulker D (1989) Specific deficits in component reading and spelling skills: genetic and environmental influences. Journal of Learning
Disabilities 22: 339–49.

Paulesu E, Frith U, Snowling M, Gallagher A, Morton J, Frakowiak R et al. (1996) Is developmental dyslexia a disconnection syndrome? Evidence from PET scanning. Brain
119: 143–57.

Plaut D, McClelland J, Seidenberg M, Patterson K (1996) Understanding normal and
impaired reading: computational principles in quasi-regular domains. Psychological
Review 103: 56–115.

Pennington BF, Grossier D, Welsh MC (1993) Contrasting cognitive defects in attention
deficit hyperactivity disorder vs reading disability. Developmental Psychology 29:
511–23.

Pennington BF, Filipek PA, Churchill J, Kennedy DN, Lefly D, Simon JH et al. (1999) Brain morphometry in reading disabled twins. Neurology 53: 723-9.

Perfetti C, Beck I, Bell L, Hughes C (1987) Phonemic knowledge and learning to read are reciprocal: a longitudinal study of first grade children. Merrill-Palmer Quarterly 33: 283-319.

Phillips G, McNaughton S (1990) The practice of storybook reading to pre-school children in mainstream New Zealand families. Reading Research Quarterly 25: 196-212.

Pinker S (1994) The Language Instinct: The New Science of Language and Mind. London: Penguin Press.

Rabin M, Wen XL, Hepburn M, Lubs HA, Feldman E, Duara R (1993) Suggestive linkage of developmental dyslexia to chromosome 1. Lancet 342: 178.

Rack J, Hulme C, Snowling M, Wightman J (1994) The role of phonology in young children's learning of sight words: the direct mapping hypothesis. Journal of Experimental Child Psychology 57: 42-71.

Rack J, Snowling M, Olson R (1992) The non-word reading deficit in developmental dyslexia: a review. Reading Research Quarterly 27: 29-53.

Ravens JC, Court JH, Ravens J (1978) Manual for Ravens Progressive Matrices and Vocabulary Scales. London: HK Lewis.

Raz IS, Bryant PE (1990) Social background, phonological awareness and children's reading. British Journal of Developmental Psychology 8: 209-25.

Renfrew C (1969) The Bus Story — A Test of Continuous Speech. Published by the author, North Place, Old Headington, Oxford.

Reznick JS, Goldfield BA (1992) Rapid change in lexical development in comprehension and production. Developmental Psychology 28: 406-13.

Reynell J (1977) Reynell Developmental Language Scales — Revised. Windsor: NFER-Nelson.

Richardson AJ, Calvin CM, Clisby C, Schoenheimer DR, Montgomery P, Hall JA et al. (2000) Fatty acid deficiency signs predict the severity of reading and related difficulties in dyslexic children. Prostaglandins, Leukotrenes and Fatty Acids 63: 69-75.

Richardson AJ, McDaid AM, Calvin CM, Higgins CJ, Puri BK (2001) Treatment with highly unsaturated fatty acids can reduce ADHD Symptoms in children with specific learning difficulties: A randomised controlled trial. Paper presented at the British Dyslexia Association International Conference, York, UK.

Rohl M, Pratt C (1995) Phonological awareness, verbal working memory and acquisition of literacy. Reading and Writing: An Interdisciplinary Journal 7: 327-60.

Rust J (1996) Wechsler Objective Numerical Dimensions (WOND). London: The Psychological Corporation, Harcourt Brace.

Rust J, Golombok S, Trickey G (1993) Wechsler Objective Reading Dimensions, WORD. London: The Psychological Corporation, Harcourt Brace.

Rutter M, Tizard J, Whitmore K (eds) (1970) Education, Health and Behaviour. London: Longmans.

Rutter M, Yule W (1975) The concept of specific reading retardation. Journal of Child Psychology and Psychiatry 16: 181-97.

Savage R (1997) Do children need concurrent prompts in order to use lexical analogies in reading? Journal of Child Psychology and Psychiatry 38: 235-46.

Sawyer D (1987) Test of Awareness of Language Segments, TALS. Austin, Tex: Pro-Ed.

Scarborough H (1990) Very early language deficits in dyslexic children. Child Development 61: 1728-43.

Scarborough H (1991) Antecedents to reading disability: pre-school language development and literacy experiences of children from dyslexic families. Reading and Writing 3: 219–33.

Scarborough H (1998) Early identification of children at risk for reading disabilities. In: Shapiro BK, Accardo PJ, Capute AJ (eds) Specific Reading Disability: A View of the Spectrum. Timonium, Md: York Press; 75–119.

Scarborough H, Dobrich W (1994) On the efficacy of reading to pre-schoolers. Developmental Review 14: 245–302.

Schneider W, Kaspert A, Roth E, Vise M, Marx H (1997). Short- and long-term effects of training phonological awareness in kindergarten: evidence from two German studies. Journal of Experimental Psychology 66: 311–40.

Schneider W, Naslund JC (1993) The impact of metalinguistic competencies and memory capacity on reading and spelling in elementary schools: results of the Munich longitudinal study on the genesis of individual competencies (LOGIC). European Journal of Psychology of Education 8: 273–87.

Schneider W, Roth E, Ennemoser (2000) Training phonological skills and letter knowledge in children at risk for dyslexia: a comparison of three kindergarten intervention programs. Journal of Educational Psychology 92: 284–95.

Schonell F, Goodacre E (1971) The Psychology and Teaching of Reading (fifth edition). Edinburgh & London: Oliver & Boyd.

Schulke-Korne G, Grimm T, Nothen MM, MullerMyhsok B, Propping P, Remschmidt H (1997) Evidence for linkage of spelling disability to chromosome 15. American Journal of Medical Genetics 74: 661.

Seidenberg M, McClelland J (1989) A distributed developmental model of word recognition and naming. Psychological Review 96: 523–68.

Senechal M, LeFevre J, Thomas E, Daley K (1998) Differential effects of home literacy experiences on the development of oral and written language. Reading Research Quarterly 33: 96–116.

Seymour PHK, Duncan L (1997) Small versus large unit theories of reading acquisition. Dyslexia 3: 125–34.

Shankweiler D, Crain S, Brady S, Macaruso P (1992) Identifying the causes of reading disability. In: Gough PB, Ehri LC, Treiman R (eds) Reading Acquisition. Hillsdale, NJ: Erlbaum Associates; 275–305.

Share D, Jorm AF, Maclean R, Matthews R (1984) Sources of individual differences in reading acquisition. Journal of Educational Psychology 76: 1309–24.

Shaywitz SE, Escobar MD, Shaywitz BA, Fletcher JM, Makugh R. (1992a) Evidence that dyslexia may represent the lower tail of a normal distribution of reading ability. New England Journal of Medicine 326: 145–50.

Shaywitz BA, Shaywitz SE, Fletcher JM (1992b) The Yale Center for the Study of Learning and Attention Disorders. Learning Disabilities 3: 1–12.

Smith SD, Kimberling WJ, Pennington BF, Lubbs HA (1983) Specific reading disability: Identification of an inherited form through linkage analysis. Science 219: 1345–7.

Snowling MJ (1981) Phonemic deficits in developmental dyslexia. Psychological Research 43: 219–34.

Snowling M (1998) Reading development and its difficulties. Educational and Child Psychology 15: 44–58.

Snowling M (2000). Dyslexia. Oxford: Blackwell.

Snowling M, Stackhouse J (eds) (1996) Dyslexia, Speech and Language. London: Whurr Publishers.

Snowling MJ, Bryant PE, Hulme C (1996) Theoretical and methodological pitfalls in making comparisons between developmental and acquired dyslexia: some comments on A Castles and M Coltheart 1993. Reading and Writing 8: 443–51.

Snowling M, Chiat S, Hulme C (1991) Words, nonwords and phonological processes: some comments on Gathercole, Ellis, Emslie and Baddeley. Applied Psycholinguistics 12: 369–73.

Snowling M, Hulme C, Goulandris N (1994) Word recognition in developmental dyslexia: a connectionist interpretation. Quarterly Journal of Experimental Psychology 47A: 895–916.

Snowling M, Stothard S, MacLean J (1996) The Graded Nonword Reading Test. Bury St Edmunds: Thames Valley Test Co.

Snowling, MJ, Wagtendonk B van, Stafford C ((1988) Object naming deficits in developmental dyslexia. Journal of Research in Reading 11: 67–85.

Spector JE (1995) Phonemic awareness training: application of principles of direct instruction. Reading and Writing Quarterly: Overcoming Learning Difficulties 11: 37–51.

Stanovich KE, Cunningham AE, Cramer BB (1984) Assessing phonological processes in kindergarten children: issues of task comparability. Journal of Experimental Child Psychology 38: 175–90.

Stanovich KE, Siegel LS (1994) The phenotypic performance profile of reading-disabled children: a regression-based test of the phonological core variable-difference model. Journal of Educational Psychology 86: 24–53.

Stanovich KE, Siegel LS, Gottardo A (1997) Progress in the search for dyslexia subtypes. In: Hulme C, Snowling M (eds) Dyslexia: Biology, Cognition and Intervention. London: Whurr Publishers; 108–30.

Stanovich KE, West RF (1989) Exposure to print and orthographic processing. Reading Research Quarterly 24: 402–33.

Stein JF (1989) Visuospatial perception and reading problems. Irish Journal of Psychology 10: 534–41.

Stein J (2001) The magnocellular theory of developmental dyslexia. Dyslexia 7: 12–36.

Stein JF, Fowler MS (1985) Effect of monocular occlusion on reading in dyslexic children. Lancet 13 July: 69–73.

Stein JF, Richardson AJ, Fowler MS (2000) Monocular occlusion can improve binocular control and reading in developmental dyslexics. Brain 123: 164–70.

Stevenson J, Graham P, Fredman G, McLoughlin V (1987) A twin study of genetic influences of reading and spelling ability and disability. Journal of Child Psychology and Psychiatry 28: 229–47.

Stuart M (1990) Processing strategies in a phoneme deletion task. Quarterly Journal of Experimental Psychology 42: 305–27.

Stuart M (1999) Getting ready for reading: early phoneme awareness and phonics teaching improves reading and spelling in inner-city second language learners. British Journal of Educational Psychology 69: 587–605.

Stuart M, Coltheart M (1988) Does reading develop in a sequence of stages? Cognition 30: 139–81.

Stuart M, Masterson J (1992) Patterns of reading and spelling in 10-year-old children related to pre-reading phonological abilities. Journal of Experimental Child Psychology 54: 168–87.

Sumbler K, Willows D (1996) Phonological awareness and alphabetic coding instruction within balanced senior kindergartens. Paper presented at National Reading Conference, Charleston, SC, December.

Swan D, Goswami U (1997) Phonological awareness deficits in developmental dyslexia and the phonological representations hypothesis. Journal of Experimental Child Psychology 60: 334–53.

Sylva K, Hurry J (1995) Early intervention in children with reading difficulties: An evaluation of reading recovery and phonological training. Report to the Schools Curriculum Assessment Authority.

Tabachnick B, Fidell L (1989) Using Multivariate Statistics. New York, NY: Harper Collins.

Tallal P (1980) Auditory-temporal perception, phonics and reading disabilities in children. Brain and Language 9: 182–98.

Tallal P, Piercey M (1974) Developmental aphasia: rate of auditory processing and selective impairment of consonant perception. Neuropsychologia 12: 83–93.

Teale WH (1986) Home background and young children's literacy development. In: Teale WH, Sulsby E (eds) Emergent Literacy: Writing and Reading. Norwood, NJ: Ablex; 173–206.

Torgesen J, Bryant B (1994) Test of Phonological Awareness, TOPA. Austin, Tex: Pro-Ed.

Torgesen JK, Wagner RK, Rashotte CA, Rose E, Lindamood P, Conway T et al. (1999) Preventing reading failure in young children with phonological processing disabilities: group and individual responses to instruction. Journal of Educational Psychology 91: 579–93.

Treiman R (1984) Individual differences among children in spelling and reading styles. Journal of Experimental Child Psychology 37: 463–77.

Treiman R (1985) Onsets and rimes as units of spoken syllables: evidence from children. Journal of Experimental Child Psychology 39: 161–81.

Treiman R, Weatherston S, Berch D (1994) The role of letter names in children's learning of phoneme–grapheme relationships. Applied Psycholinguistics 15: 97–122.

Tunmer WE (1989) The role of language-related factors in reading disability. In: Shankweiler D, Liberman IY (eds) Phonology and Reading Disability: Solving the reading puzzle, IARLDM. Ann Arbor, Mich: University of Michigan Press; 91–131.

Tunmer WE, Chapman JW (1998) Language prediction skill, phonological recoding, and beginning reading. In: Hulme C, Joshi R (eds) Reading and Spelling: Development and disorders. Mahwah, NJ: Erlbaum Associates; 33–67.

Turner M (1997) The Psychological Assessment of Dyslexia. London: Whurr Publishers.

Van Ijzendoorn MH, Bus AG (1994) Meta-analytic confirmation of the non-word of the non-word reading deficit in developmental dyslexia. Reading Research Quarterly 29: 267–75.

Vellutino F, Scanlon D (1991) The pre-eminence of phonologically based skills in learning to read. In: Brady S, Shankweiler D (eds) Phonological Processes in Literacy: A tribute to Isabelle Y. Liberman. Hillsdale, NJ: Erlbaum Associates; 237–52.

Vellutino FR, Scanlon DM, Sipay E, Small S, Pratt A, Chen R et al. (1996) Cognitive profiles of difficult to remediate and readily remediated poor readers: towards distinguishing between constitutionally and experientially based causes of reading disability. Journal of Educational Psychology 88: 601–38.

Wagner RK, Torgesen JK (1987) The nature of phonological processing and its causal role in the acquisition of reading skills. Psychological Bulletin 101: 192–212.

Wagner RK, Torgesen JK, Rashotte CA (1994) The development of reading-related phonological processing abilities: new evidence of bi-directional causality from a latent variable longitudinal study. Developmental Psychology 30: 73–87.

Wagner RK, Torgesen JK, Rashotte CA, Hecht SA, Barker TA, Burgess SR et al. (1997) Changing relations between phonological processing abilities and word-level reading as children develop from beginning to skilled readers: a 5-year longitudinal study. Developmental Psychology 33: 468–79.

Wagner RK, Torgesen JK, Rashotte CA (1999) CTOPP: Comprehensive Test of Phonological Processing. Austin, Tex: Pro-Ed.

Walley A (1993) The role of vocabulary development in children's spoken word recognition and segmentation ability. Developmental Review 13: 286–350.

Wechsler D (1967) Wechsler Pre-School and Primary Scale of Intelligence — WPPSI. London: Psychological Corporation, Harcourt Brace.

Wechsler D (1990) Wechsler Pre-School and Primary Scale of Intelligence — Revised (WPPSI-R). London: Psychological Corporation, Harcourt Brace.

Wechsler D (1992) Wechsler Intelligence Scale for Children III UK. London: The Psychological Corporation, Harcourt Brace.

Wendon L (1997) Letterland. London: Collins.

White KR (1982) The relation between socio-economic status and academic achievement. Psychological Bulletin 91: 461–81.

Whitehurst G, Lonigan C (1998) Child development and emergent literacy. Child Development 69: 848–72.

Wilkins AJ, Evans BJW, Brown JA, Busby AE, Wingfield AE, Jeanes RJ et al. (1994) Double masked placebo-controlled trial of precision spectral filters in children who used coloured overlays. Ophthalmic and Physiological Orthoptics 14: 365–70.

Willows D, Ryan E (1986) The development of grammatical sensitivity and its relationship to early reading achievement. Reading Research Quarterly 21: 253–66.

Wimmer H (1993) Characteristics of developmental dyslexia in a regular writing system. Applied Psycholinguistics 14: 1–34.

Wimmer H, Landerl K (1998) How learning to spell German differs from learning to spell English. In: Perfetti CA, Rieben L, Fayol M (eds) Learning to Spell: Research, theory and practice across languages. Mahwah, NJ: Erlbaum; 81–96.

Wimmer H, Landerl K, Schneider W (1994) The role of rhyme awareness in learning to read a regular orthography. British Journal of Developmental Psychology 112: 469–84.

Wimmer H, Mayringer H, Landerl K (1998). Poor reading: a deficit in skill automatisation or a phonological deficit? Scientific Studies of Reading 2: 321–40.

Windfuhr K (1998) Verbal Learning, Phonological Processing and Reading Skills in Normal and Dyslexic Readers. University of York: DPhil thesis.

Windfuhr K, Snowling M (2001) The relationship between paired associate learning and phonological skills in normally developing readers. Journal of Experimental Child Psychology 80: 160–73.

Wise B, Olson R (1995) Computer-based phonological awareness and reading instruction. Annals of Dyslexia 45: 99–122.

Wolf MA (1982) The word retrieval process and reading in children and aphasics. In: Nelson K (Ed.) Children's Language. Hillsdale, NJ: Erlbaum Associates; 437–92.

Wolf M (1997) A provisional, integrative account of phonological and naming speed deficits in dyslexia: Implications for diagnosis and intervention. In Blackman B (eds) Foundations of Reading Acquisition in Dyslexia. Hillsdale, NJ: Erlbaum & Assocs: 67–92.

Wolf M, Bowers P (1999) The double deficit hypothesis for the developmental dyslexias. Journal of Educational Psychology 91: 1–24.

Wolf M, O'Brien B (2001) On issues of time, fluency and intervention. In Fawcett A (Ed.) Dyslexia: Theory and Good Practice. London: Whurr Publishers; 124–40.

Yopp H (1988) The validity and reliability of phonemic awareness tests. Reading Research Quarterly 23: 159–77.

Index